ROPNER'S NAVY

Billy McGee
Dis. A. UK066942
Merchant Navy
1980-1992

'ROPNER'S NAVY'

Author : Billy McGee

Published in Great Britain by Cormorant Publishing Hartlepool
Copyright © 2008 Billy McGee
1st Edition

First published in 2008 by
Cormorant Publishing Hartlepool,
5 Teesdale Ave,
Hartlepool. TS26 9QD
cormorantpublishing@yahoo.co.uk
www.riddlewrites.co.uk

ISBN No. 978-0-9558593-5-9

Typeset, Printed and bound in Great Britain by
Connoisseur Crafts Ltd
Hartlepool Enterprise Centre, Brougham Terrace
Hartlepool, TS24 8EY
United Kingdom
concrafts@surfree.co.uk

Acknowledgements

Special thanks to Mr. Roger Griffiths for his hours of help during his many visits to The National Archives at Kew unearthing files for me and teaching me how to navigate the digital online service. Mr. Ted Finch from the Rootsweb forum for all his emails sent when I could not find information on certain ships. Maureen Annette from the Commonwealth War Graves Commission for the records regarding casualties. My friend Mr. Simon Thomas for proof reading the following pages. A special thanks to those members of the Ropner family who have contacted me. Capt. Colin Tingle (retd.), a friend and neighbour who spent thirty years with the Ropner Shipping Co. Mr Geoff Morton MBE, a survivor from Fort Pelly for his account on the sinking. Eddie Sands who sadly crossed the bar in February 2006, a survivor from SS Warlaby and finally to all those individuals who gave me the encouragement and support to finish these pages. Photographs are from my personnel collection and include photographs purchased from Fotoflite, South African & Welsh Maritime Museums.

Dedication

Dedicated to Merchant Seamen of all nations past and present. To those who belong to this brotherhood who have experienced the power of the sea and the dangers it brings. For all those still in peril on the sea, I admire and salute you, and for those who sleep beneath the sea I honour you.

Introduction

In 2005 my son Callum appeared in a play written by Mr. Robert Smith entitled "A Park Supreme" detailing the early life of Sir Robert Ropner and Stockton towns affiliation with Ropner Park. Speaking to people afterwards, I realized that the majority of people had no idea of the huge impact in the world of shipping Sir Robert played in not just the North-East, but on the whole world of shipping. A legacy, which would last some 123 years as a major ship owner as well as ship builder. As a former Merchant Seaman, I was well aware of the Ropner Shipping Co. having served on two of their ships, the Ravenscraig & Appleby in the mid 80's. I was also well aware of the enormous losses incurred by the Ropner & Pool Shipping Co., another fact that the general public seemed to know very little of. As 2005 was the official "Year of the Sea" coinciding with the 60th anniversary VE & VJ celebrations, I approached a local group "Friends of Ropner Park" with the idea to have a bronze Memorial Plaque dedicated to recognise the sacrifice of over 700 men lost while serving on Ropner's Merchant ships in two World Wars. I was then introduced to the Park Ranger, Mr Tony Raine to put forward my idea for official approval by the council. When permission was granted I set up the "Ropner Navy Memorial Fund" to raise the £1,500 needed to cover the cost of the plaque. The Memorial was unveiled in Ropner Park in a ceremony on 30th October 2005, attended by over 100 people, including veterans, survivors, 16 Standard Bearers and the Rgt. Hon. Dari Taylor MP who laid a wreath. So successful was this event I decided to set about tracing the history of all the ships Ropner owned and managed and put it in writing to preserve for posterity. If you are reading this, then I've succeeded in my task.

Billy McGee Dis. A. UK066942 Merchant Navy 1980-1992.

4

ROPNER'S NAVY

In 1857 a young 18-year-old stowaway landed at West Hartlepool onboard the ship *Gitania*. His head, which had been full of dreams of becoming a sailor, lay in tatters as his first trip across the cruel North Sea brought on the dreadful Mal-de-Mer (Seasickness). His name, *Robert Ropner*, born 16th December 1838 at Magdeburg, Germany, the son of a Prussian army officer John Henry Ropner and Emilie Ropner (nee Bessel). Little would Robert have thought or known at the time, but his destiny was already being written.

With his sea going dream gone, and no knowledge of the English language the young Ropner needed to seek work. At this period of time it was fairly common to find German & Scandinavian's working the North-East ports as the industrial expansion and the growing coal trade attracted men from all corners of Europe, so he would not of been totally alone. Robert had received a good education in Germany where he attended grammar school at Helmstedt while living with his aunt after both his parents had died from cholera in 1848 when Robert was only nine. He was fluent in both Latin & French; so it was not long before he took a grasp of the English language and soon found himself work in a local Hartlepool bakery on the High Street not far from the docks. There he met *Mary Ann Craik*, the daughter of the bakery shop owner who helped with his English and who was to become his wife a year later.

In 1858, now proficient in the English language Robert took on the job of junior clerk with a local colliery fitter and coal exporter named *Geipels* and was soon working as a go between for Giepels to secure contracts for coal export with German businesses. By 1860 Robert was becoming well known locally as a man with acute business sense and in 1860 he was offered a post with the firm of *Thomas Appleby & Co.,* another coal exporter based at Hartlepool. His job once again was to expand the company's coal business, which saw him visit the continent on several occasions seeking contracts. 1860 would also see the birth of his first of ten children, *John Henry Ropner*.

In 1861, four years after first landing on British soil Robert applied for and was granted British citizenship. Business continued to expand, as did his family with the birth of his second son, *Hugo Oscar Robert Ropner Jnr.* in 1862 followed by *William Ropner* in 1864. By 1866 the Thomas Appleby Co. had become so successful largely due to Robert's initiative he was offered a partnership and the name was changed to the *Appleby & Ropner Co.* In 1867 Robert was elected a member of the Hartlepool Town Council and with business at an all time high the company decided to capitalise on their success. Instead of chartering ships to export their coal it was decided the company would export its own cargo in its own ships. An inquiry was made with the local ship builder *Denton, Gray & Co.* and a delivery date of August 1868 was made for the 800dwt *SS Amy*, named after Robert's daughter born the previous year. Delivered a month early, the ship was tragically lost on her second trip after stranding at Winga in the Grecian Archipelago under the command of *Captain. David Rooke*. A number of other ships were soon ordered for the company.

By 1874 Robert had fathered three more children, *Walter Ropner* born 1868, *Leonard Ropner* 1873 & *Lillian Ropner* in 1874. By 1874 the *Appleby & Ropner Co.* partnership was terminated by mutual consent with the ships being split between the two men and so was born what was to be the biggest tramp steamer fleet known and named *R. Ropner & Co.* The same year Robert ordered his first new ship the *SS Renpor* (Ropner spelt backwards) built by Short Brothers of Sunderland. With the large economical growth at the end of the nineteenth century, which was taking place, the Ropner Co. had no problem exporting vast amounts of coal and returning with cargoes of pit props & timber. 1876 & 1877 saw the birth of his eighth and ninth children *Eveline Ropner* and *Mabel Ropner*. In 1879 he opened an office in Cardiff to tap into the South Wales market, which was growing as a coal exporter and by 1880 the company had acquired a further 11 ships into the fleet.

In 1882 Robert purchased *Preston Hall* as the family home on the outskirts of Stockton-on-Tees for £27,500, which contained 117 acres of land. The ship building boom of the 1870's continued into the 1880's and in the five years up to 1885 saw a rise in British steamer tonnage from 2,949,282 net tons to 4,308,643, which caused a slump in the trade market between 1884-1885 due to more ships biding for trade. Robert being a very shrewd business man though had learned to conserve his profits whilst still building new tonnage at a cheaper price due to the depressed market. In 1886 his eldest Son was taken into partnership and his tenth child *Elsa Ropner* was born. By 1887 The Ropner Co. opened an office in London as well as purchasing the Stockton ship-yard of *M. Pearce & Co.*, which was placed in control of his two son's Robert & Leonard. This year would also see the first steel built vessel brought into the fleet as all previous had been of iron construction. Robert's family shipyard went on to design and build tramp steamers most suitably for the world ports they would be chartered to visit and the *"Trunk Decker"* design became synonymous with the name Ropner. Designed by Robert Jnr., the first one *SS Trunkby* was built in Stockton in 1896. The ships had a steel trunk built along their main deck running the length of the ship. The earlier ships trunk decks stopped either side of the amidships bridge and accommodation section. This was later changed to run the full length of the ship. The design

6

improved overall stability once a ship had been fully loaded with cargo, while giving greater protection to hatch coverings from huge seas breaking over the ships deck while sailing in heavy weather and also gave a greater cargo capacity. The design also exempted the ships trunkspace from the tonnage tax measurements for passage through the Suez Canal. The way ships were measured at the time; this method of construction gave a tonnage figure that was low for the ships carrying capacity. As various dues, such as that for using the Suez Canal, were based on the tonnage figure, this reduced costs dramatically, which made them cheaper to run for the Far East and Australian shipping market. The only set back being when in ballast the ships had a low draft, which caused them to lose stability. In all Ropner's Stockton yard would launch 22 of these type of ships until the design was discontinued in 1907.

Robert now approaching his sixties began to slowly hand over the day to day running of the company business side to his son's Robert Jnr & William, which left Robert more time to pursue other interests in local politics and the wider affairs concerning the shipping industry. In 1889 he became Chairman of the Stockton Conservative Party. In 1890 he donated 36 acres of land to the borough of Stockton to be used as a public park, providing the local authorities looked after the upkeep. In 1893 Ropner Park was officially opened by the *Duke & Duchess of York*, later to become *King George V & Queen Mary*. (In 2005/2006 the park underwent a 2.65 million pound restoration, funded largely by the Heritage Lottery Fund to restore the park back to its former glory). In 1891 the Hartlepool Ship owners Society had him elected to the General Committee of Lloyds Register of Shipping in London. A popular figure in Stockton, Robert was elected Mayor of the town in 1893 and a year later became a member of the Tees Conservancy Commission, followed in 1896 by becoming Deputy Lieutenant for County Durham and High Sheriff. Since 1889 he had been a member of the Hartlepool Port & Harbour Commission and was elected Chairman in 1898. The same year he became Chairman of the Hartlepool Shipping Federation and the following year became a Justice of the Peace for the North Riding of Yorkshire. Robert never forgot about the local people of Stockton all this time and donated a convalescent home to the workmen of Stockton & Thornaby as well as a gift of £10,000 to local hospitals and the same year became a member of the executive council for the Chamber of Shipping, which had been founded in 1878 to represent and protect the interests of shipowners and by 1900 he was vice-president and a year later president. The shipping side was still being well run by his son's and by 1900 the company had a fleet of 34 deep-sea tramps. In 1902 Robert was knighted for his services to shipping and two years later was made a Baronet.

By 1903 Robert was no longer involved in the running of the R. Ropner Shipping Co. but still maintained a watchful eye on what was going on. The same year it was decided to form a limited company named Pool Shipping Co., which was formed to wholly own and acquire ships while still being managed by Sir R. Ropner & Co. All these ships would carry the suffix *Pool*, with the first two *Heronspool* & *Troutpool* being launched that same year from their Stockton yard and made to the trunk deck design of *Robert Ropner Jnr*. The same year the company also took over the management of the SS *Therese Heymann* which had been built at the Stockton yard for the *Therese Heymann SS Co. Ltd*. 1907 and 1908, and again between 1910 and 1911 saw a severe slump as the price of coal fell. With many of the smaller shipping companies laying up ships. Two small shipowners from West Hartlepool, Leask, Clarke & Co. & J.A. Wood & Co. were especially hit and were forced to sell one of their ships apiece, which were snapped up at a reduced market price by Ropner's who did not seem to feel the effects of the slump and still managed to build another nine ships between 1907 to 1911. Between 1912 to 1914 a further nine ships were completed at the Stockton yard bringing the total amount of ships to 57 flying the Ropner House Flag by the time WWI started.

The company's first casualty of the war was not through enemy action but by the stranding of the SS *Hawnby* off Montrose in September 1914, blamed due to lack of shore lights. The SS *Selby* became their first war loss after hitting a mine 30th September 1914. On 16th December 1914, the battle cruisers Blutche, Moltke & Seidlitz, units belonging to the German High Seas Fleet bombarded the East coast at Whitby, Scarborough & Hartlepool damaging the company's office, luckily without loss of life. A shell also exploded in William Ropner's home killing one of the kitchen staff. William's eldest sons Leonard & Guy were part of the Hartlepool artillery battery who were returning fire on the German ships causing considerable damage, preventing the German's main objective to cause damage to the docks & steelworks. SS *Saxilby* was launched in November 1914. The SS *Therese Heymann* after leaving the Tyne on Christmas Day 1914 disappeared and nothing was ever found of the ship and her 21 crew. The ship was not officially classed as missing/untraced until 3rd March 1915, though it is believed she was one of several ships mined off Filey around Christmas time. 1915 would see a further seven Ropner ships sent to the bottom. They were SS *Willerby*, SS *Oakby*, SS *Coleby*, SS *Gadsby*, SS *Glenby* SS *Kirkby* & SS *Scawby*. Two being sunk by the German raiders *Printz Eitel Frederick* & *Kronprinz Wilhelm* and five by German U-boats. Only 2 crew were lost from all seven ships, both these coming from the SS *Glenby* who were killed when the U-boat which attacked them continued shelling the ship as the crew were abandoning ship. At this time most of the Germans followed the rules of war engagement towards Merchant shipping and would first stop a ship allowing the crew to abandon ship before sinking any vessel. This would all change in February 1915 when the German government declared the seas around the British Isles a war zone and any ship found there on or after 18th February faced sinking without warning: unrestricted U-boat warfare began for the first time in history and any neutral flag was considered to be no guarantee for safety. This descision would ultimately see the loss of the passenger liner *Lusitania* causing the death of American citizens, provoking anger in the USA. The American government brought pressure to bear on Germany after the loss and demanded an end to sinking without warning. On 30th August 1915 Germany prohibited further action of this type. The Germans, in an attempt to reduce further damage to American shipping, withdrew all U-boats from the English Channel area. 1916 would see this lull come to an end as unrestricted warfare started up again, which would see the loss of Ropner & Pool ships *SS Dromonby, SS Thornaby, SS Trunkby & SS Salmonpool. SS Ashby* would also be lost after being wrecked at Ushant on the 15th February 1916.The Ropner ship *SS Newby* which had been sold the year before to the Temple-Thompson & Clark Co. was also sunk in 1916. On the 24th March 1916 with the sinking of the passenger liner *Sussex* which again resulted in the loss of US citizens, the Germans were once again pressured into restricting their submarine warfare. By 1917 Germany was becoming desperate, as the British Naval blockade of the North Sea tightened its grip and German supplies and raw materials needed for war became more depleted. In a final attempt to starve Britain into submission and with America likely to become involved in the European war, unrestricted submarine warfare was again declared on the 1st February 1917. Two days later America broke off diplomatic relations with Germany and by April 6th America had declared war on Germany. The previous months had seen the loss of the Ropner ships *SS Wragby, SS Martin, SS Burnby, & SS Daleby* all sunk by U-boats, but things were about to change and Ropner's were about to fight back and the legend of *"Ropner's Navy"* was born. (The term "Ropner's Navy" was not termed until WWII, but the seeds had been sown on 2nd April 1917).

The *SS Wandby* under the command of *Captain David Simpson* on voyage from Bilbao to La Rochelle, France in convoy was forced to stop for repairs in the Bay of Biscay due to broken steering chains. The convoy was unable to stop and help, leaving the *Wandby* drifting alone. During the night a gale blew up severely hampering the repairs, but by the morning of the 2nd April 1917 the ship was under way once more and making speed of 8 knots to try and catch up with the convoy. Shortly after a bright flash was seen astern of the ship followed by a huge white splash of a shell bursting in the sea. This was followed by a further five shells bursting around the ship into the sea before the cause was spotted by the ships lookouts. It turned out to be one of the latest German U-boats mounted with two 4-inch deck guns. By 1917 a number of Merchant ships had begun to be armed and were known as DEMS (Defensively Equipped Merchant Ship). The *Wandby* was one such ship and a small single mounted stern gun had been added. The *Wandby* began to return fire at a lot less slower pace made even more difficult due to the heavy seas. By now the U-boat was firing off shrapnel and explosive rounds, with the shrapnel rounds peppering the ships decks and the explosive rounds beginning to home in closer. About two miles off the *Wandby's* stern the U-boats 36th shell found its mark, striking the port quarter just above the water line severely wounding a crewmember. The damage to the ship was only superficial as it had only been a shrapnel round. The *Wandby* continued to return fire and her 15th round struck the U-boat, which was last seen with its bow high in the air sinking fast by the stern. The whole action had last forty five minutes. Captain Simpson and three of his crew were later decorated for their action while the crew were rewarded with sums of money. Sadly Captain Simpson was to lose his life on the Ropner ship *Empire Merlin* sunk during WWII on the 25th August 1940.

The same month as the *Wandby's* action another of the companies ship took on a U-boat. SS *Thirlby* under the command of *Captain Thomas Morgan Hill*. When WWI had been declared *Thirlby* had been caught at the Russian port of Cronstadt on the small island of Kotlin in the Gulf of Finland in the Baltic Sea. The ship was held for two years until the company managed to get her out of the Baltic, which proved to be a very expensive affair to the Ropner Co. The British government decided to let the company run this ship free of requisition until the end of the war. This however was to be short lived. On the 24th April 1917 *Thirlby* was on voyage from Bombay to Dunkirk, sailing alone and unescorted in the Bay of Biscay. At 07.00 hours the unmistakable track of a torpedo was seen crossing the ships bow. *Thirlby* had earlier been fitted with a small 12-pounder Vickers gun on her stern and her gun crew were called to action stations. Diligent lookouts were posted and Captain Hill eagerly awaited the U-boats next move. This came forty minutes later when the track of another torpedo was sighted. Captain Hill issued the ships wheel swung hard over and the torpedo passed harmlessly across the ships stern. Another ten minutes passed and a third torpedo was sighted and once again the helm hard over the torpedo failed to hit. The U-boat now surfaced astern of *Thirlby* and was met by a shell from her 12-pounder which caused the U-boat to crash dive. The U-boat then resurfaced three mile astern of the ship, out of effective range of the ships gun and opened up with both four inch deck guns. Evasive zig zagging was taken up by the merchantman as shell after shell rained in. Around one hundred shells had been fired at *Thirlby* when she was finally hit in one of her cargo holds, the shell exploding amongst her cargo though sustaining little damage. Encouraged by the hit the U-boat began to close in only to be driven back time and time again, as *Thirlby's* 12-pounder fired off round after round. This game of cat and mouse continued for four and a half hours with the U-boat firing some 150 rounds and only finding her mark once. *Thirlby's* 57th round found its mark exploding on the U-boats conning tower. The Germans had had enough and broke off the action dropping further astern until she disappeared over the horizon. Captain Hill was awarded the Shipping Federations Gold Medal and diploma while three other crewmembers were awarded the Silver Medal. The success was to be short lived as on her very next trip on the 2nd July, still under the command of Captain Hill, *Thirlby* was torpedoed and sunk off Fastnet by a German U-boat killing two crewmembers. The U-boat then came along side the survivors in their lifeboats and removed all the lifeboat sails. Despite this Captain Hill and his crew were picked up by a patrol boat and landed ashore in Ireland. This would not be the last Captain Hill would see of the war. The previous month had also seen the loss of SS *Westonby* & SS *Brookby*.

On Captain Hill's safe return to Britain he was requested to join the *SS Teesdale*, which had been torpedoed and damaged in the English Channel on the 15th June 1917 on voyage to Gibraltar with a cargo of coal. The ship had remained afloat and the ships Master & crew managed to beach the ship at Salcombe Bay, South Devon. After receiving temporary repairs Captain Hill was ordered to bring the ship back to the River Tees where permanent repairs would take place. On the 2nd August about three miles off Saltburn Pier the temporary repairs gave way and the ship started taking on water very quickly and sank shortly after taking two of her crew with her. Captain Hill and the remainder of his crew spent some twelve hours in their lifeboats in very rough seas before safely being landed ashore. The war would still not be over for Captain Hill, as he would see more action during 1918. 1917 would see the loss of two more Ropner ships SS *Rollesby* torpedoed 15th September & SS *Romanby* which was lost after a collision with the *SS Romera* in the North Atlantic. The only good news of 1917 was that the convoy system was finally put into full effect; this would dramatically reduce shipping losses. The first Ropner ship since 1914 was launched in SS *Swainby*.

February 1918 saw the successful launch of the SS *Sedgepool*, which was soon overshadowed by the loss of the SS *Maltby* at the end of the same month. Earlier in the same month, Captain T. Hill formerly of SS *Thirlby* & SS *Teesdale* fame was in command of the SS *Pikepool* on voyage from Rouen to South Wales in an escorted convoy. Somehow a U-boat managed to penetrate the escort screen and torpedoed *Pikepool* in number two hold, which caused flooding in the engine room and bunker hold. Captain Hill ordered his ship abandoned. As the crew waited in their lifeboats for the ship to sink, *Pikepool* had settled in the water and showed signs of staying afloat and was re-boarded. Tug assistance was called for and the ship arrived at Portland the following day and was later put back into service. The beginning of March would see no let up and *SS Rockpool* was lost to a U-boat and her Master, *Captain John White* taken prisoner. In May *SS Saxilby* was damaged but survived an attack off Malta. With the war fully in the Allies favour and better convoy protection nearly three months would pass before the next Ropner loss, the *SS Mountby* who had earlier in the year escaped from a U-boat by using smoke floats and an evasive zig zagging action to lose the enemy. Her luck ran out on the 10th June 1918 when she was torpedoed off the Lizard on voyage from Cardiff with a cargo of admiralty stores. The 28th September 1918 would see the last Ropner loss of WWI when *SS Baldersby* was sunk in the St George Channel on voyage from Montreal to Avonmouth. To help the struggling company cope with such severe losses, in 1918 the British Shipping Controller handed over two ships for the Ropner Company to manage for them, *SS War Deer* & SS *War Hind*. *War Deer* would be damaged by a torpedo but would survive the war.

When the Armistice was signed on the 11th November 1918 the Ropner Company had lost 26 of their tramps to enemy action, one other had been seriously damaged causing loss of life and three others lost through various marine causes. Although the ships losses were severe the death rates amongst their crews were surprisingly low, mainly due to the restricted submarine warfare. WWII would be a very different story and would see the death rate amongst the Ropner crews rise almost ten fold due to the unrestricted war fare directed at all Merchant shipping. One of these to die would be *Captain Thomas Morgan Hill*, who after surviving three Ropner sinkings during WWI would lose his life at the age of 61 while Master of the *SS Fishpool* which was severely damaged by incendiaries in the first fourteen months of the Second World War. *Captain David Simpson* who had been Master of the *SS Wandy* which sank a U-boat in 1917 would not survive WWII either and would be killed on the Ropner ship *SS Empire Merlin* eleven months into the second world war at the age of 69. One man who would have more luck than most would be *Captain John Kenny*. Having already survived the sinking of one ship the *SS Oakfield* belonging to the Doughty Shipping Co. during WWI before joining Ropner's in 1918, he would survive the sinking of the *SS Maltby* in 1918 and a further two Ropner ships sunk in WWII, *SS Wandby* & SS *Empire Rainbow*. He would later become Commodore of the Ropner fleet.

In 1919 the first of Sir Robert's grandsons, *Colonel Leonard Ropner* and *Major William Guy Ropner* joined the company. Although more than 50% of the Ropner fleet had been lost during WWI and there was a post war boom up until about 1921, no more ships were built or added to the Ropner fleet at this time. Two German ships taken as war prizes by the Shipping Controller *SS Germanicus & SS Hornfels* were put under Ropner management in 1919; the *Germanicus* was lost the same year after stranding in the Gulf of St Lawrence and *Hornfels* was sold a year later. 1919 saw the Diamond Wedding Anniversary of Sir Robert & Lady Ropner who made it a quiet affair, donating £500 to a local charity instead of the planned garden party. The slump in shipbuilding continued into the 1920's with many companies selling up and disappearing altogether. In 1914 there had been some forty-four tramp companies registered at West Hartlepool, owning some 232 ships between them. This was now down to ten companies with only forty-four ships between them. Sir Robert's old partner Thomas Appleby was one of the companies forced into voluntary liquidation. (It is not for these pages to go into detail and explain the technical side of the shipping market. It can be explained to a much better degree in *Ian Dear's* book *"The Ropner Story"* ISBN 0091638100). In 1921 Lady Ropner passed away and *SS Wandby* was wrecked of Portland, Maine. 1923 as things could not seem to get much worse they did when both Ropner ships *SS Troutpool & SS Somersby* were lost within two months of each other after both ships stranded and became total losses. This blow was some what softened by the purchase of a ship on the stocks at their Stockton yard from a company, which had recently gone bankrupt. The ship was launched as the *SS Roxby (2)*. On the 26th February 1924 *Sir Robert Ropner* passed away at his final residence at *Skutterskelfe Hall* near Hutton Rudby at the age of 86 and was buried in the nearby Hutton Rudby Churchyard. It had been fifty-six years earlier that a young penniless immigrant had landed on the shores of West Hartlepool and through sheer hard work, a self determined astute business mind and self belief, that Sir Robert's legacy would live on through the company he founded. A family business now left in the capable hands of his sons, grandsons & eventually his great grandsons. A legacy which also left a gross unsettled estate value of £3,615, 828, with net personality £3,600,200 15s 3d (figures quoted taken from Evening Gazette article dated 26th July 1924).

The tonnage price and shipbuilding had fallen so low by 1923 as it had done before in the late 1800's. The Ropner directors decided to act on the same policy, which Sir Robert had done in his time, and take a gamble and build the fleet up again despite the state of the freight market. Five new tramp steamers where put on order to be completed in 1924, three of which would be built in the family yard at Stockton. In 1925 the *SS Willowpool* was launched from the

Stockton yard, which would prove to be the last ship delivered from the yard as it was decided to close the yard down. In the thirty seven years the family had run the yard they had successfully launched no less than seventy one ships for their company as well as vessels for many other companies. The site was left idle and during the depression of 1930-31 and it was demolished as part of the shipbuilding industries national plan to reduce shipping capacity. One more ship *SS Ainderby* would be launched in 1925 from the William Gray yard and William's third Son Mr. *John Raymond Ropner* (affectionately known as Jock) joined the company. In 1926 despite the General Strike, which took place that year a further, two more ships *SS Firby* & *SS Otterpool* were built. 1927 a number of the older ships in the fleet were sold of to gain extra capital for the six ships the company ordered that year. John & William Ropner seemed to of inherited the optimistic strength and conviction of their late father and went in the total opposite direction to other shipping companies who could see no light a the end of the tunnel and were laying their ships up due the rapidly deteriorating world economy, which was having a devastating effect on the international trade and freight rates. 1928 would see no let up in John & William's building plans and a further eleven ships were built and added to the fleet, with one other placed under their management. In 1929 a further four ships were built and delivered for the company from West Hartlepool's William Gray & Co. Ltd, the last one *SS Yearby* delivered a month after the infamous Wall Street Crash which caused the Great Depression to sweep across America and eventually throughout Europe and the rest of the capitalist world. Although Britain was less affected than most due to the continuing benefits of her Empire, though its industrial and export sectors remained seriously depressed until the beginning of World War II. Even the Ropner fleet could not avoid the knock on effect this had and as many as thirteen of their ships were laid up during 1932 to 1933 with a further seven laid up for short periods of time. Even those ships which they managed to keep running were barely making a profit and in some cases ran at a loss. William's fourth son Mr. *Robert D Ropner* joined the company in 1930. By 1933 the company had a fleet of fifty ships and even though the depression was biting deeper and deeper they had still managed to have a further five ships built and added to the fleet between 1930-1932. One of the reasons for this was due to the negotiations set up between Ropner's and the Dominion Coal Co. for time-chartering ships for the Canadian coal & ore trade. Two twenty odd year old tramp steamers were purchased for the charter, plus *SS Domby* was specially constructed for the charter. Once again shrewd buisness was responsible for the company to remain afloat in these hard times whilst many other companies around them sank without trace.

The North Atlantic winters of 1933 & 1934 were some of the most atrocious on record and were responsible for the loss of the SS Saxilby & SS Millpool. Distress signals were picked up from both ships but nothing was ever found of either ship or their crews. Legend has it that a crew member from the Saxilby named Joe O'Kane wrote a goodbye note to his brother, sister and fiancee telling them the ship was sinking off the coast of Ireland. The letter was then sealed in a water tight container and thrown overboard, only to be washed up on the beach at Aberavon in Swansea Bay three years later where it was found by some young boys playing along the beach who took it to the town mayor and amazingly it was found to be less than a mile from Joe's family home. The Ropner ship SS Ainderby was caught in the same storm as the Millpool but was unable to offer assistance as she was fighting for her own life as giant seas had swept away the bridge & engineroom telegraphs rendering the man at the wheel unconsious and stoving in the No. 1 hold. A young cadet was also washed overboard by a moutainous sea and was never seen again. Only by sheer skill, courage and seamanship shown by her ships Master, Captain E. Bestell and his crew was the Ainderby able to safely limp into Swansea.

Between 1934 to 1936 a number of the older ships in the fleet were sold off for scrap while seven new more modern ones were built to replace them. On the 13th July 1936 at the age of 76 Sir Robert's eldest son Sir John Henry Ropner, senior director of the company passed away quite suddenly at the same place as his Father at Skutterskelfe near Hutton Rudby. William Ropner was now appointed senior director of the company, though he was only attending the office on a morning daily basis as the main business was being run by his four sons. Like their Grandfather before them, the four sons of William had also become well established in their own careers, Leonard had become a well known and respected Member of Parliament for Barkston Ash, Tadcaster. Guy & Robert both had an interest in the Chamber of Shipping while Jock chose to place his full attention on the running of the shipping side of the business.

In 1937 Sir Robert's youngest son Leonard passed away. He was the last of the Ropner family to reside at the family home at Preston Hall, which was later leased by the family to the local company of Ashmore, Benson & Pease to be used as offices. In 1944 it had been intended to develop Preston Hall into a housing estate after the land was bought by a firm of builders. The development plans were later abolished after new building restrictions were brought in after WWII. The land was later purchased in 1947 by Stockton Corporation who turned the former Ropner home into a museum, which was officially opened in 1969. In 1974 the museum came under the control of

Stockton Borough Council and today is still one of the most popular visited local attractions, which has helped retain part of the Ropner legacy.

By 1937 a marked recovery in world trading conditions had been taking place and the forsight taken by the Ropner family during those lean years to carry on building new tonnage was now beginning to bear fruit as ships could once more be ran profitably. One more ship *SS Danby* was built for the company and another purchased and renamed *SS Eastpool* was added in 1937, *Eastpool* being sold within a year. Once again the clouds of war were looming across Europe and Ropner's would once again be thrust to the forefront of a war at sea which was to see total unrestricted warfare mounted from day one against Merchant shipping and would once again decimate the Ropner fleet to near extinction and far surpass the losses of WWI.

On the 3rd September 1939, the day WWII was declared by Britain against Germany, the first British & Commonwealth casualty of the war occurred a few hours later with the sinking of the British Donaldson Line passenger liner *SS Athenia,* sunk by U-30 with the loss of 112 passengers and crew. The *Battle of the Atlantic* had begun. While Britain was living in what became known as the *"Phoney War"* between September 1939 to May 1940 177 British Merchant ships were sunk with the loss of hundreds of Merchant Seamen. In the near six years of war in between, some 32,000 British Merchant Seamen gave their lives with a further 4,654 missing presumed dead, 4,707 wounded and 5,720 held prisoners of war from 2,500 British ship flying the Red Ensign, lost to U-boats, mines, E-boats, aircraft, commerce raiders, pocket battleships, those who died in captivity as well as those lost from the forces of nature in supplying the world with food and raw materials. Over 650 of these men would be from *"Ropner's Navy"* When war was declared the Ropner & Pool companies had 45 ships in their fleet and during the war a number of ships would also be built by the Ministry of Shipping (MOS), which later became the Ministry of War Transport (MOWT) and placed under Ropner management. Later America & Canada would also supply Merchant ships to the British government under the *"Bareboat Charter"* and some of these ships would be placed under Ropner management. The day after war was declared the Ropner shipping office in West Hartlepool was quickly moved inland to a large derelict house in Sedgefield called "The Whins" The war would come to Ropner's doorstep eight days after the first shots were fired.

On the 11th September 1939 *SS Firby*, sailing independently and unescorted from the Tyne to Hudson Bay to pick up a cargo of grain was intercepted by a German U-boat West of the Hebrides, who commenced to shell the unarmed merchant ship. Evasive zig zagging was the only thing *Captain Thomas Prince* could do. This was to little avail as the U-boat closed in and began finding her mark scoring five hits on *Firby*. After several of his crew were injured, Captain Prince orderd *Firby's* engine stopped and ordered his men to take to the lifeboats. U-48 under the command of *Korvettenkapitan Herbert Schultze* came along side Captain Prince's lifeboat and removed him for questioning. Sometime later he was returned to his boat and was given some bread and bandages for the wounded. Shultze then did something that would very rarely repeated during war time. In an open transmission he sent the following message which could be picked up easily by any other ships in the area. *"Transmit to Mr. Churchill. I have sunk British steamer Firby position 59' 40N 13' 50W. Save the crew if you will please. German submarine."* The message was intercepted by an American Merchant ship who in turn passed the message on which was then relayed to the Admiralty and *Firby's* crew were picked up fifteen hours later by the Royal Navy and landed at Thurso, Scotland. *Captain Thomas Prince* was to lose his life while serving as Master of the *SS Otterpool* just over eight months later when his ship was torpedoed and sunk on voyage to Middleborough from Africa.

In October 1939 *"Ropner's Navy"* was to be truly cemented into the history books. On the 6th October 1939 *SS Heronspool* left Swansea with a cargo of coal for a port on the St Lawrence and joined up with the outward bound eleven ship Convoy OB-17, which also included the Ropner ship *SS Stonepool*. Both these ships had been fitted with four inch guns on their poop deck. During the crossing due to severe bad weather *Heronspool* had lost her station in the convoy and became a straggler. By the 12th October the day the convoy was due to disperse no other ship from the convoy could be seen by the ships lookouts. Suddenly during early evening at a distance of about six miles a lookout on *Heronspool* sighted a burning ship. A closer look revealed a German U-boat was shelling a tanker, which turned out to be the French ship *SS Emile Minuet* on voyage from the West Indies to the UK. The U-boat attacking her was U-48 under the command of *Korvettenkapitan Herbert Schultze* who had sunk the *SS Firby* a month earlier. In accordance with standard procedure at the time *Captain Sidney Batson* had no choice but to turn his ship away and make her own escape and hope she had not been sighted herself. As the evening slowly drew in and darkness enveloped the sea on a moonless night, Captain Batson thought he had evaded the enemy. He was wrong. U-48 had sighted *Heronspool* long before and had been stalking the ship for a couple of hours awaiting for an opportunity to strike. At around 20.00 hours a signal light was seen flashing astern of *Heronspool* ordering the ship to heave to. *Herbert Schultze* on U-48 was once again showing compassion to his fellow seafarers hoping to avoid unnecessary bloodshed if possible. Instead Captain Batson ordered the engine room to give him every ounce of steam they could and hopefully lose the U-boat in the dead of night while at the same time ordering an SOS to be sent. Intercepting the SOS U-48 fired a shell from her deck gun only to have fire returned at her from *Heronspool's* gunners who had been on stand by all this time. Taken aback by this Schultze was forced to dive. Two hours later the U-boat resurfaced on *Heronspool's* port quarter and commenced firing once more. *Heronspool's* gunners managed to fire off a single round and the U-boat once again submerged. An hour later the same routine was repeated. Unknown to Captain Batson U-48 had also fired off four torpedoes at his ship and all had missed. Just before midnight a hugh explosion occurred just off the ships beam. A torpedo had prematurely exploded about ten yards off the ships side. U-48 again resurfaced and zig zagging across the ships stern from quarter to quarter began shelling the ship as she went, with every shot falling short of her mark as *Heronspool's* four inch gun fired off her reply, again forcing the U-boat to dive. Just after 01.00 hours the inevitable happened. U-48 had managed to get the *Heronspool* beam on through her periscope and a torpedo was fired detonating in No. 1 hold breaking the ships back. Nothing more could be done. Captain Batson rang down to the engine room finished with engines and the ship was ordered abandoned. All hands got away safely and as the sun came up on the morning of the 13th October Captain Batson and his crew watched *Heronspool* slip beneath the waves. Soon after the American passenger ship *President Harding* came across the survivors, picking them up and landing them at New York. Captain *Sidney Batson* was later awarded the OBE and gunner *George Pearson* the MBE.

SS Stonepool who had been part of the same convoy as *Heronspool* had dispersed as ordered from the convoy and was making her own way South to the Cape Verde Islands with her cargo of coal and machinery parts. About the same time as the *Heronspool* crew were being rescued a U-boat was sighted by a lookout on *Stonepool*. *Captain Albert A. White* ordered his ship to immediately alter course away from the U-boat and send an SOS. The U-boat sighted was U-42 under the command of *Korvettenkapitan Rolf Dau* who immediately opened fire. As *Stonepool's* stern swung around to face the U-boat she returned fire with her small stern mounted gun. Two shells from U-42 quickly found their mark, one smashing the port lifeboat to pieces while the other slammed into the ships hull just above the waterline. *Stonepool* continuing to return fire forced U-42 to then dive beneath the waves. Shortly afterwards the unmistakable wake of a torpedo was seen heading straight at *Stonepool* and Captain White ordered hard over just in time as the torpedo passed harmlessly close by. U-42 again surfaced and the two adversaries commenced shelling each other and a shell exploded close by *Stonepool's* other lifeboat shattering it into pieces. U-42 now began an erratic zig zagging manoeuvre across *Stonepool's* port & starboard quarter inadvertently showing her full beam to the ships gunners whose 15th round was seen to hit the side of the U-boat causing it to crash dive. Fifteen minutes late U-42 resurfaced in about the same position. On closer inspection through his binoculars Captain White could see clearly that the U-boats deck gun was hanging part way over to the side of the submarine at a strange angle and realised the shell fired from his ship had scored a direct hit on the U-boats gun platform. Slowly the U-boat began to drop astern of the ship until she disappeared from site only to reappear later about five miles off *Stonepool's* port quarter. For about an hour the U-boat steamed along keeping the ship in her sights but when the ship altered course away from it, she again disappeared over the horizon and the pursuit was finally ended. With the threat of U-42 out of the way, Captain White could now concentrate on the plight of his ship which now noticeably down by the head. The shell, which had holed the ship above the waterline, had been slowly flooding No. 1 hold, which was found to have ten foot of water in it when a sounding was taken. Volunteers entered the hold and began to dig the coal away until the hole was exposed and temporarily patched up enabling the ships pumps to clear the water away. The ships carpenter and other crewmembers began to patch the remaining damaged lifeboat in case they had to abandon ship at short notice.

Captain White decided it was too dangerous to carry on his voyage to the Cape Verde Islands and ordered the ship to return to the Bristol Channel. Shortly after swinging the ship around and setting course for home a British destroyer who had picked up *Stonepool's* SOS hove in sight and U-42's last known position was relayed between ships and the destroyer sped of to intercept. (The mist of time has clouded over what happened next to U-42. Certain reports state she was sunk by depth charges from the British destroyers *HMS Imogen* & *HMS Ilex*. Other reports state that the ship had been so badly damaged by *SS Stonepool's* action that the U-boat was unable to manoeuvre and scuttled herself as soon as the destroyers hove into sight). A few hours later one of the destroyers returned to escort *Stonepool* home with a number of German prisoners onboard from U-42 including *Korvettenkapitan Rolf Dau,* who would eventually be interned in a Canadian PoW camp. Now with her own personal escort the *Stonepool* felt relativly safe until a lookout spotted another U-boat surfacing on the port quarter at such an angle as the U-boats site was restricted and did not see the destroyer escort. The alarm was quickly raised and the destroyer sped off to engage the enemy forcing the U-boat to crash dive. (Again history is unclear as to what happened next. Claims were put forward that the U-boat was sunk, but German U-boat records show no U-boat was lost at this time or position). Two days after the U-42 incident

Stonepool again sailing alone after her escort had been obliged to leave, found herself once more at the mercy of the North Atlantic. Severe weather pounded the ship endlessly and a huge sea partially carried away the only surviving patched up lifeboat. No. 1 hold began to flood again and the pumps were kept constantly running to stem the flow of sea water. On the morning of 16th October 1939 *Stonepool* finally limped into Barry Roads and dropped anchor. Captain White was later awarded the OBE for his actions and gunner *Frederick Hayter* the BEM. Congratulations were also sent and received from the Commander in Chief of the Western Approaches on *Stonepool's* actions. *SS Stonepool's* luck would run out on the 11th September 1941 when she was torpedoed and sunk by U-207 sinking in less than three minutes with the loss forty-two crew while sailing in the sixty-four ship Convoy SC-42 which was partially decimated with the loss of sixteen merchant ships.

On the very same day *Stonepool* fought her gallant action, on the other side of the North Atlantic the Ropner ship *SS Rockpool (2)* was in trouble of her own. The ship had left Halifax, Nova Scotia with a cargo of iron ore in the ten ship homeward bound Convoy HX-4 which sailed from Halifax on the 8th October 1939. During the crossing due to trouble with her boilers she was unable to maintain the 9 knots required to keep her station in the convoy and found herself straggling the main convoy. A severe Atlantic gale was in full swing and the *Rockpool* was in danger of her cargo shifting if she held her same course as a huge sea had already partially carried away her port lifeboat. The ships Master, Captain *William H. Harland* tried to make signal contact with the Convoy Commodore ship *SS Rothermere* to ask permission to heave to until the weather subcided. Due to the severe weather and darkness this proved impossible and so for the safety of his ship and crew he hove too without permission. By doing so the crew were able to retrieve the lifeboat and secure properly. The following morning *Rockpool* was sailing alone and the rest of the convoy were no where to be seen. Bringing his ship back on course Captain Harland had no choice but sail on. By the 19th October *Rockpool* had entered the *Western Approaches* where U-boat activity was known to be rife. Around midday Captain Harland was on the bridge when he spotted the unmistakable silhouette of a U-boat and raised the alarm, ordering the ships wheel over hard to port and advising the ships Radio Officer to send an SOS. *Rockpool* had been spotted and five shells were fired at his ship in quick succession, all missing their target. *Rockpool* began to return fire and the U-boat crash dived after a third shot was fired from *Rockpool*. After a few minutes the U-boat began to resurface and was met by gunfire once more and returned fire, firing shrapnel rounds at the ship. For nearly two hours the fighting went on when Captain Harland ordered smoke floats to be thrown over the ships side with the hope of making her escape. This action proved very successful and *Rockpool* eventually arrived home safely. Captain Harland was later awarded the OBE for his actions and the ships main gunner *Tom Watkins* the BEM. Captain Harland was later informed by the Admiralty that he has caused such damage to the U-boat that it was unable to submerge and was subsequently sunk by the Royal Navy. (Again the mists of time come into play here. Although the actions of Captain Harland and his ship can be confirmed. The statement by the Admiralty that a U-boat was sunk has to be thrown into some doubt today as German records released after the war reveal no U-boats were lost on that date or in that area. This in no way should deflect against *Rockpool's* distinguished actions in the face of the emeny and in times of grave danger. Nor should the reliabilty of Admiralty be brought into question at what was a fearful time in the early days of WWII for Britain).

Far away from the sea a debate in the House of Commons on how best to operate the Merchant fleet during war time was being argued and a statement was made in regard of the vast amount of profits which would be made by shipowners unless the Ministry of Shipping was given complete control of the Merchant fleet. Listening to this, *Mr. Leonard Ropner* was instantly on his feet and sharp to the point stating. *"That in spite of the increased freight rates there was no profit and in many cases substantial and heavy losses. Long detention of ships had been experienced in every case. The convoy system effcient as it was, led to delays and voyages were taking twice as long as in normal times.* He also went on to say. *"While all these conditions existed, neutral tramp ships where being chartered by the Government at fantastically high rates of freight and that the British Mercantile Marine was in a position entirely inadequate to the needs of the nation".* He went on to pay tribute to the help given to merchant shipping by the Royal Navy and explained that two of his companies ships had been lost and two others had given such a good account of themselves that they had disabled two German submarines. His closing words gave birth to the legend of *Ropner's Navy"* when he stated *"At the Admiralty, Ropner's Navy was almost as well known as that of his Majesty's"* This last statement brought loud bursts of laughing & cheering across the house.

In the last two months of 1939 *SS Deerpool* was wrecked while trying to navigate the Humber after dark without the aid of navigation lights. Her Master had been informed U-boats were in the area and thought it safer to try bring his ship into port. *SS Willowpool* was also lost to a mine. Three ships that had been ordered by the company before the war were delivered in 1940, *SS Seapool*, SS *Wandby* & *SS Fishpool*. The life of *SS Wandby* was to be short lived as she was torpedoed and sunk returning home from her maiden voyage. *SS Fishpool* did not have much of a charmed life either. She was attacked and damaged by German aircraft on her maiden voyage with loss of life. After being repaired she was later damaged during an air raid in 1941 and was eventually blew up during another air raid in 1943. April 1940 would prove a bad month for the company. Two of their ships *SS Romanby (3)* & *SS Salmonpool* were captured by the German's during the invasion of Norway. *Romanby* would be sunk alongside the quay partially loaded with iron ore. The captured crew from *Romanby* were later force marched to the neutral border of Sweden in severe cold weather which resulted in one member of the crew suffering from frost bite. Once at the border the men were released. After spending two years as internees in Gothenburg thirteen of *Romanby's* crew including her Master *Captain Harry Nicholson* joined two Norwegian Merchant ships in an attempt to run the German blockade and try to deliver her vital cargo of special steels and ball-barings to Britian in a ten ship convoy codenamed *"Operation Performance"* which sailed on 31st March 1942. Hugging the Swedish coast within the three mile limit until such time as they thought it safe, the ships suddenly made a dash across the North Sea under the cover of a fog bank. Unfortunately the fog bank lifted and the convoy came under attack from German forces in which five ships were sunk, one scuttled, two returned to Gothenburg while the remaining two reached Britain safely. The thirteen men from *Romanby* were picked up by a German armed trawler and locked in the fish hold without food for two days until landed at Frederickshaven. They were eventually sent to the Merchant Navy prisoner of war camp *Marine Internierten Lager* (which was christened *Milag Nord* by the inhabitants) in Germany for the duration of the war until the camp was finally liberated on the 28th April 1945. *Romanby's* Captain Nicholson died in the camp in 1942. *Salmonpool* would not be returned to her owners until after the war and thirty-seven of her crew who were captured also became prisoners at *Milag Nord*. One Irish AB from *Salmonpool* was sent to camp Ilag VIII in Poland and escaped to Britain in 1942. *Salmonpool's* Master *Captain Christopher Yare* who was one of the senior officers in charge of the distribution of Red Cross food parcels at Milag was awarded the OBE after the war for his work in the camp. Although it was against the rules of the Geneva Convention to take Merchant Seamen prisoners of war because of their civilian status, the Germans realised that a short supply of qualified seamen could only help their cause. At times only the most senior Officer was taken by a U-boat, other times a full crew were taken if captured by a commerce raider. Merchant Seamen were first interned at the *Sandbostel Concentration Camp* up until 1942 when they were forced to build their own separate camp of which over 5,000 Allied Merchant Seamen were incarcerated at some point. *SS Swainby* was lost to a U-boat, *SS Hawnby* under the command of *Captain William H. Harland* was lost to a mine and *SS Haxby* was sunk by the commerce raider *Orion* in the same month. The survivors from *Haxby* were taken prisoner onboard the *Orion* and spent three month as prisoners before being rescued by the Royal Navy after they had been transferred over to a Norwegian ship which had been taken as a war prize and was intercepted while trying to make the occupied port of Bordeaux. A number of Norwegian Merchant ships that were at sea or managed to escape from Norway before the invasion and came over to Britain and were immediately taken over by the British MOS. Seven of these ships were put under Ropner management while retaining most of their own native Norwegian crews. Two would be lost during the course of the war, the others to be returned their original owners following the wars end. The two Norwegian ships lost were carrying part British crew. One of them the *SS Aust* sunk by the German raider Thor had a number of her crew held captive by the Japanese which resulted in the death of one of the British seamen. The following month Holland fell and eleven Dutch Merchant ships that had escaped or been at sea at the time were also taken over to be managed by Ropner's for the MOS. Seven of these would be lost and four handed back in 1945.

The War in May & June 1940 was going from bad to worse for Britain as the the German Blitzkreig swept across Europe and the British Expeditionary Force was being pushed back into the sea at Dunkirk. The war for Ropner's had been fairly quiet for the month of May and it was not until June 1940 when their next loss occurred with the sinking of the *SS Otterpool* on voyage from West Africa to the Tees sunk by German U-boat, U-30 commanded by *Kapitänleutnant Fritz-Julius Lemp*, the man responsible for the opening shots of WWII against the *SS Athenia*. This was followed a month later by the loss of *SS Troutpool* which had sailed from Rosario on the River Plate to the Belfast Lough with a cargo of grain without incident when she set of a German magnetic mine after her degaussing gear had been temporarily switched off while entering the Lough. The ship sank almost immediately taking eleven men with her.

The next three months would see al lull in the losses incurred by the Ropner Co. though overall Merchant shipping losses were growing at an alarming rate as the noose tightened around Britain. The pace of new ships being built compared to losses was widening at an alarming rate as shipyards struggled to breaking point to keep up with daily losses. The last five months of 1940 would see a total of 315 British Merchant ships sent to the bottom. Ropner's *SS Wandby, SS Sedgepool & SS Pikepool* would be amongst these losses, as well as the *Empire Bison & Empire Merlin* who had been renamed and placed under Ropner management. These two ships were American; both built in 1919 and purchased by the British MOS in 1940. *Empire Bison* had been under the command of *Captain William H. Harland OBE* who had been both Master of the *SS Rockpool* during an engagement with a German U-boat and Master on *SS Hawnby* when sunk was killed along with most of his crew when the *Empire Bison* went down. The German High Command had calculated that an average loss of 800,000 tons of Allied shipping per month would be enough to ensure an Axis victory by starving Britain into submission. Shipping losses to December 1940 to U-boats alone were 2,606,000 tons, and when mines, bombers, surface raiders and E-boats were included the total rose to 4,523,000 tons. Although Britain's shipyard output had been dramatically increased from the pre-war slump, their output was limited to a maximum of 1,250,000 tons per year. A further four old American Merchant ships were purchased by the MOS in 1940 and all renamed with the prefix Empire and handed to the Ropner Co. to manage.

Two months before *SS Pikepool* was lost to a mine in which she lost seventeen crew, with the survivors left adrift on a liferaft for days before rescue, *Pikepool* had been involved in the dramatic rescue of over eighty Merchant seamen from two torpedoed ships. In September 1940 *Pikepool* who was six days outward bound from the UK heading westwards intercepted radio signals that a homeward bound convoy was under attack on their designated course. The Convoy was HX-72 consisting of forty-two Merchant ships and five naval escorts, which had left Halifax, Nova Scotia on the 9th September. Over a two-day period from the 21/22 September U-boat attacks managed to sink ten British and one Norwegian Merchant ships, damaging a further three before the attack broke off from HX-72. *Pikepool* who had been picking up and listening to the unfolding nightmare almost ran into the remains of the convoy. Two of the radio messages *Pikepool* received from the *SS Blairangus* & *SS Elmbank* stated the ships were somewhere in her area. Extra lookouts were posted and her gun crew closed up for action. *Captain J. B. Atkinson* of *Pikepool* was about to break a golden rule of warfare given to ships Master's. He was going to search for and if found, pick up any survivors he could by stopping his ship in the middle of a war zone. About two hours later at daybreak *Pikepool* came across the *Blairangus* whose stern had been blown off and was only probably still afloat due to her cargo of timber giving extra buoyancy. Two lifeboats were spotted nearby and her twenty-eight survivors were picked up. Captain Atkinson even had one of the ships derricks rigged to lift the lifeboats onboard. Shortly afterwards the *Elmbank* came into site and was also seen in a state of sinking. On approaching the survivors in three lifeboats a German U-boat was sighted. Unperturbed by this Captain Atkinson manoeuvred his ship into a position as to put her stern facing the U-boat where her gun crew were awaiting to fire. The survivors totalling fifty-five men including the body of the only casualty, the ships Master *Captain*

Harold T. Phillips were quickly brought onboard and the lifeboats abandoned. *Pikepool* then made off at speed using evasive zig zagging until the U-boat disappeared over the horizon. Captain Phillips from *Elmbank* who had lost both legs in the attack was committed to the deep that evening and all the survivors were eventually landed at St. John's, Newfoundland. Ropner ship *SS Ullapool* had also been sailing home in Convoy HX-72 and arrived in port unscathed.

1941 would see no let up to Merchant shipping losses, which would include the loss of the Ropner, ships *SS Rushpool, SS Warlaby, SS Mansepool, SS Boulderpool, SS Hindpool & SS Ullapool* all within the first three months of 1941. *SS Rockpool (2)* became a constructive total loss after running aground on a voyage from St. John's, Newfoundland to the Clyde. The loss of the *SS Warlaby* epitomised just how vulnerable Merchant shipping was especially when convoy's had to sail without naval protection due to lack of escort vessels. *Warlaby* had loaded a cargo of general stores in Alexandria and was to sail to Oban, Scotland for orders in the nineteen ship unescorted Convoy SL-64S, which left Freetown on the 30th January 1941. On the morning of the 12th February a war ship suddenly appeared and sailed between the centre columns of the convoy. Thinking the ship to be the British cruiser *HMS Renown* arriving to escort the convoy home, men lined the ships rails and watched in awe at the size of the cruiser in their midst. The ship then suddenly declared herself raising the Nazi battle ensign; it was the German cruiser *Admiral Hipper* and focused her first salvo at the *Warlaby* devastating the ship at close range. When the smoke settled the *Warlaby* had already rolled over and disappeared within two minutes of the first shot being fired taking thirty-eight of her crew with her. Only two survivors were found where the ship had once been. By the time the *Admiral Hipper* had left the scene in case any distress signals had been sent, seven Merchant ships had gone to the bottom.

In the March of 1941 although Yugoslavia had joined the Axis alliance with Germany, the Yugoslav government was soon toppled by an anti-German military coup, which took place on the 25th March 1941. Germany followed this up by invading the Balkan countries of Yugoslavia and Greece in early April 1941. Once again the Merchant ships from these countries able to escape headed for Allied ports, those reaching British ports were taken over by the now formed MOWT. Thirteen of these Yugoslav ships would be put under Ropner management while retaining their native crew, five would be lost due to enemy action during the course of the war, the remainder eventually returning to their country of origin.

On the 20th March 1941 Convoy SC-26 made up of twenty-three Merchant ships and her single escort slipped into the North Atlantic bound for Liverpool and numerous other British ports. Amongst the heavy-laden ships were the Ropner ships *SS Thirlby (2)* & *SS Alderpool*. On the 1st April nearing the Western Approaches where four more naval escort ships were to meet the convoy for the last leg of the journey, U-76 had the convoy in her sites and was relaying messages for other U-boats to form a patrol line. The following evening at 23.29 hours Central European Time *(CET was used by all U-boats no matter where in the world they were. All Merchant shipping used GMT)* on the 2nd April the attack begins and the British tanker *British Reliance* is torpedoed and sunk. The attack begins in earnest and shortly after *Alderpool* laden with 7,000 tons of wheat under the command of *Captain Thomas V. Frank* is hit by a torpedo fired from U-46 and begins to settle in the water but does not sink. The attacks go on relentless over several hours and more ships are hit and sunk including the only escort vessel, *HMS Worcestershire* an *Armed Merchant Cruiser*, which is damaged by a torpedo from U-74.

The convoy is now in disarray and ships are starting to lose station and beginning to disperse on their own initiative fighting for their own survival. Just after *Alderpool* had been hit *Thirlby (2)* who was the ship directly behind her under the command of *Captain Peter E. Birch* was hit one minute later by a torpedo from U-46, but it failed to go off. Captain Birch ignoring the standing orders that no ship should stop to pick up survivors from any other torpedoed ship no matter what, did just the opposite and manoeuvred his ship and brought her to a stop to pick up *Alderpool's* crew. While doing this a German U-boat was sighted on the surface and *Thirlby* brought her stern mounted gun to bare and manoeuvred such as to leave the sinking *Alderpool* between herself and the U-boat while hauling the survivors onboard. With this done Captain Birch rang down for full ahead to make his escape just as two torpedoes passed by. Thirty-five minutes after *Alderpool* was first hit a second torpedo fired from U-73 sent her to a watery grave. *Thirlby* was now making speed in the region of twelve knots and an evasive zigzagging pattern was taken up. In just over four hours since the attack began six Merchant ships are sent to the bottom, while the only escort ship is rendered useless.

The remaining ships are running for their lives and right behind them are eight U-boats preparing to attack again. At 06.01 hours (CET) U-69 reports a torpedo hit on *Thirlby* and is seen to sink almost immediately. This is not true though, *Thirlby* may have been hit again but she certainly did not sink. Later in the afternoon of the 3rd the escorts finally arrived consisting of the destroyers *HMS Wolverine* & *HMS Havelock*, the sloop *HMS Scarborough* and the corvette *HMS Arbutus*. The convoy is still slightly scattered and U-76 sinks the Finnish Merchant ship *SS Daphne* who had tried to make a run for it on her own. Late that evening and early the following morning of the 4th April, U-94 & U-98 sink three more ships between them and U-76 sinks another but is then sunk by two of the naval escorts on the 5th April after the U -boat was caught by surprise on the surface while recharging her batteries. On the 8th April the remains of Convoy SC-26 arrived off Liverpool and *Thirlby* along with *Alderpool's* survivors headed North about for her discharge port of Hull.

On the 10th April 150 miles North-West of the Butt of Lewis, Isle of Lewis a German aircraft suddenly appeared from no where and began raking the *Thirlby* with cannon and machine gun fire causing damage to the ships bridge. A stick of two bombs were dropped but both missed their target with *Thirlby* returning fire with her Hotchkiss 13.2mm anti-aircraft gun. The plane came around for a second attack and a stick of two bombs were dropped with one finding its mark hitting the forward well deck, blowing the foremast away and damaging the bridge. A third attack saw a direct hit on the ships fo'c'sle. Captain Birch ordered his ship abandoned in the hope the bomber would then think the ship was about to sink and leave without any further attacks. Whether this ruse worked or not is not truly known, but on circling the ship one more time the bomber flew off. A short time later the ship was re-boarded and although on fire and number one hold taking in seawater through the ships side where her steel plates had split, it seemed possible to Captain Birch she may stay afloat. The fire was brought under control and the ships side patched up. Thing were looking up when all of a sudden the German bomber again reappeared and Captain Birch ordered his crew back into their lifeboats. Passing over the ship one last time the bomber flew off and did not return. To be on the safe side the men stayed in the lifeboats for a further hour until they were sure the plane would not return. With the weather now turning rough the ship was re-boarded once more and nearly five hours after the first attack *Thirlby* had ceased to take on water and was in a fairly stable condition. At 14.45 Captain Birch ordered the lifeboats be raised back into their davits and he would attempt to make port under their own steam. As the weather began to worsen the ship could only manage to make a speed of around five knots but the following day limped into Loch Ewe where she received temporary repairs before sailing to the Clyde for a full refit. Despite everything the ship had been through only two of *Thirlby's* crew were killed. This would not be last action seen by the *Thirlby*.

The next ships to be sent to the bottom were the *SS Somersby* sunk after becoming a straggler from her convoy; *SS Ainderby* which had survived the terrible Atlantic storm of 1934 was lost on the return leg of her voyage sailing

27

alone and unprotected heavy laden with iron ore and *SS Swiftpool* also laden with iron ore for the steel works on the River Tees sank like a stone after being torpedoed taking all but two of her crew with her. *SS Clearpool* was also damaged by German aircraft and was eventually brought safely in tow into the River Tees the day after the attack.

On the 28th June 1941 *SS Rudby* sailed from Methil Roads in ballast in a coastal convoy and was routed to Oban for further instructions. The following day in foggy conditions the convoy Commodore ship signalled for an emergency turn to be executed. *SS Rudby* blew her whistle to indicate to the ship directly behind her that she was about do a 180 degree turn. When the turn had been almost completed it was seen through the fog that another ship *SS Yorkwood* (Constantine SS Line Ltd) was on a collision course and both ships collided off their starboard bows. *SS Rudby's* own anchor tore through her crew forward accommodation crushing three men to death in an instant. One crewmember *Henry Wharton* was pulled from the wreckage and was transferred to a destroyer for medical treatment where he unfortunately died from his injuries and was buried at sea. The ship was then rerouted to Aberdeen where two of the bodies were returned home for burial, the other being buried at sea.

The end of November 1941 would see the last Ropner ship sunk that year in *SS Ashby (2)*. The *Ashby* was unlucky enough to find herself left behind her convoy due to engine trouble. The ship had sailed from Middlesbrough up to Oban, Scotland and had joined up with a Freetown bound convoy with orders to sail to the African port of Pepel to load a cargo of iron ore. Apart from tankers the ore carriers were the next most vulnerable type of Merchant ship to be in. The sheer weight and density of iron ore and the known fact it's habit of shifting in bad weather had caused the loss of many a ship without the threat of enemy attack, which could cause a ship to sink within seconds rather than minutes if hit by a bomb or torpedo. The ship was in ballast outward bound, which gave the crew a feeling of less apprehension for this part of the voyage for the time being anyhow. Eleven days out of Liverpool the *Ashby* suddenly developed engine trouble and was forced to stop. The rest of the convoy had no choice but to sail on, but luckily the convoy was fairly well escorted and a British destroyer had been ordered to stay with *Ashby* while undertaking her repairs. As the destroyer steamed around to perform a defensive screen the men on the *Ashby* worked frantically to get her engine working. After six hours the ship was still dead in the water and the destroyer signalled she could no longer stay and bid the *Ashby* "good luck" as she steamed off at full speed to catch the rest of the convoy up. Throughout the night the ships engineers carried on repairs until finally the following morning

28

the ship was again under way at her top speed of nine knots. With no chance of catching the convoy up the *Ashby* proceeded alone and vulnerable. Suddenly without warning a huge resounding crack echoed throughout the ship lifting the boilers from their bedding. The *Ashby* had been struck aft by a torpedo blowing the ships stern completely off and she was going down fast. The men below in the engine room who had survived the initial explosion raced up the flights of steps onto the main deck, which was already ankle deep in water. There was nothing to do but go over the side. *Bill Linskey*, one of the ships firemen who had been in the engine room with his friend *Joe Beck* stood on the handrail and stepped into the sea calling for his friend Joe to follow. Joe did not move, he was rooted to the spot with fear and could only shout out to Bill that he could not swim. In the panic to get out of the engine room no one was wearing a life jacket. As Bill swam away he turned and saw Joe who was now up to his chest in water and still had not moved. Continuing to swim away the next time he turned around Joe and the main part of the ship had gone and he watched the poop deck disappear below the sea. The sinking had taken only two minutes from the first impact of the torpedo. Bill recounts for a few seconds there was silence then he was sucked into a whirlpool and was being dragged down with the ship unable to do anything. Then the ships boilers exploded propelling him away from the danger zone. Dazed and surrounded by falling debris and narrowly missed by one of the ships hatch-boards, which he now desperately clung to. Due to the sea swell Bill could see nothing but could hear the desperate cries of other men in the water around him. As he rose and fell with each swell amazingly he sighted a lifeboat some distance off. Two of the *Ashby's* crew had taken an axe to one of the boats davits releasing the lifeboat, which floated free as the ship went down. The boat was desperately going around pulling men from the water and after what seemed like an eternity Bill was hauled aboard. Only two more men were picked after Bill and then the sharks arrived in a feeding frenzy.

When a final head count of survivors was taken it revealed the ships Master, *Captain Tom Valentine Frank OBE*, eleven crew and five DEMS gunners were missing which included all the ships Engineers who had taken the brunt of the torpedo impact. The sharks had soon taken anyone else that was left. The ships Chief Officer, *Lancelot Henderson* being the most senior surviving officer in the boat, which included seven crew under the age of eighteen, took control of the boat and stock of their situation, finding most of the lifeboat stores had been lost during the launching including the compass. Dropping the boats sea anchor it was decided to sit tight until the weather died down and the Chief Officer had chance to take a bearing by the stars during the night. Most of the men in the boat although suffering from shock were in fairly good shape though the ships Carpenter had lost a finger. During the night one of the ship's Radio Officers had to be restrained. He was severely traumatised as he had stayed at his radio sending an SOS as the ship went down. He had still been onboard the ship as it slipped beneath the waves and was only hurled to the surface when the ship's boilers exploded. The men in the boat made him as comfortable as possible by huddling together and letting him lie down in the bottom of the boat. The following morning the Chief Officer explained he would try to hit the Azores by dead reckoning using the sun and stars to plot his course. If he got it wrong and they missed the Azores, there were another thousand miles of ocean to cross before reaching the coast of Africa. The following morning course was set and the first of the meagre rations were dispensed. To keep their spirits up the men sang songs and asked quiz questions amongst themselves. It was during these questions that the ships Cook *William Humble* raised the point which not all the men in the boat were aware of in the fact that once the ship had been sunk, all pay was stopped. This caused many an argument, which only ceased when the Chief Officer reluctantly nodded in agreement when the question was put to him. Their minds were soon distracted away from this as the sharks had returned. Several sharks circled the boat in curiosity but after a while swam away. One day their hopes were suddenly raised as far off in the distant the outline of a ship could be seen. Shouting and waving to attract the attention of their would be rescuers, their hearts sank as the ship slowly disappeared over the horizon. Later that day someone said they could see land ahead and what looked like a shoreline. Chief Officer Henderson knew better, he knew there was no land to where their position was and explained what they could see was merely a cloud formation, which was later to proved correct. On the fifth day land was spotted in the distance. It turned out to be the mountainous Island of Pico in the Azores, but with the mountain having an elevation of 7,713 feet above sea level it was a lot further away than they realised and it would still take another two days to reach. During the sixth night a brightly lit ship was seen which had to represent a neutral ship in these waters, so flares were fired only to cause he ship to black her lights out totally and ignore them. It turned out later to be a local ferry running between the Azores, Madeira & Portugal. The ferry Captain with a full compliment of passengers at the time did not want to put his ship or passengers in danger as these were perilous times for all ships so had his ship blacked out and carried on his course, though he had radioed the lifeboats position. On the seventh day exhausted through the searing heat and lack of sufficient food and water, the men in the boat could see hundreds of people lining the cliff tops and two longboats heading their way. They were now safe after seven days adrift. *Bill Linskey* survived the war and would later write a book about his war experiences called *"No Longer Required"* (ISBN 0953728501), the ships cook *William Humble* did not survive and was lost at sea when his ship the *SS Newton Ash* was torpedoed and sunk in 1943.

During 1941 a further eight Empire built ships were put under the Ropner management. 1941 would also see a major turning point in the war at sea. On 9th May 1941 U-110 under the command of *Fritz J Lemp* (Athenia & Otterpool sinking), attacked a convoy along with U-201. After being spotted by the convoy escort ships *HMS Aubretia*, *HMS Bulldog*, and *HMS Broadway*, U-110 was forced to the surface after depth charges were dropped. Believing he was about to be rammed Lemp ordered his U-boat to be abandoned. At the very last moment *HMS Bulldog* turned to evade the collision when her Commander realized he could capture the U-boat. The story goes that Lemp dove into the sea and tried to board his vessel to scuttle her, and was subsequently shot and drowned. On board U-110 was the latest German Enigma machine used to send and receive coded messages. With this the British could now decipher all messages and warn of impending U-boat positions and attacks. Over a long period of time this would be very effective to the Allied war cause, but not so much noticed by the men at sea as 1942 continued to see a devastation on merchant shipping and men, which would see a Ropner ship lost on average one every four weeks.

In 1942 ten Empire ships and two Canadian built Fort boats were put under the Ropner management. The first loss of 1942 was the *SS Thirlby (2)* who having survived two previous attacks in 1941 was sunk by a U-boat on the 23rd January 1942 killing three crew. The ship had been under the command of *Captain Peter E. Birch* who had been Master during her previous exploits. After her previous attack by German aircraft *Thirlby (2)* had been fitted with the Mark III Holman Projector. This was a crude form of mortar, which propelled a hand grenade using compressed air or steam at low flying attacking enemy aircraft and could reach a height of 600 to 650 feet. It had been successfully used in driving off a German Focke-Wulf Condor aircraft. When practising the use of the Holman Projector, grenades were substituted for potatoes to save ammunition. They were also quite dangerous to the men firing these contraptions when not enough steam pressure was built up and in one incident Middlesbrough *Captain Henry Crackles* (Buried in Middlesbrough's Linthorpe Road Cemetery) was mortally wounded in such an incident. At the time of *Thirlby's* loss she had left her convoy for the last part of her voyage when torpedoed. The next to go was the *SS Carperby*. The ship had detached from her convoy and was sailing independently to South America when she was intercepted by a German U-boat and sunk with the loss of all forty-one crew and her compliment of 6 DEMS gunners. April 1942 would see the first of five of the Empire ships under Ropner management lost that year as well as the *Empire Moonrise* which was damaged by enemy aircraft after arriving at Colombo. The *Empire Starlight* had been built the previous year in Hong Kong for the MOWT and handed over to the Ropner management. Her Master, *Captain William H. Stein* a local West Hartlepool man was given command of the ship which had a compliment of fourteen British officers, twelve DEMS gunners and fifty-one Hong Kong Chinese crew. Having loaded a cargo of Hurricane fighters and military trucks the ship was ordered to Loch Ewe, Scotland to await orders. When they came Captain Stein found his ship had been assigned to the Russian Convoys and was ordered to sail from Loch Ewe on the 10th March 1942 for Reykjavik, Iceland where he would join up with the rest of Convoy PQ-13 bound for Murmansk. Departing Reykjavik on the 20th March a gale blew up on the first night and the convoy was having trouble keeping all the ships in station hampered further by frequent snow squalls. The weather worsened and a full Arctic storm erupted. With this type of weather the ships were in no danger of enemy attack, but due to the ships and deck cargo icing up the possibility of the merchantmen simply capsizing was just as big a danger. By the third day out the weather eased slightly and *Empire Starlight* found herself in a small convoy of seven ships as to the twenty merchant ships that started out, but now these ships had no escort and with the weather improving by the hour the possibility of attack from below and the air was imminent, and sure enough the same morning the scattered convoy came under its first air attack. Worse was to come as the ships closest the *Empire Starlight* became trapped in pack ice unable to move. Without a second thought for the safety of his own ship Captain Stein ordered full ahead and for the next four hours ground his way through the ice pack cutting channels to free the trapped ships. Once this was done he manoeuvred his own ship into open waters, but now found his ship was now all alone. Captain Stein decided his best option was to continue on his own and the ship arrived in Murmansk two days later on the 27th March seven days after leaving Reykjavik. Slowly but surely the remaining ships from PQ-13 slowly entered Murmansk though five had not made it and were sunk from a combination of U-boat, air attack and German destroyers. The ordeal for the *Empire Starlight* and the other ships was far from over as the German airbase at *Petsamo, Finland* was only fifty mile away and the attacks started almost immediately the ship was along side. During the first attack the *Empire Starlight* suffered slight damage from a near miss causing leaks in her engine room plating. The attacks continued relentlessly some times as many as four of five a day. During one of these raids a 500lb bomb exploded in the ships No. 1 hold causing a fire in No. 2 hold, killing a number of Russian dock workers and destroying part of the ship valuable cargo. Once the fires had been brought under control it was decided to move the ship to a safer anchorage up river. This made little difference as wave after wave of enemy bombers continued their destruction of the port. The *Empire Starlight* again seemed to be the central focus of the attacks and again she was damaged by near misses. The attacks had now been continuous for three weeks as the ship slowly unloaded her cargo. She was also fighting back and her DEMS gun crew managed to shoot down three enemy bombers. The Germans seemed to have had enough and the attacks ceased up to the end of April only to begin again on the 4th May and continue none stop for two weeks. Once again leaking badly from so many near misses the *Empire Starlight* was moved to shallow water in case she finally sank and still the bombers came. Eventually suffering from four more hits the ship finally settled on the bottom on June 1st 1942 after nearly eight weeks of constant bombardment. Miraculously only one crew member was killed and he had been ashore taking refuge in an air raid shelter, which had received a direct hit on the 15th April. His body was later recovered and he was buried in the Murmansk Russian Cemetery. Captain Stein and his crew were eventually repatriated and in January 1943 Captain Stein and his Chief Engineer were awarded the OBE.

Around the same time of *Empire Starlight* incident, the Ropner ship *SS Kirkpool* under the command of *Captain Albert Kennington* had dispersed from the Freetown bound Convoy OS-19 and was making her way independently to Lourenco Marques, Mozambique to load a cargo of iron ore for the UK via a brief stop off in Cape Town. A couple of days out of Cape Town the distinctive shape of a periscope was spotted by one of the ships lookouts. *Kirkpool* was equipped with a stern mounted 4 inch gun and unusually for a merchant ship, three depth charges. The U-boat quickly crash dived and no further echo soundings were picked up so *Kirkpool* proceeded without further incident. On reaching Cape Town the ships orders were changed and she was ordered to Durban where she would pick up a cargo of coal for Montevideo. With her cargo fully loaded the ship was underway by the 31st March and was to proceed to Uruguay sailing independently and without escort with only a four inch deck gun as her main armament. Ten days out the *Kirkpool* slowly edged her way across the South Atlantic unbeknown just over the horizon and out of sight the ships lookouts she was being monitored by radar from the German commerce raider *Thor*. On the same evening of the 10th April *Kirkpool* was suddenly rocked by a huge explosion as a 5.9-inch shell from one of the *Thor's* six main guns slammed into the ship. All hell broke loose as round after round impacted into the ship hull and accommodation. After only eleven minutes the ship was ablaze from stem to stern and going down by the head. *Kirkpool's* gun crew had not even time to man their own gun when the order to abandon ship was given. Even as the crew were abandoning ship *Thor* continued to pour shells into the hapless ship as well as raking the ships boat deck with machine gun fire. On the aft well deck the DEMS gunners were pinned down taking cover from the shelling and machine gun fire and could see no way of escape. Captain Kennington on seeing the plight of the gunners went to the fo'csle head with a number of crew members, releasing a cargo net containing buoyant material which floated down the port side of the ship enabling the gunners to jump overboard an cling to it while at the same time carrying them away from the burning wreck. Once the shelling had subsided *Thor* then went around pulling the survivors from the water for the next three and a half hours. The survivors were eventually transferred to the German supply ship *Regenburg* and then onto the German ship *Dresden*. Sailing in an Easterly direction and after a short stop off at Borneo, Java & Sumatra, the prisoners worst fears were confirmed, they were on their way to Japan and were officially handed over to the Japanese authorities over four months after being first sunk. Here the prisoners were split up and a number of *Kirkpool's* crew including Captain Kennington were transported to the *No.1 Camp Kawasaki* at Yokohama near Tokyo where they would spend the next three years as forced labourers. Captain Kennington would not survive and he would die on the 14th March 1944. Official records state his cause of death was from pneumonia having succumbed at the *Shinigawa Hospital*, Tokyo. He is now interned at the Yokohama War Cemetery. Official documents also show an Indian Fireman & Trimmer named *Eboe Ullah* from *Kirkpool* died at Kawasaki on the 21st April 1945. He became sick and refused all food and died from the effects and was later buried in the Indian section of the Yokohama War Cemetery.

June 1942 would reach the second highest peak in regard to Merchant shipping losses with the loss of 190 British, Allied and neutral ships of 843,455grt, ironically not one Ropner ship was amongst them. *SS Empire Dryden* had been lost in April 1942 ten days after the *Kirkpool,* while May & June saw a respite for the fleet losses. This was short lived as *SS Empire Rainbow* outward bound from the UK to Halifax, Nova Scotia was sunk on the 26th July 1942 after only being launched the previous year. This was *Captain John Kenny's* fourth ship sunk from under him, but luckily he and all his crew were rescued by two naval escorts 300 miles East of Race and landed safely in Canada. On the 4th August the *Empire Arnold* was intercepted and sunk by a U-boat after dispersing from her convoy. Her Master *Captain Frederick Tate* although wounded was taken from his lifeboat by the Germans as a prisoner of war and was eventually sent to *Milag Nord*. Nine of his crew perished. Also lost in July was the former Ropner managed ship *Empire Johnson* which had been handed over the Dutch Government and renamed *Paulus Potter* and was one of the ships lost from the infamous Russian Convoy PQ-17, which was abandoned by her escorts on orders from *Admiral Dudley Pound* at the Admiralty, which saw twenty-four of the thirty-five Merchant ships decimated by Luftwaffe & U-boat attacks from the 4th to 10th July 1942.

Four days after the loss of the *Empire Arnold* another Ropner managed ship *Empire Moonbeam* was involved in a bizarre incident while crossing the North Atlantic. *Empire Moonbeam* had left Sydney, Cape Breton in the thirty-six ship Liverpool bound Convoy SC-94 on the 31st July 1942, which was accompanied by six naval escorts. On the 5th August part of the convoy is sighted by U-593 consisting of six ships and two escorts which have romped away from the main convoy because of fog. The U-593 attacks and manages to sink a small Dutch steamer before being chased off by the escorts. A total of seventeen U-boats now descend upon the convoy and on the 8th August all hell breaks loose. In less than two hours five merchantmen had been sent to the bottom in two separate attacks. In the second attack three ships were simultaneously hit and is possibly what caused the following incident. Three ships which had not been hit suddenly began to be abandoned by their crew in the sheer terror and confusion going on around them, one of the ships being abandoned was *Empire Moonbeam*. After sometime two of the ships including *Empire Moonbeam's* crew were persuaded to re-board their vessels, unfortunately not before the sea had taken seven of her crew to a watery grave. The attack was eventually called off on the 10th August with eleven ships sunk and a further two damaged, with the convoy reaching port three days later. One explanation given by the Second Officer of another ship in the convoy who was on watch at the time may explain what caused the men to abandon ship. At the time he recalls his own ship being hit by a resounding thump causing the ship to heave over. Believing his own ship had been torpedoed (of which he had previous experience), he was surprised to see after inspection the ship had not been hit, but the crew also believing they had been torpedoed were preparing to release their own lifeboats and were subsequently ordered to secure the boats. It is believed that what all the ships may have felt had been caused by a huge underwater explosion from one of the munitions ships cargoes which had been already been torpedoed, exploding under water. The *Empire Moonbeam* was lost on her very next voyage just over a month after the above incident.

On the 20th September *SS Reedpool* was intercepted by a U-boat 240 miles South-East of Trinidad and sunk. Her Master *Captain William J. Downs* was taken prisoner and landed in France two month later and interned at *Milag Nord*. The first week of November 1942 would see the last two company losses that year in the sinking of *SS Daleby* torpedoed off Cape Farewell, fortunately without loss of life. Three days later *SS Roxby* outward bound for Canada was torpedoed and sunk taking her Captain and thirty-three of her crew with her. November 1942 recorded the highest tonnage loss for the whole of WWII with Merchant shipping losses recorded at 136 ships for 848,129grt sent to the bottom.

1943 would see a further four Empire ships join the Ropner fleet as well as seven Canadian built Liberty ships with the prefix Fort added. One of these Empire ships handed over to Ropner's was *Empire Tide* who had originally been managed by Royal Mail Lines for the MOWT and had been one of the few ship to survive Convoy PQ-17. The war was now definitely going in favour of the Allies as greater convoy protection had grown; radar detection and code breaking had steadily eased the plight of the merchantmen and subdued the U-boat menace. However none of this would help the next Ropner loss in *SS Lackenby*. The ship had left New York in the homeward-bound twenty-one ship Convoy SC-117 on the 12th January 1943. Sometime during the crossing the ship became detached from the main convoy and found herself a straggler and totally unprotected. Thirteen days after leaving New York *Lackenby* was intercepted by U-624 South of Cape Farewell and hit by two torpedoes and sunk. It is not known how many survived the actual sinking, but her Master *Captain William Arthur Allon MBE* and all forty-three men onboard were never seen again.

It would be several months before the next Ropner ship was lost and a major turning point in the *"Battle of the Atlantic"* was about to take place in the outward bound Convoy ONS-5 in April and May of 1943 which included the Ropner ship *SS Yearby*. The convoy mostly made up of ships in ballast formed up on the 21st April 1943 and headed out into the North Atlantic. The convoy and her escorts were ordered to take a Northerly course in order to keep the convoys air escort as long as possible which were using Allied air bases in Iceland. Recent codes deciphered by the British would also direct the ships away from known U-boat activity elsewhere. However on the 25th April the Germans suddenly changed their codes and a temporary black out occurred leaving the British Admiralty virtually blind to all German U-boat movements. During this black out a number of U-boats had formed up a patrol line in what they expected was a Westerly bound convoy heading their way. This movement was not detected by the British to reroute the convoy and ONS-5 is heading straight into the path of the U-boats. On the 28th April the convoy is sighted by U-650 and the information relayed to the German BdU (BdU was the German U-boat Operational Dept.). In total four wolfpacks consisting of some forty-one U-boats are directed to engage the convoy. Some of the convoy escorts are fitted with HF/DF (High Frequency Direction Finder) commonly known as Huff Duff and are picking up signals between the U-boats and are now well aware of an impending attack. On the evening of the 28th an unsuccessful attack is made on the convoy and the escorts damage two U-boats who are forced to return to port. The following day an American Merchant ship is lost.

The weather began to deteriorate making it almost impossible for the U-boats to attack but this also affects the convoy as her escorts can no longer refuel at sea and the convoy is beginning to break up into smaller groups. The *Yearby* finds herself in one of these small groups made up of five ships. The next sinking occurs on the 4th May when a lone British straggler is lost. By the 5th May the U-boats finally penetrate the protective screen of the convoy and manoeuvre between the columns of ships and the devastation begins in earnest. By the end of the day eight British, two American and one Norwegian are sunk with the loss of over one hundred and thirty men. The *Yearby* was lucky to have fallen out of the main convoy when she did. The *Yearby* had originally been stationed as the first ship in the tenth column when the convoy first left port. The Merchant ships that had been on either side of her as well as the ship directly astern of her were all lost in the attack. The remainder of the convoy now runs into a fog bank, but with the aid of new radar fitted to the escort ships they easily detect the U-boat movements and repel a further twenty-five attacks and the following morning begin to drive off the U-boats as further escorts arrive at the scene. The BdU finally call off the attack when they find six U-boats have been sunk with a further seven so badly damaged they were unable to continue in the engagement. Over the next week the surviving Merchant ships sailed into Halifax, Nova Scotia, with the *Yearby* arriving in port on the 9th May along with three other stragglers and her escort *HMS Pink*. Back at the BdU *Admiral Karl Dönitz* finally had to recognize defeat was inevitable and on the 23rd May 1943 he halted all convoy operations and recalled his U-boats from the North Atlantic convoy routes as no further successful attack on any convoy in following three weeks took place while still continuing to suffer severe losses amongst his U-boats. It was later stated by *Winston Churchill* that *"The Battle of the Atlantic was the only thing that really frightened me."* Merchant shipping would continue to be lost to U-boats right up to the final day of the war in Europe though never to the alarming rate prior to May 1943.

On the night of 9/10 July 1943, an Allied armada of over 2,500 US, Royal & Merchant Navy vessels launched one of the largest combined operations of World War II, the invasion of Sicily in *"Operation Husky"*. Over the next thirty-eight days, half a million Allied soldiers, sailors, and airmen fought against their German and Italian counterparts for control of this small rocky Island of Hitler's *"Fortress Europe."* Amongst them were the next two Ropner ships to be sunk. *Fort Pelly* who had been delivered to the MOWT on the Bareboat Charter and handed over to the Ropner Co. as managers in August

1942 left Alexandria four days before the invasion with a volatile cargo including ammunition and cased petrol, arriving to discharge her valuable cargo in the seized harbour at Port Augusta on the 18th July. Two days later the German Luftwaffe counter-attacked the ports of Augusta & Syracuse relentlessly for a week and on the early morning of the 20th July German Heinkel 111's supported by Italian SM79 heavy bombers attacked and found their mark on *Fort Pelly*. Two direct hits, one in number five hold detonating the contents of the ships hold demolishing the whole aft section including the crew accommodation, the other exploding in the engine room killing all the engineers and a number of the ships Firemen & Greasers. When the planes left the ship had sunk in the dock and thirty-eight men onboard lay dead, one of them being a first trip Deck Apprentice who had not long since celebrated his seventeenth birthday. A further nine men were injured, the most serious being a sixteen year old first trip Deck Apprentice named *Geoff Morton* who suffered a double skull fracture and a perforated knee. The injured were eventually shipped to Tripoli and on to Algiers before returning home. Four days later the *SS Fishpool* entered the harbour at Syracuse loaded with a cargo of petrol and ammunition and was given the berth where the Ropner managed ship *Fort George* had successfully discharged her cargo during the air raids for which her Master, Captain *Clifford H. Churchill* was later mentioned in dispatches. Captain Churchill had always considered himself a lucky man during the war as he had already survived sixteen North Atlantic convoy crossings. His luck was to stay with him, as the berth he left now occupied by *Fishpool* became the focus of an air attack on the morning of the 26th July by German JU-88's & FW-190's attacking the port in two waves. *Fishpool* received a direct hit amidships causing a fire amongst the drums of petrol and ammunition. This was soon followed by a further two direct hits igniting the cargo blowing the ship to pieces. Amazingly eighteen of her crew survived. These would be the only two Ropner ships lost in 1943.

The constant threat of an attack was a stress and fear known only to those who have lived through it, though this was not the only enemy to be feared by those at sea. The sea itself is unforgiving and as deadly as any torpedo or bomb and will show no mercy. This combination of severe stress and gale lashed seas would have devastating consequences for three of the crew from the Ropner ship *Empire Trent*.

On the 13th July 1943 *Empire Trent* having loaded a cargo of iron ore in Pepel left Freetown in the homeward bound Convoy SL-133 with orders to sail to Loch Ewe to await further orders. The *Empire Trent* had originally been built as the Ropner ship *SS Rockpool* and had ran aground on the Clyde back in 1941 and was abandoned as a total loss. The ship was later re-floated and repaired by the MOWT and placed back under Ropner management on their behalf. Convoy SL-133 rendezvous with Convoy MKS-18 for the last leg of the journey which sees only one Merchant ship damaged by a U-boat.

By the 31st July the convoy is encountering severe North Atlantic weather and heavy seas and the *Empire Trent* is only making speed of three knots. Constant heavy seas are sweeping and rolling over the forecastle head causing constant flooding within the forward crew accommodation. At 18.00, the Captain orders all crew to make their way aft amidships and to stay under cover until the weather subsides. At 18.30 as the crew struggle along the rolling deck of their ship a huge sea swamps the ship and the ships Carpenter *William Byrne* is seen from the bridge to be carried away and over the ships side. Desperate attempts were made by throwing life buoys and lifebelts overboard and the ships Third Mate launched the Starboard liferaft all to no avail and within second the sea had claimed another victim. He is reported in the ships Log Book as lost in position 50' 54N 15' 15W.

On the evening 4th August 1943 *Empire Trent* arrives safely in Loch Ewe where upon a doctor is summoned to the ship as it would seem a couple of crew members are suffering from Malaria and the Chief Engineer is found in a confused state talking incoherently. He is diagnosed as suffering from "nervous exhaustion" and would die five days later. One of the crewmen being treated for malaria died on the 6th August from heart failure. Both these men were buried ashore and granted full war grave status; *William Byrne* was not and has been forgotten (until now!). (A HMSO study of 1955 *"Merchant Shipping & the Demands of War"* states that as many as 11,600 Merchant Seamen between 1942-1944 died shortly after leaving their ship, or whose lives were permanently damaged, either physically or mentally. The vast majority of those who died were never registered with CWGC or granted war grave status).

1944, the German's were retreating on all fronts and only sinking on average one Merchant ship a day over any given month. One more Empire ship is handed over to Ropner's by the MOWT plus five American liberty ships with the prefix SAM (Structure Aft of Midships) are placed under their management. Two of these SAM boats would be the last casualties of Ropner's wartime escapades. *Samsylarna* had loaded a cargo of general stores and explosives in Baltimore & New York for ports in Bombay, Colombo & Calcutta via the Mediterranean. After an uneventful crossing of the North Atlantic the ship made her way through the Bay of Biscay and through the Strait of Gibraltar into the Mediterranean. On the 4th August 1944 off North Africa the ship was hit by a German aerial torpedo, which blew most of the ships stern off flooding the engine room through the propeller shaft and opening No.5 hatch up to the incoming sea. Her Master *Captain William G.S. Hewison* who had earlier survived the sinkings of the *SS Kirkby* in WWI plus *SS Rushpool* in 1941 & *Empire Moonbeam* in 1942, ordered his ship abandoned as the after deck became awash. After a while the ship settled in the water and Captain Hewison decided to re-board the ship where assistance was called for. The ship was eventually beached off Benghazi where she was partially discharged and patched up enough to be towed to Alexandria where she remained until the end of the war. For saving the ship and her valuable cargo Captain Hewison was awarded the OBE and his Chief Engineer received a commendation.

Captain *Clifford H. Churchill* who had a lucky escape at Sicily on the *Fort George* in 1943 now found himself in command of the Ropner managed ship *Samsuva* in late 1944. The ship had arrived safely in the Kola Inlet on her first Russian Convoy JW-59 discharging her war stores and then loading up a cargo of pit props for the return journey to Loch Ewe in Convoy RA-60, which sailed from Russia on the 28th September 1944. The following day the convoy is sighted by U-310 who fires a spread of torpedoes into the convoy hitting an American Merchant ship in front of the *Samsuva*, who is then hit in the engine room killing three crew and injuring a number of others. Abandoning ship, Captain Churchill, thirty-six crew and twenty gunners were picked up by the *Convoy Rescue Ship Rathlin* and later landed in the Clyde. *Samsuva* stubbornly refused to sink and it was decided that she would be sunk by part of the naval escort to prevent capture or cause a hazard to shipping. *HMS Bulldog* & *HMS Musketeer* dually sent her to the bottom.

The war in Europe would continue for another eight months and a further one hundred and seventy British, Allied and neutral Merchant ships would be lost before the very last ship *SS Avondale Park* being the last casualty of the war in Europe sunk by U-2336 on the 7th May 1945 who stated he had not received the surrender signal sent by *Dönitz* days earlier.

It was now time for Ropner's to count the cost of nearly six years of war. Thirty-three ships belonging to the Ropner & Pool Shipping Co. lost as well as numerous others ships under their management sunk. Over 650 men including seventeen ships Masters dead and hundreds of others injured, maimed and scarred for life, both physically and mentally. The men of *"Ropner's Navy"* had certainly done "their bit". During those war years no less than 13 OBE's, 3 British Empire Medals & 2 Lloyds War Medals were awarded to the Officers & crew of the Ropner fleet. The original company ships, which survived the war, were *Bridgepool Cragpool, Drakepool,*

40

Gullpool, Seapool, Stagpool, Wearpool, Danby, Domby, Moorby and *Yearby*. *SS Stagpool's* war service is well due an extra mention. The ship had left the UK in October 1940 after being converted into a water distilling ship to supply the Royal Navy in the Middle East. The ship would not return home for six years, steaming over 200,000 miles replenishing her Royal Navy counterparts and was affectionately known as *Gunga Din* after Rudyard Kipling's water carrier character from the poem of the same name.

On the 8th June 1946, just over one year after the end of the war in Europe, Britain held a national Victory Parade in London in which three of Ropner's Senior Officers were in attendance to represent the Co. as well as an apprentice chosen from the Co. to act as a Standard Bearer for the Merchant Navy contingent.

Once again it was time for Ropner's to begin rebuilding its fleet. This was initially done by purchasing some of the ships the Co. had managed for the MOWT as well as leasing other ships from the *Bareboat Charter* on a five-year time charter with the option to purchase at a later time in the future. A number of changes began to take place in the post-war period, firstly by moving from the temporary office at Sedgefield to a permanent office at Greylands situated on Coniscliffe Road, Darlington. A new colour scheme of green replaced the original black hull and funnel as well as the drab wartime grey. The Co. house flag of red and white checks with the logo R. R. & Co. which occupied the four corners of the flag were removed and later replaced by the family coat of arms consisting of a black and yellow shield with three stars and three stags heads within the shield. During 1946 the biggest change came when the Co. decided to break into the passenger/cargo liner service between Europe and the US Gulf of Mexico and so was born the Ropner Line, which was to be run by *Robert Ropner* with the help of a Mr. Bill Gidley from the Company London Office, while Jock would concentrate on the tramp shipping operations. The first of these new ships *Daleby (3)* would be launched in 1950, followed by four more *Deerpool (2), Somersby (3), Swiftpool (2) & Troutpool (3)* over the coming years.

On the 17th March 1947 age 82 *William Ropner*, senior director of the Co. passed away after more than fifty years service to the family business. Like his father before him he had been an astute businessman whose other achievements included membership and eventually becoming Chairman of the Hartlepool Port & Harbour Commission as well as duties as a County Magistrate. He was also President of the Hartlepool Crippled Children's League for whom he bought and furnished property in Elswick where local children in the area could be sent for holidays.

William's oldest son *Sir Leonard Ropner* (later to become Baronet in 1952) took over as senior director. 1947 would also see William's second son *William Guy Ropner* knighted as well as the first of the fourth generation of the family to join the company with the appointment of *David Ropner* who was later joined in 1952 by *Jeremy V. Ropner* another of the fourth generation to enter the firm. With the death of *William Ropner* brought the family heavy estate duties, which left the company little choice but to seek a quotation on the stock market to form a public holding company. In December 1948 the *Ropner Holding Ltd* was registered to acquire the shares from both the Ropner & Pool companies and kept the same directors as the parent managing company of *Sir R. Ropner Co.* This way the company remained a private company having a management agreement with the public company. In 1950 the name of the management company was changed to *Sir R. Ropner & Co. Management Ltd.*

The 1950's unbeknown at the time were probably the beginning of the end of the British registered fleet of the Merchant Navy. Between 1939-1950 the British tramp fleet had reduced by some 600.000grt and dramatically dropped by another 400.000grt between 1950-1952. The valuation of ships decreased dramatically possibly due to the excess amount of Liberty ships built during the war years, which had now entered trade under various foreign countries flags to fight for competition, though to be fair freight rates had continued to be good at the time. The biggest post-war problem caused to British shipping was simply down to high taxation which made it almost impossible for company's such as Ropner's to set aside funds from their profits to replace new ships for old. Figures revealed show that 40% of British dry cargo & tramp ships in 1954 were actually built before or during the war and would need to be replaced within the next few years. The British Government unlike their competitors abroad offered no help whatsoever to British shipowners with subsidies, loans or tax remissions. January 1954 *Bruce Ropner* another of the fourth generation of the family joins the firm after completing his National Service in the Welsh Guards. 1954 would also see the last of the pre-war built Ropner ship *SS Wearpool* sold to Sweden where she continued in service ending up under the Greek flag and continued trading until 1972.

Another real concern for the British shipping industry were the post-war strikes, go slows and walkouts by the likes of the ships dockers, railway workers and miners, causing excessive delays and berthing fees as well as a backlog of shipping awaiting berthing, all losing money by the day. *Guy Ropner* who at the time was President of the Chamber of Shipping stated in an earlier speech that the Ropner Co. if using North Continental ports to discharge could save around three weeks delays at the cost of £20.000 after just two of their ships had been stuck on the Mersey due to industrial action. The Ropner ships that were involved in the US Gulf Line trade, he added were losing one round trip each a year on the sole basis of British port delays.

In the mid 1950's another success of the Ropner directors was to enter the oil freight and tanker market. Once again astute business focused minds were going to step onto unsteady ground and come out on top. The first half of the 1950's had seen a successful rise in the oil freight market, but the market was becoming flooded as figures show that from 1948 to 1957 the tanker market doubled in tonnage to 32.000.000grt and many ships coming off the slip way went straight to be laid up idle. So why were Ropner's different. One reason was the company directors chose to enter the market with only two ships (a third was ordered but later cancelled). In 1955 the first of the tankers *Thornaby* (2) entered the fleet followed by *Thirlby (4)* in 1958. Another reason for the success of these two ships was both ships were chartered. *Thornaby* became time-chartered to British Petroleum on an initial five-year charter, which meant BP would be responsible where the ship went and what cargo to transport while Ropner's still retained possession of the ship. *Thirlby* while staying under the Ropner management would go on bare-boat charter to Shell Oil. In a bare-boat charter, the owner gives possession of the ship to the charterer and the charterer hires its own master and crew. So successful was the bare-boat charter of *Thirlby* it lasted over twenty years until the ship was sold to the Greeks in 1982. Also between 1954-1957 three ships of the Western Canada Shipping Co. came under Ropner management and the 1957 built *Romanby (4)* entered the fleet.

By 1957 while at its peak it was announced the Ropner Gulf Line was to be discontinued. Although still in a competitive market, new overseas competition was becoming fiercer and a further series of crushing strikes in British ports lead to *Jock Ropner* announcing to the shareholders the decision to fold while at it's height of success. The ships of the Gulf Line were integrated into the Ropner tramp fleet and gave good service up until the last one was sold in 1964, apart from the *Somersby (3)* which was sold in 1958 to the British Admiralty and converted into an Air Store Support Ship, serving the Royal Fleet Auxiliary for nearly twenty years. The late 1950's would see thirteen of the fifteen ships built during the war period, acquired by the company after the war being sold, many after being laid up during 1958 after freight rates fell to a disastrous new low. The *Wandby (3)* launched October 1959 being the only high point of that year.

43

As early as 1947 Ropner's had entered a diversification period outside that of the ship owner & management business it was renowned for and a ships chandler service supplying ship stores from the family owned Elton Stores to the fleet and to other ships began. Through the 1950's & 60's these diverse tactics would lead to the company entering the Engineering, Insurance Broking and Property Divisions within the group. (It is not for the pages of this book to go into the detail of these additions to the company and can again be explained better in Ian Dear's book "The Ropner Story" I merely wish to concentrate on the shipping side). 1960 would see only one ship *Willowpool (2)* launched for the company. The same year the company took management of the Bonny Co. Shipping Ltd refrigerated cargo ship *Golden Comet*, followed a year later by the sister ship *Silver Comet*. Both ships belonging to a *Mr. Antonio Bonny* a well-known Canary Islands tomato grower who was a friend of *Jeremy Ropner*. In 1961 as part of a development deal arranged by *Sir Leonard Ropner*, the company ordered a ferry to be built named *Lady Esme* for service between the Seychelles Islands which was later sold to Seychelles Government. (This ferry was still known to be in service in October 2005).

The most prolonged slump in the market since WWII took place in the early 1960's and the Ropner directors decided to sell the last two steam ships purchased from the MOWT after the war and the *SS Levenpool* & *SS Swainby* ended another era of the Ropner legacy both being sold in 1962 followed a year later by the *Troutpool (3)* which was only seven years old. In 1960 a French company had chartered *Troutpool (3)* after one of their own ships suffered serious engine failure while fully loaded. Transferring all cargo from one ship to another at anchor at Rotterdam. 1964 the ten-year-old *Swiftpool (2)* was sold to the *British India SN Co. Ltd.*

With such a market slump as well as the Merchant Seamen's unofficial strike of 1960 and the selling off of fairly new ships, many with less than half their life span used, it would seem strange to those in the shipping business to order new ships at this time. Nevertheless this is exactly what this fourth generation of Ropner directors did, just like their great grandfather policy of buying and building while all others seemed to be failing and the *Barlaby (2)* & *Bridgepool (2)* both entered the fleet in 1962 just when it seemed that the market could go no lower. By 1966 the *Stonepool (2)* entered service, with the tanker *Thornaby (2)* being sold on. The same year *Jock Ropner* decided to relinquish the day to day running of the shipping operations after twenty-seven years and this responsibility was now passed onto Jeremy & Bruce, with David taking responsibility of the London based business.

44

In 1966 the Ropner fleet consisted of just eight owned ships *Barlaby (2)*, *Bridgepool (2)*, *Romanby (4)*, *Rushpool (2)*, *Stonepool (2)*, *Thirlby (4)* *Wandby (3)* & *Willowpool (2)* and the managed ships for Mr. Antonio Bonny. A far cry from the early days, though all the dry cargo ship ships were lucky enough to be on charter even if only short term and the *Thirlby (4)* was still on long term charter to Shell. The world of shipping was changing and the old tramp ships of the golden era of Britain's maritime heritage were slowly disappearing as the winds of change saw the introduction of the now more familiar site of container ships and the quick turnaround.

On 16th May 1966, the National Union of Seamen (NUS) launched its first national strike since 1911. The strike aimed to secure higher wages and to reduce the working week from 56 to 40 hours. It was widely supported by union members and caused great disruption to shipping, especially in London Liverpool and Southampton. The political importance of the strike was enormous: the disruption of trade had an adverse effect on the United Kingdom's precarious balance of payments and threatened to undermine the Government's attempts to keep wage increases below 3.5%. The Labour Prime Minister, Harold Wilson, was strongly critical of the strike, alleging that it had been taken over by Communists whose aim was to bring down his administration. On 23rd May, a week after the outbreak of the strike, the Government declared a state of emergency although emergency powers were not used . The strike finally came to an end on 1st July.

The same year *Jeremy Ropner* was introduced to members of the Norwegian Skaugen Shipping family who together with a number of other companies were members of the Norwegian Bulk Carriers Consortium (NBC), who were highly successful in the iron ore and bulk cargo trade for the European steel producers. The consequences of this meeting would see the Ropner Shipping side well into its centenary year and beyond. After lengthy meetings and negotiations for the construction and chartering out of two large bulk carriers including an element of profit sharing to Ropner's based on the voyages undertaken on behalf of the consortium, finally an order for the *Rudby (3)* & *Iron Somersby* were placed on order at Harland & Wolff for delivery in 1971.

From 1967 to 1970 the fleet was again reduced to an all time low with the sale of *Willowpool (2)*, *Barlaby*, *Romanby (4)* & *Rushpool (2)* as well as both the Bonny Shipping Co. Ltd being sold to the Dutch. While the remaining four ships traded profitably the company was now focusing on the long-term market and eagerly awaiting delivery of the two new ships on order. In 1970 Ropner took over management of a brand new 14,833grt bulk carrier *Norse Viking* for the Cardigan Shipping Co. Ltd.

In 1971 *Sir William Guy Ropner* passed away and the *Rudby (3)* & *Iron Somersby* were launched with the *Rudby (3)* entering straight into the coal & iron ore delivery for the European steel producers, while the *Iron Somersby* was placed on bare-boat charter for the Australian Broken Hill Proprietary Co. to carry iron ore from Port Hedland to Port Kembla, New South Wales. 1972 saw the sale of *Wandby (3)* and two years later this was followed by the sale of *Bridgepool (2)*. The latter being sold even though she had been a profitable run ship, this being brought about by the decline in world trade through the 1973 oil crisis. Because the ship had been built during the slump of the early 1960's the directors still managed to sell her at a book profit.

In 1977 both *Sir Leonard & Sir Robert Desmond Ropner* passed away and the 64,640grt *Lackenby (3)* was launched at Belfast as *Otterpool*, originally for the Norwegian Bulk Carriers Consortium but was instead put on a fifteen-year charter to the British Steel Corporation and renamed after the steel works on Teesside. The following year the sister ship *Appleby* was purchased while still being built at Harland & Wolff for a Norwegian company and placed on a similar long term charter as *Lackenby (3)*. In 1979 a third sister ship *Ravenscraig* joined the fleet also on charter to British Steel, as well as the *Farland* which was placed under Ropner management from the Skaarup Shipping Corporation of Greenwich, USA on behalf of her Swedish owners.

In 1980 the *Rudby (3)* even though only nine years old was sold to Liberia as the market was, if only for a short period of time was having a relative prosperous period and her charterers saw an opportunity to take advantage of selling her for a profit above her book price. In 1981 the oldest ship in the fleet, the twenty-three year old *Thirlby (4)* which, had been on charter to Shell Oil all those years, finally out grew her usefulness to the tanker company and she was released from her charter and returned to Ropner. Unable to find any source of revenue for the ship she was sold to the Greeks the following year. 28th December 1982 the *Stonepool (2)* arrived at Tilbury on her last voyage after being sold to Liberia. When she went to scrap four years late she still carried the Ropner name. This ship was soon replaced the same year by one of around the same tonnage named *Salmonpool (3)*, purchased on the stocks in Greece. Two older ships *Iron Kirby & Iron Kestrel* who were half way through a bare-boat charter to the Broken Hill Property of Australia were purchased for the company. These ships were mainly employed on the Australian and Far East run and as such were manned by Australian crew and served the Ropner fleet well until being sold in the early 1990's.

Unbeknown at the time the last ship purchased by the Ropner Co. to be given a traditional Ropner name was *Otterpool (2)*, purchased in 1991 from Worldwide Shipping and placed on charter for a series of voyages loading grain in South America for the UK. Two more ships *Eastern Bridge & Western Bridge* being built in Japan for the British Steel Corporation under the supervision of Ropner's were launched in January & April 1991 with the management contract undertaken by Ropner and placed on long-term charter to supply the raw material for British Steel in the UK.

In 1996 the shipping and transport group *Jacobs Holdings PLC* who had built up a 10% stake in the Ropner Co. made an offer to buy the remaining 90% stake of the Ropner Shipping Co. and engineering concern and in February 1997 an estimated £34.000.000 completed the deal. The focus thereafter concerning Ropner's was more on ship management than direct ownership and the Dart Line fleet of Roll on Roll vessels was put under their management as part of the Bidcorp Shipping Division, of which Ropner Ship Management was an integral part of.

Prior to the Jacobs Holdings takeover in 1997, the Ropner Shipping Co. and Moor Investments, a company controlled by Runciman Investments, acquired a 50% stake in a 305,000dwt VLCC (Very Large Crude Carrier) to be delivered in the first quarter 1999. The vessel was ordered by Golden Tide Corporation of Liberia, a 50-50 venture between Ropner/Runciman Investments and Golden Ocean Tankers Ltd, and it was intended to be built by Mitsubishi Heavy Industries. After the takeover for whatever reasons the deal was never completed by Jacobs Holdings or Runciman Investments and the ship was eventually launched as the *New Circassia* for Frontline Ltd and Golden Tide Corporation.

By 1999 the last three ships *Appleby, Lackenby & Ravenscraig* had all been sold for scrap and in October 2000 the Ropner head office was closed in Darlington and re-located to Dartford in Kent. From 1st March 2006, Ropner Ship Management ceased to trade as a Ship Management Company. EuroShip Services Limited based within the port of London is now undertaking business previously performed by Ropner's.

Epilogue

I don't think any amount of words can really do justice to show just how much the Ropner Shipping Co. and name has played in our maritime history. They were only one of hundreds of tramp ship company's that have disappeared over the years, never to return, but unlike most, stood the test of time through the depression, two World Wars and the ever changing world of shipping. Not always the Merchant Seamen's favourite company either, often referred to as "Ropey Ropner's" by their crews. Never the less these ships were once the backbone of Britain's sea trade for more than a century and should be remembered as such.

"Now all the capstans and the cargo boats and Stevedores are gone. To where all the old ships go but memories, just like the sea live on......" (Jimmy Nail, "Big River")

Fleet List

The following is a complete history of all the ships owned and managed by the Ropner & Pool Shipping Co. until the Co. was taken over by Jacobs Holdings in 1997. This includes ships managed by the company for the WWI Shipping Controller. The list also includes all the WWII ships with the prefix EMPIRE, which were owned, built or taken as war prizes by the MOS/MOWT and put under the management of the Ropner Company. Other ships included are those supplied on the WWII "Bareboat Charter" from Canada & America with the prefix SAM, FORT & OCEAN, transferred over to Britain's MOWT and put under Ropner's management. Ships owned and managed by Ropner in both World Wars, if lost due to enemy action are marked "War Loss" only and the full details are in the section on WWI & II Losses.

SS Ainderby

AINDERBY, 4,860grt, built 1925 (Wm. Gray & Co., West Hartlepool) for the Ropner Shipping Co. Ltd. 1941 War Loss.

AISALBY, 2,745grt, built 1889 (Ropner & Son, Stockton) for R. Ropner & Co. 1912 sold to Roth Bros., London renamed DODDSWELL. 1914 sold to Japan not renamed, 1916 sold renamed YEITAI MARU, 1933 sold same name. 1934 scrapped in Japan.

ALDERPOOL, 4,313grt, built 1930 (William Pickersgill & Sons, Sunderland) Built as NORTHWICK but laid up unfinished. 1936 purchased by Ropner and renamed ALDERPOOL. 1941 War Loss.

ALICIA, 1,428grt, built 1880 (E. Withy & Co., West Hartlepool). 1887 purchased by the R. Ropner & Co. from Middleton & Co. not renamed. 1895 foundered after collision with SS NETLEY ABBEY off Cromer on voyage from Middlesbrough to Bilbao in ballast.

AMY, 583grt, built 1868 (Denton, Gray & Co., Hartlepool). Completed for Appleby, Ropner & Co., 1868 stranded at Winga, in the Grecian Archipelago on only her second voyage.

M V Appleby

APPLEBY, 64,124grt, built 1978 (Harland & Wolff, Belfast) as GOLDEN MASTER. 1978 purchased from Norway renamed APPLEBY. Placed on British Steel Charter, managed by Ropner Shipping Co. Ltd. February 1999 arrived China for scrapping.

ASHBY (1), 2,606grt, built 1896 (Ropner & Son, Stockton) for R. Ropner & Co. 15th February 1916 driven ashore during a severe gale and wrecked near Ushant on voyage to Cardiff in ballast. Captain Samuel Green and 1 seaman drowned.

SS Ashby

ASHBY (2), 4,871grt, built 1927 (Cowpen Dry Docks & Shipbuilding Co., Blyth) for the Ropner Shipping Co. Ltd. 1941 War Loss.

BALDERSBY, 3,613grt, built 1913 (Ropner & Son, Stockton) for R. Ropner & Co. 1916 registered under the Sir R. Ropner & Co. Ltd. 1918 War Loss.

MV Barlby

BARLBY (1), 2,489grt, built 1895 (Ropner & Son, Stockton) for the R. Ropner & Co. 1926 sold to D.A. Mango, Greece renamed NOEMI. 1930 sold to Noemijulia SS Co. renamed NOMEMIJULIA. 1942 sold to Irish Shipping Ltd renamed IRISH HAZEL. 1943 taken over by Ministry of War Transport renamed EMPIRE DON. 1945 reverted back to Irish Shipping Ltd and again renamed IRISH HAZEL. 1949 sold to Turkey renamed UMAN. 6th January 1960 ran aground and became a complete total loss at Kefken Point, Turkey.

BARLBY (2), 16,565grt, built 1962 (Sir J. Laing & Sons, Sunderland) for the Ropner Shipping Co. Ltd. 1968 sold to Greece renamed AGIOS GEORGIS, 1980 sank near Japan after flooding in No. 5 hold.

BELLERBY (1), 3,097grt, built 1898 (Ropner & Son, Stockton) for the R. Ropner & Co. 1916 registered under the Sir R. Ropner & Co. Ltd. 1927 sold to Greece renamed DZEKA. 1928 sold renamed KATE. 1933 scrapped in Italy.

SS Bellerby (2)

BELLERBY (2), 7,071grt, built 1944 (Wm. Gray & Co., West Hartlepool). Built as EMPIRE IRVING for the MOWT, 1946 purchased from Ministry of War Transport and renamed BELLERBY. 1960 sold to Iranian Lloyd renamed PERSIAN CAMBYSES. 1964 sold renamed IRANIAN TRADER. 1964 renamed SHIRAZ. 1970 sold to Bahrain renamed SAYHET. 1972 scrapped at Karachi.

BLACKHALLS, 1,142grt, built 1880 (Wm. Gray & Co., West Hartlepool) for the R. Ropner & Co. 1888 stranded off the Dutch Schiermonnikoog, West Frisian Island, sailing from Archangel to Amsterdam with a cargo of wood and became a total loss.

BOULDERPOOL, 4,803grt, built 1928 (Smith's Dock Co., Middlesbrough) for the Pool Shipping Co. Ltd. 1941 War Loss.

SS Boulderpool

BRIDGEPOOL (1), 4,845grt, built 1924 (Ropner Shipbuilding & Repairing Co., Stockton) for the Pool Shipping Co. Ltd. 5th November 1943 damaged by a mysterious explosion in No. 1 hold. 1946 sold to Ford S.S. Co. renamed WANFORD. 1950 sold to Egypt renamed RAMSES II. 23rd March 1951 grounded on a sandbank proceeding to Sharpness Docks with 7,000 tons of Russian maize. Broke in two whilst salvaging cargo.

M V Bridgepool

BRIDGEPOOL (2), 11,428grt, built 1962 (Austin & Pickersgill, Sunderland) for the Pool Shipping Co. Ltd. 1969 registered under the Ropner Shipping Co. Ltd. 1975 sold renamed EKTON. 1982 laid up. 1985 scrapped at Huangpu, China.

BROOKBY, 3,679grt, built 1905 (Ropner & Son, Stockton) for R. Ropner & Co. 1916 registered under the Sir R. Ropner & Co. Ltd. 1917 War Loss.

BURNBY, 3,665grt, built 1905 (Ropner & Son, Stockton) for R. Ropner & Co. 1916 registered under the Sir R. Ropner & Co. Ltd. 1917 War Loss.

BUSBY, 3,256grt, built 1894 (Ropner & Son, Stockton) for the R. Ropner & Co. Sailing on her maiden voyage from Newport to Civita Vecchia, Italy with a cargo of coal became stranded in Pendeen Cove, Cornwall on 24th June 1894. Refloated 16th July but foundered a mile off shore.

CANBY, 4,804grt, built 1911 (Short Bros. Ltd Sunderland) as WABANA for British & Chilian S.S. Co. 1931 purchased by Ropner from Wabana S.S. Co. and renamed CANBY. 1934 grounded East of Guion Island, Cape Breton sailing from St. John's, New Brunswick for coal to Louisburg, Cape Breton and became a total loss.

SS Carperby

CARPERBY (1), 2,104grt, built 1895 (Ropner & Son, Stockton) for the R. Ropner & Co. 1926 sold to Sweden renamed JUPITER. 1940 seized by Germans and used as an accommodation vessel to house Norwegian prisoners of war. Later renamed SCHIFF III and used as a minelayer and depot ship from 1941. 1945 found at Kiel and handed to Great Britain. 1949 arrived Stockton-on-Tees and broken up.

CARPERBY (2), 4,890grt, built 1928 (Wm. Gray & Co., West Hartlepool) for the Ropner Shipping Co. Ltd. 1942 War Loss.

MV Cedarpool

CEDARPOOL, 7,031grt, built 1942 (Wm. Gray & Co., West Hartlepool) as EMPIRE CLARION for MOWT, Ropner managers. 1946 purchased from Ministry of War Transport and renamed CEDARPOOL 1959 scrapped at Hamburg.

CLEARPOOL (1), 4,237grt, built 1907 (Ropner & Son, Stockton) for the Pool Shipping Co. Ltd. 1933 scrapped at Rosyth.

CLEARPOOL (2), 5,404grt, built 1935 (Wm. Gray & Co., West Hartlepool) for the Pool Shipping Co. Ltd. 10th June 1941 damaged in an air attack and towed to the River Tees for repairs. 4th June 1944 wrecked on Skitter Sands, Humberside sailing from Hull to Algiers.

CLEARPOOL (3), 6,715grt, built 1941 (Wm. Gray & Co., West Hartlepool) as EMPIRE CABOT. 1942 MOWT, Ropner mngrs. 1945 purchased from Ministry of War Transport and renamed CLEARPOOL. 1954 sold to Cardigan Shipping Co., Cardiff renamed GRELMARION. 1959 sold to Germany renamed RACHEAL. 1959 scrapped at Hong Kong.

COALBY, 4,903grt, built 1911 (Armstrong, Whitworth & Co., Newcastle) as KAMOURASKA for Sydney, Cape Breton & Montreal S.S. Co. 1916 sold to Laurentian SS Co. Ltd. 1921 bought by Kamouraska Shipping Co. Ltd. 1931 purchased by Ropner from Kamouraska and renamed COALBY, 1935 sold to St. Quentin Shipping Co., Cardiff not renamed, 1936 sold same name, 1937 sold to Japanese shipbreaker.

COLEBY, 3,824grt, built 1907 (Ropner & Son, Stockton) for R. Ropner & Co. 1915 War Loss.

CRAGPOOL, 5,127grt, built 1928 (Cowpen Dry Docks & Shipbuilding Co., Blyth) for the Pool Shipping Co. Ltd. 1947 sold renamed LEANDROS. 1950 sold to Panama renamed ACROPOLIS. 1960 scrapped at Hong Kong.

CRATHORNE, 2,752grt, built 1888 (Wm. Gray & Co., West Hartlepool) for R. Ropner & Co. 1912 sold to Norway not renamed. 1917 torpedoed and sunk off Alicante on voyage from Norfolk to Genoa with a cargo of sugar and grain.

CRIMDON, 1,710grt, built 1878 (Wm. Gray & Co., West Hartlepool) for the R. Ropner & Co. 1899 sold to P. Rowe & Sons, Cardiff not renamed. 1911 sold to Sweden not renamed. 27th July 1918 torpedoed and sunk by German submarine of Whitby sailing from the Tyne to Rouen with a cargo of coal.

SS CRITON, 4,564grt, built 1927 (Wm. Gray & Co., West Hartlepool) for Cie. de Navigation d'Orbigny, La Rochelle. 9th May 1941 intercepted by Armed Merchant Cruiser HMS CELICIA and taken into Freetown. 1941 taken over by MOWT, managed by Ropner Shipping Co. Ltd. 1941 War Loss.

SS Daleby

DALEBY (1), 3,628grt, built 1900 (Ropner & Son, Stockton) for the R. Ropner & Co. 1916 registered under the Sir R. Ropner & Co. Ltd. 1917 War Loss.

DALEBY (2), 4,640grt, built 1929 (Armstrong, Whitworth & Co., Newcastle) as KITTY TAYLOR. 1934 purchased by Ropner from Eros Steamships and renamed DALEBY. 1942 War Loss.

DALEBY (3), 5,171grt, built 1950 (Sir J. Laing & Sons, Sunderland) for the Ropner Shipping Co. Ltd. 1961 sold to Jugoslavenska Oceanska Plovidba and renamed KUPRES. 1972 scrapped at Split.

DANBY, 4,258grt, built 1937 (Wm. Gray & Co., West Hartlepool) for the Ropner Shipping Co. Ltd 1952 sold to Spain renamed ASTRO. 1971 sold renamed GOPEGUI. 1976 scrapped.

DEERPOOL (1), 5,200grt, built 1930 (Wm. Gray & Co., West Hartlepool) for the Pool Shipping Co. Ltd. On the evening of 12th November 1939 stranded near Spurn Point bound for Hull and declared a total loss. There had been warnings of U-boat activity in the area and DEERPOOL had tried after dark to enter the Humber without the aid of navigation lights.

DEERPOOL (2), 5,169grt, built 1950 (Sir J. Laing & Sons, Sunderland) for the Pool Shipping Co. Ltd. 1961 sold to Jugoslavenska Oceanska Plovidba and renamed KORDUN. 1972 scrapped at Split.

M V Deerpool

DEERPOOL (3), 37,340grt, built 1982 (Tsuneishi, Namakuma, Japan) as SHANNON VENTUE. Ex DEBORAH L. 1986, ex ALPHA FLAME 1986, ex DELPHIC FLAME 1990. 1995 purchased by Ropner renamed DEERPOOL. 1996 sold to Panama renamed KONKAR LYDIA. No further detail known to 2003.

SS Domby

DOMBY, 5,582grt, built 1932 (Wm. Gray & Co., West Hartlepool) for the Ropner Shipping Co. Ltd. 1951 sold renamed CIBOU. 1955 sold to Finland renamed CALEDONIA II. 1956 sold renamed PETER. 1960 sold to Lebanon renamed KETTARA V. 1960 scrapped in Japan.

DRAKEPOOL, 4,838grt, built 1924 (Ropner Shipbuilding & Repairing Co., Stockton) for the Pool Shipping Co. Ltd. 1946 sold to Kenfig S.S. Co.,

London renamed SAN ANTHONY. 1951 sold to Japan renamed KINUGASA MARU. November 1951 damaged during a storm sailing from Nanaimo, Vancouver Island to Yokohama with iron ore. Abandoned about 1200 miles East of Yokohama and sank two days later.

DROMONBY, 3,627grt, built 1900 (Ropner & Son, Stockton) for R. Ropner & Co. 1916 War Loss.

EASTERN BRIDGE, 55,695grt, built 1991 (Hashihama Zosen, Tadotsu, Japan) under Ropner supervision for British Steel and placed under Ropner management. Sold 2000 renamed YEOMAN BRIDGE, for V. Ships management on behalf of Foster Yeoman. 2006 still in service.

EASTPOOL, 3,709grt, built 1925 (John Readhead & Sons, South Shields) as EASTVILLE. 1937 purchased from Balls & Stansfield and renamed EASTPOOL. 1938 sold to Turkey not renamed. 1938 sold renamed DEMIR. 1941 sold same name. Sold again 1952 & 1955. 1963 scrapped at Kalafat, Turkey.

EDEN, 1,446grt, built 1879 (Wm. Gray & Co., West Hartlepool) for the R. Ropner & Co. 1899 sold to R. Brown & Sons, South Shields not renamed. 1908 sold to Norway same name. 1917 sold same name. 1917 torpedoed and sunk by U-boat 10 miles South-West of Worthing Pier on voyage from the Tyne to Rouen with a cargo of coal.

EGGLESTONE, 4,695grt, built 1928 (William Gray & Co., West Hartlepool) to Ropner's own account and placed under management of Ropner Shipping Co. Ltd. Sold to Greece same year and renamed PELEUS. On the 13th March 1944 while sailing independently from Freetown to Buenos Aries the ship was intercepted by U-852 500 miles North of the Ascension Islands and sank rapidly after being hit by two torpedoes. Only 3 crew survived and were picked up by a Portuguese Merchant ship and landed at Lobito, Angola.

ELPIS, 2,010grt, built 1878 (Wm. Gray & Co., West Hartlepool) for R. Ropner & Co. 1899 sold to J.A. Parker, Cardiff not renamed. 1900 sold to Norway renamed STADT. 1903 disappeared on passage from the Black Sea.

ELTON, 2,461grt, built 1888 (Wm. Gray & Co., West Hartlepool) for R. Ropner & Co. 1912 sold to W. Coupland, & Co., Newcastle not renamed. 1915 sold to the Admiralty and used as a blockship at Scapa Flow.

EMPIRE ARNOLD, 7,045grt, built 1942 (William Gray & Co., West Hartlepool) for the MOWT managed by Ropner Shipping Co. Ltd. 1942 War Loss.

Empire Bison

EMPIRE BISON, 5,972grt, built 1919 (South Western Ship Building Co.) as WEST CAWTHON for the US Shipping Board. 1920 sold to the Green Star SS Corp. 1921 sold to the Imperial SS Corp. 1923 reverted back to US Shipping Board. 1926 sold to American South African Line Inc. 1940 purchased by the MOS renamed and managed by Ropner Shipping Co. Ltd. 1940 War Loss.

EMPIRE CABOT, see CLEARPOOL (3)

EMPIRE CHAPMAN, 8,194grt, built 1942 (Harland & Wolff Ltd, Belfast) for the MOWT managed by Ropner Shipping Co. Ltd. 1944 taken over by the British Tanker Co. Ltd. 1954 renamed BRITISH COMMANDO same company. 1959 scrapped at Ghent.

EMPIRE CHEETAH, 5,673grt, built 1918 (Skinner & Eddy Corporation, Seattle, Washington) as WEST LIANGA. 1940 purchased by the MOS renamed and managed by Ropner Shipping Co. Ltd. 1942 transferred to the Dutch government and renamed HOBBEMA. On the 4th November 1942 while sailing in Convoy SC-107 the ship was torpedoed by U-132 and hit by one torpedo on the starboard side in the engine room. The engine stopped and the ship immediately began to sink. 16 survivors launched the port lifeboats and some rafts and were later picked up by the American tugs UNCAS and PESSACUS. The Captain and 27 of her 44 crew including seven British DEMS gunners were lost.

EMPIRE CLARION, see CEDARPOOL.

EMPIRE DRYDEN, 7,164grt, built 1942 (William Doxford & Sons Ltd, Sunderland) for the MOWT managed by Ropner Shipping Co. Ltd. 1942 War Loss.

EMPIRE ELGAR, 2,847grt, built 1942 (William Gray & Co., West Hartlepool) for the MOWT managed by Ropner Shipping Co. Ltd. Same year transferred over to Dover Navigation Co. Ltd. 1947 bought from the MOWT by the same Co. and renamed SEA MINSRTRAL. 1951 sold renamed MARANDELLAS. 1956 sold to Norway renamed EDWARD JANSEN. 1960 sold renamed SPLITAN. 1961 sold to Bulgaria renamed PIRIN. 1965 scrapped.

EMPIRE ELY, 6,112grt, laid down 1944 as GRIEFSWALD for Germany, but not completed. 1945 seized by the Allies at Lubek. 1948 completed (Luber Flenderwerke A.G., Lubeck) for the MOT, managed by Common Brothers, Newcastle. 1949 taken over for the MOT, managed by Ropner Shipping Co. Ltd. Had an option to buy and she was to be renamed SWIFTPOOL (2). In the end this never came to fruition and the ship was taken over by for the MOT, managed Macklay & McIntyre Ltd, Glasgow in 1950. 1951 MOT, managed Stott, Mann & Fleming Ltd, Newcastle. 1954 sold to Liberia and renamed MARIBELLA. 1955 sold to Germany and renamed GANGES. 1959 sold to Greece and renamed ELENI. 1971 damaged during collision with Norwegian ferry PRINSESSE RAGNHILD. Considered a total loss the ship was sold for breaking up. 1972 scrapped at Santander, Spain.

EMPIRE FRIENDSHIP, 7,058grt, built 1943 (Short Brothers Ltd, Sunderland) for the MOWT managed by Ropner Shipping Co. Ltd. 1945 sold to the French government and renamed MATELOTS PHILLIEN ET PEYRAT. 1962 broke her moorings and driven onto the breakwater at Port de Bouc. Considered a total loss and scrapped at La Seyne.

EMPIRE GRANGE, 6,981grt, built 1943 (Harland & Wolff Ltd, Belfast) for the MOWT managed by Ropner Shipping Co. Ltd. 1946 sold to King Line renamed KING ROBERT. 1961sold Hong Kong renamed ARDGEM. 1967 sold Gibraltar renamed KELSO. 1969 scrapped at Kaohsiung, Taiwan.

EMPIRE GRENFELL, 7,238grt, built 1941 ((William Doxford & Sons Ltd, Sunderland) for the MOWT managed by Ropner Shipping Co. Ltd. 1942 transferred to the Norwegian government and renamed KONG SVERRE. 1946 sold renamed MARTHA KLEPPE. 1959 sold renamed REINA. 1960 sold renamed MIAMI. 1964 sold renamed IMPALA. 1968 scrapped at Kaohsiung, Taiwan.

EMPIRE JOHNSON, 7,168grt, built 1942 (Joseph L. Thompson & Sons Ltd, Sunderland) for the MOWT managed by Ropner Shipping Co. Ltd. Same year transferred over to the Netherlands Shipping & Trading Committee Ltd and renamed PAULUS POTTER managed by Van Ommeren. 5th July 1942 damaged by aerial torpedo in Convoy PQ-17 West of Nova Zembla and abandoned. 13th July found drifting by U-255 who boarded the ship and tried to restart her engines. When this failed any useful items were removed from the ship and she was sunk by a coupe de grace.

EMPIRE KINGSLEY, 6,996grt, built 1941 (Greenock Dockyard Co. Ltd) for the MOWT managed by Ropner Shipping Co. Ltd. 1944 management taken over by Christian Salvesen & Co. 22nd March 1945 torpedoed and sunk by U-315 sailing from Ghent to Manchester in the coastal Convoy TBC-103, killing 8 crew.

EMPIRE KITTIWAKE, 5,834grt, built 1919 (Ames Shipbuilding & Dry Dock Co., Seattle, Washington) as WAR HECTOR, but completed as WESTERN ALLY. 1929 renamed FORBES HAUPTMANN. 1940 purchased by the MOS renamed and managed by Ropner Shipping Co. Ltd. Transferred to the Norwegian government and renamed NORFALK. 20th July 1944 mined and sunk while on the way to the Normandy beaches to be used as a blockship.

EMPIRE LARK, 4,971grt, built 1921 (Deutsche Werke A.G., Kiel) as MARTHA HEMSOTH. 1926 sold renamed KIRSTEN MILES. 1939 interned at Las Palmas. 1945 handed over to British MOWT as a war prize renamed and managed by Ropner Shipping Co. Ltd. 1947 scuttled 400 miles West of Ireland with a cargo of war surplus gas shells.

EMPIRE LIONEL, see LEVENPOOL (2).

EMPIRE MERLIN, 5,680grt, built 1919 (Ames Shipbuilding & Dry Dock Co., Seattle, Washington) as WEST ISLETA for US Shipping Board, Seattle. 1926 sold to American South African Line, New York. 1940 purchased by the

Empire Merlin

Ministry of Shipping renamed EMPIRE MERLIN, MOS, managed by Ropner Shipping Co. Ltd. 1940 War Loss.

EMPIRE MOMBASA, 7,319grt, built 1946 (Shipbuilding Corporation Ltd, Sunderland) for the MOT, managed by Ropner Shipping Co. Ltd. Same year sold to India SS Co. Ltd renamed INDIAN ENTERPRISE. June 1950 sank in the Red Sea after an explosion on voyage from Bremen to Calcutta via London with a cargo of general stores and 538 tons of explosives. Captain and 72 crew killed, 1 survivor. Explosion believed to have been caused by spontaneous combustion.

EMPIRE MOONBEAM, 6,849grt, built 1941 (Hong Kong, & Whampoa Dock Co. Ltd) for the MOWT, managed by Ropner Shipping Co. Ltd. 1942 War Loss.

EMPIRE MOONRISE, 6,854grt, built 1941 (Hong Kong, & Whampoa Dock Co. Ltd) for the MOWT, managed by Ropner Shipping Co. Ltd. 1942 damaged in an air raid at Colombo and later repaired. 1942 taken over by J.D. McLaren & Co. 1945 purchased from MOWT by same company and renamed HARTLAND POINT. 1947 sold to Burness Shipping Co. Ltd renamed BURMOUNT. 1954 sold to Panama renamed MARILENA under Costa Rican flag. 1957 sold renamed ATHAMAS. 1959 transferred under Panamanian flag. 1963 sold to Greek owners. 1966 scrapped at Whampoa China.

EMPIRE MOUFLON, see PRESTON (3)

EMPIRE OUTPOST, 6,978grt, built 1943 (Harland & Wolff Ltd, Belfast) for the MOWT managed by Ropner Shipping Co. Ltd. 1945 sold to the French government and renamed PILOTE GARNIER. 1960 sold to Panama renamed KYRA HARIKLIA. 1966 ran aground outside Malmo. Towed to Hamburg but was declared a total loss and scrapped.

EMPIRE OYKELL, 2,623grt, built 1930 (Flensburger Schiffsbau Gesellschaft, Flansberg) as ADELE TRABER. 1945 seized by the Allies at Kiel and given to the British MOT as a war prize and managed by Ropner Shipping Co. Ltd. 1946 sold to the Norwegian government and renamed BRUSE. 1958 renamed HOEGH BRUSE. 1959 renamed HOEGH COLLIER. 1961 sold to Finland renamed POMO. 1967 renamed TOMI. 1968 scrapped at Spezia, Italy.

EMPIRE PTARMIGAN, 6,076grt, built 1920 (G.M. Standifer Construction Corporation, Vancouver) as ABERCOS. 1941 purchased by the MOWT, managed by Ropner Shipping Co. Ltd and renamed EMPIRE PTARMIGAN. 1942 transferred over to the Norwegian government and renamed NORELG. 1946 sold to Panama. 1948 sold renamed NEW ASIA. 1955 was reported as sailing under the name CHUNG HSING I. 1967 deleted from Lloyds Register as whereabouts unknown.

EMPIRE RAINBOW, 6,942grt, built 1941 (Greenock Dockyard Co. Ltd) for the MOWT managed by R. Ropner & Co. 1942 War Loss.

EMPIRE SALMONPOOL, see SALMONPOOL (2).

EMPIRE SOAR, 2,740grt, built 1924 (Blyth Shipbuilding & Dry Docks Co. Ltd) as TULLOCHMOOR for W. Runciman & Co., Newcastle. 1936 sold to Germany and renamed BRIGITTE. 1945 seized by the Allies at Hamburg as a war prize, renamed by MOT, managed by Ropner Shipping Co. Ltd. 1946 sold to the Greek government and renamed PREVEZA. Sold 1948 renamed ARMONIA. 1959 sold to Panama renamed KEANEYEW. 1960 renamed CHARLIE. 1960 scrapped at Hong Kong.

EMPIRE STARLIGHT, 6,854grt, built 1941 (Hong Kong, & Whampoa Dock Co. Ltd) for the MOWT, managed by Ropner Shipping Co. Ltd. 1942 War Loss. 1945 salvaged by Russian government renamed MURMANSK. Last reported in 1979 at Nakhoda, Russia as a converted storage barge.

EMPIRE SUNBEAM, see SWAINBY (4)

EMPIRE TIDE, see THIRLBY (3)

EMPIRE TRENT, see ROCKPOOL (2)

EMPIRE WEAVER, 2,822grt, built 1939 (Lubecker Maschb. Ges, Lubeck) as DALBEK. 1945 seized by Allies at Rendsburg. Renamed for the MOT, managed by Ropner Shipping Co. Ltd. 1946 handed over to the U.S.S.R. and named TCHERNIGOV. 1969 scrapped at Split.

EMPIRE WOODCOCK, 5,572grt, built 1918 (Ames Shipbuilding & Dry Dock Co., Seattle, Washington) as WEST CAPE. 1940 purchased for MOS, managed by Ropner Shipping Co. Ltd. 1942 handed over to the Greek government renamed EPIROS. 1948 sold same name. 1951 sold to Costa Rica renamed SAN ANDREA. 1953 broken up at Stockton-on-Tees.

M V Farland

FARLAND, 64,077grt, built 1974 (Rheinstahl Nordseewerke, Emden) as FERNBAY. 1978 renamed NEWALA. 1979 taken over by Ropner Management Ltd from Skaarup Shipping Corporation of Greenwich, USA on behalf of Swedish owners and renamed. 1994 scrapped at Alang.

FIRBY (1), 4,868grt, built 1926 (Wm. Gray & Co., West Hartlepool) for the Ropner Shipping Co. Ltd. 1939 War Loss.

FIRBY (2), 7,173grt, built 1942 (Todd Bath Iron S.B. Corp., Portland, Maine) as OCEAN FAME. 1947 purchased from Ministry of War Transport and

SS Firby

SS Firby (2)

renamed FIRBY. 1955 sold renamed IRENE K. 1958-sold not renamed. 1964 renamed WINCHESTER QUEEN. 1966 scrapped at Biboa.

SS Fishpool (1)

FISHPOOL (1), 4,533grt, built 1912 (Ropner & Son, Stockton) for the Pool Shipping Co. Ltd. 1938 sold to Atlantic & Mediterranean Trading Co., London renamed ATLANTIC SCOUT. 1939 sold not renamed. 1940 ran aground on voyage from Algiers to River Tees at Cap Gris-Nez. Refloated and beached at Boulogne as a complete total loss. In 1949 broken up by explosives.

FISHPOOL (2), 4,950grt, built 1940 (Sir J. Laing & Sons, Sunderland) for the Pool Shipping Co. Ltd. 1943 War Loss.

FORT BEAUSEJOUR, 7,151grt, built 1943 (Marine Industries Ltd, Sorel P.Q., Canada) for bareboat charter to the British MOWT and managed by Ropner. 1946 management taken over by Goulandris Bros., Ltd, London. 1948 sold to Panama renamed THEOGENNITOR. 1952 sold same name. 1961 transferred under Greek flag. 1962 back to Panama renamed LILLIAN K. 1964 renamed GOLDEN LILY. 1967 sold same name. 1967 scrapped at Uchiumi, Shodo Island, Japan.

FORT BRULE, 7,133grt, built 1942 (West Coast Shipbuilders Ltd, Vancouver) for the United States War Shipping Administration for bareboat charter to the British MOWT and managed by Ropner. 1947 returned to America. 1948 sold to Scindia SN Co. Ltd, renamed JALAMOTI. 1961 sold to Panama, renamed ADAWIND. 1963 sold renamed ISLAND VENTURE. 1966 taken over by the Wah Kwong Co. 1967 scrapped at Kaohsiung, Taiwan.

FORT CADOTTE, 7,128grt, built 1943 (Burrard Dry Dock Co., Vancouver) for the United States War Shipping Administration for bareboat charter to the British MOWT and managed by Ropner. 1945 ownership transferred to Canada. 1946 management taken over by Cunard White Star Line Ltd. 1950 sold renamed FRY HILL. 1957 sold to Liberia renamed AKTI. 1959 transferred under Greek flag. 1961 sold renamed GLORIA. 1964 sold renamed HELEN. 1967 scrapped at Kawajiri, Japan.

FORT COULONGE, 7,136grt, built 1943 (United Shipyards Ltd, Montreal) for the Dominion of Canada for bareboat charter to the British MOWT and managed by Ropner. 1949 management transferred to W.H. Cockerline & Co. Ltd. 1950 sold renamed ANDOVER HILL under various management. 1961 sold to Liberia renamed LOURIA 1964 sold renamed SURABAJA STEER. 1965 sold renames BEYRL. 1970 scrapped at Hirao, Japan.

FORT FINLAY, 7,134grt, built 1943, (West Coast Shipbuilders Ltd, Vancouver) for the United States War Shipping Administration for bareboat charter to the British MOWT and managed by Ropner. 1948 returned to America. 1959 scrapped at Beaumont, Texas.

FORT GEORGE, 7,129grt, built 1942 (Burrard Dry Dock Co., Vancouver) for the United States War Shipping Administration for bareboat charter to the British MOWT and managed by Ropner. 1948 returned to America. 1959 arrived Baltimore and laid up. 1962 scrapped.

FORT HENLEY, 7,138grt, built 1943 (United Shipyards Ltd, Montreal) for the Dominion of Canada for bareboat charter to the British MOWT and managed by Ropner. 1950 sold to Counties Ship Management Co., renamed PINE HILL. 1964 sold renamed NEWMOAT. 1969 scrapped at Spezia, Italy after being laid up at Piraeus.

FORT PELLY, 7,131grt, built 1942 (Yarrows Ltd, Victoria B.C.) for the United States War Shipping Administration for bareboat charter to the British MOWT and managed by Ropner. 1943 War Loss.

FORT STAGER, 7,132grt, built 1943, (West Coast Shipbuilders Ltd, Vancouver) for the United States War Shipping Administration for bareboat charter to the British MOWT and managed by Ropner. 1948 returned to America. 1958 scrapped at Baltimore

FORT WELLINGTON, 7,131grt, built 1943 (United Shipyards Ltd, Montreal) for the Dominion of Canada for bareboat charter to the British MOWT and managed by Ropner. 1948 sold to Canada renamed HALIGONONIAN QUEEN. 1950 transferred back to UK register, renamed MUSWELL HILL. 1967 scrapped Kinoura, Japan.

GADSBY, 3,497grt, built 1899 (Ropner & Son, Stockton) for the R. Ropner & Co. 1915 War Loss.

GERMANICUS, 3,967grt, built 1901, (Ropner & Son, Stockton) for C. Andersen, Germany. 1919 taken as a war prize by the British Shipping Controller and handed over to R. Ropner & Co. On the 8th November 1919 wrecked off the North-West reef near Biquette Island in the Gulf of St. Lawrence, Canada on voyage from Rotterdam.

GLENBY, 2,196grt, built 1900 (Ropner & Son, Stockton) for the R. Ropner & Co. 1915 War Loss.

GLENHOLT, 1,689grt, built 1883 (E. Withy & Co., West Hartlepool). 1899 sold to Sweden renamed HILDA. Wrecked at Ambromer Point in the White

Sea on 28th July 1899.

GOLDEN COMET, 1,280grt, built 1960 (Schps. De Waal, Zaltbommel, Netherlands) for the Bonny Shipping Co. Ltd and placed under the management of the Sir R. Ropner Co. 1968 sold to the Netherlands, Antilles renamed Golden Star. 1969 sold to the Netherlands renamed SHAMROCK REEFER and managed by Irish & Continental Shipping Co. Ltd. On the 2nd October 1970 on voyage from Rotterdam to the Cape Verde Islands the ship developed flooding in her engine room and ran aground 40 miles North of Lisbon. The ship was abandoned and declared a complete total loss.

GRANBY, 1,891grt, built 1895 (Ropner & Son, Stockton) for R. Ropner & Co. 31st July 1895 wrecked at Imbetiba, River Plate sailing on her maiden voyage.

GREYSTOKE, 2,119grt, built 1885 (E. Withy & Co., West Hartlepool) for R. Ropner & Co. 1892 wrecked on Gross Voge Islands on the Frisian Coast on voyage from Odessa to Hamburg.

SS Gullpool

GULLPOOL, 4,870grt, built 1928 (Cowpen Dry Docks & Shipbuilding Co., Blyth) for the Pool Shipping Co. Ltd. 1950 sold to Italy renamed SAN FELICE. 1959 renamed SANTO EMILIO. 1959 scrapped at Osaka, Japan.

HARDWICK (1), 978grt, built 1873 (M. Pearse & Co., Stockton). Completed for Appleby, Ropner & Co., 1874 transferred to T. Appleby. 1880 foundered 18 lives lost.

HARDWICK (2), 1,122grt, built 1880 (E. Withy & Co., West Hartlepool). 1898 sold to Sweden renamed LIZZIE. 1899 sold same name, 1916 sold same name. 1917 sold to Sweden. 1920 sold. 1921 sold to German Government. 1922 sold to E. R. Retzlaff renamed HELMWIGE. 1930 sold renamed CLARA HINTZ. 1937 scrapped in Germany.

HARSLEY, 1,729grt, built 1879 (Wm. Gray & Co., West Hartlepool) as HARLSEY. 1879 purchased from Callender, White & Hunter by R. Ropner & Co., not renamed. 1893 disappeared after sailing from Gibraltar.

HARTBURN, 1,928grt, built 1882 (E. Withy & Co., West Hartlepool) for R. Ropner & Co. 1898 sold to Sweden renamed EOL. 1913 wrecked near Gelfe, Sweden on voyage from Gelfe to Soderham, Sweden with a cargo of iron ore.

HARTLEPOOL, 4,409grt, built 1904 (Ropner & Son, Stockton) for the Pool Shipping Co. Ltd 1918 converted into a tanker. 1920 sold to Anglo Saxon Petroleum Co. not renamed. 1921 renamed PURPURA. 1931 scrapped at Osaka, Japan.

SS Hawnby

HAWNBY (1), 2.136grt, built 1895 (Ropner & Son, Stockton) for R. Ropner & Co. 1914 wrecked off Johnshaven, Montrose on voyage from Hull to Archangel with a cargo of coal. An inquiry blamed the absence of any coastal lights for the loss.

HAWNBY (2), 5,404grt, built 1936 (Wm. Gray & Co., West Hartlepool) for the Ropner Shipping Co. Ltd. 1940 War Loss.

HAXBY (1), 3,445grt built 1892 (Ropner & Son, Stockton) for R. Ropner & Co. 1919 sold to Watts, Watts & Co., London renamed FINCHLEY. 1920 registered with the Britain SS Co. Ltd. 1926 scrapped at Gateshead.

SS Haxby

HAXBY (2), 5,207grt, built 1929 (Wm. Gray & Co., West Hartlepool). 1940 War Loss.

SS Heronspool

HELMSTEDT, 1,586grt, built 1877 (E. Withy & Co., West Hartlepool) for R. Ropner & Co.1890 struck rock off Mandali Island and foundered.

HERONSPOOL (1), 3,276grt, built 1903 (Ropner & Son, Stockton) for the Pool Shipping Co. Ltd 1928 sold to Greece renamed EUGINIA M. GOULANDRI. 1933 scrapped in Italy.

HERONSPOOL (2), 5,202grt, built 1929 (Wm. Gray & Co., West Hartlepool). 1939 War Loss

HERENSPOOL (3), 7,174grt, built 1942 (Todd California Iron S.B. Corp., Richmond) as OCEAN VALOUR for MOWT. 1946 placed under Ropner management. 1947 purchased from Ministry of War Transport and not renamed. 1949 renamed HERONSPOOL. 1955 sold to Achille Lauro, Italy renamed LIANA. 1967 scrapped at La Spezia, Italy.

HESLEDEN, 1,536grt, built 1876 (Wm. Gray & Co., West Hartlepool) for R. Ropner & Co. 1899 sold to R. Jobson & Co., West Hartlepool not renamed.

SS Hindpool

1905 sold to Sweden renamed PHYLLIS. 1917 taken over by the British government and managed by Casper, Edgar & Co. 1918 wrecked off the coast of Devonshire.

HINDPOOL, 4,897 built 1928 (Wm. Gray & Co., West Hartlepool). 1941 War Loss.

HOLTBY, 3,675grt, built 1909 (Ropner & Son, Stockton) for R. Ropner & Co. 1916 registered under the Sir R. Ropner & Co. Ltd. 1919registered under the Ropner Shipping Co. Ltd. 1936 sold to Greece renamed POSEIDONA. 1939 sold to Egypt renamed SAMIR. 1942 torpedoed and sunk by German submarine U-658 on voyage from Cristobel to Guantanamo Bay in ballast.

HORDEN, 1,633grt, built 1877 (Wm. Gray & Co., West Hartlepool) for R. Ropner & Co. 1899 sold to R. Jobson & Co., West Hartlepool not renamed and resold to Zerssen & Co., Germany renamed KATHE. 1906 sold to Spain renamed JUAN. 1916 sold renamed JACINTO. 1918 sold same name, 1926 sold same name. 1927 sunk in collision near Gibraltar on voyage from Malaga to Huelva.

HORNFELS, 3,417grt, built 1912, (Craig Taylor & Co. Ltd, Stockton) for H.C. Horn, Germany. 1919 taken as a war prize by the British Shipping Controller and handed over to R. Ropner & Co. 1920 sold to W.J. Williams, Cardiff, renamed TEMPESTUOUS. 1922 sold to William Bros. Ltd, renamed NORTHWAY. 1925 sold, renamed CHARTERHULME. 1931 sold to Finland, renamed WIIRI. On the 17th July 1940 the ship was sunk during an air attack by Italian bombers off Malta on voyage from the Tyne to Piraeus via Gibraltar. Abandoned and re-boarded twice over the day after eight separate attacks, the crew were forced to abandon for the third and last time as the ship sank rapidly bow first. Captain and crew landed at Malta.

HURWORTH (1), 2,387grt, built 1888 (Wm. Gray & Co., West Hartlepool) for R. Ropner & Co. 1912 sold to G. Payavlas & Co., Greece renamed THRASYVOULOS. 1927 sold renamed KYDARIS. 1928 sold same name. 1929 stranded at St. Eustratios, refloated and scrapped at Genoa, Italy.

HURWORTH (2), 7,238grt, built 1944 (Bethlehem Fairfield Shipyard Inc., Baltimore) as SAMLISTAR for United States War Shipping Administration. 1947 purchased by Ropner and renamed HURWORTH. 1954 sold to Costa Rica renamed SUERTE. 1962 sold to Lebanon same name. 1962 ran aground at Halifax, Nova Scotia, refloated the following day and scuttled.

73

SS Ingleby

INGLEBY (1), 3,815grt, built 1907 (Ropner & Son, Stockton) for R. Ropner & Co. 1916 registered under the Sir R. Ropner & Co. Ltd. 1929 sold to Greece renamed ATLAS. 1934 scrapped in Italy.

INGELBY (2), 7,174grt, built 1942 (Todd California Iron S.B. Corp., Richmond) as OCEAN VENGEANCE for the MOWT. 1947 purchased from Ministry of War Transport and renamed INGLEBY. 1960 sold to Nassau renamed MARTHA ENTERPRISE. 1966 sold to Panama renamed WELCOME. 1969 scrapped at Kaohsiung, Taiwan.

IRON KESTREL, 16,819grt, built 1974 (Hakodate Dockyard) as STAR KESTREL. 1982 purchased from Kulukundis and renamed IRON KESTREL. 1990 sold to Greece renamed AGHIA TRIAS. 1993 sold, renamed VIENNA SKY. 1996 sold, renamed PANAGIOTIS. 2003 scrapped at Alang, India.

IRON KIRBY, 16,819grt, built 1974 (Hakodate Dockyard) as STAR KERRY ex (IRON KERRY 1975). 1982 purchased from Kulukundis and renamed IRON KIRBY. 1991 sold renamed SEAJOY. 1993 sold to Turkey renamed AYNUR KALKAVAN. 1998 Scrapped at Gadani Beach, Pakistan.

IRON SOMERSBY, 40,088grt, built 1971 (Harland & Wolff, Belfast). 1986 renamed SOMERSBY (4). 1987 sold renamed CHIA YUN. 1993 sold, renamed CHI KUNI. Scrapped same year at Nantong, China.

KIRKBY, 3,034grt, built 1891 (Ropner & Son, Stockton) for R. Ropner & Co. 1915 War Loss.

KIRKPOOL, 4,840grt, built 1928 (Sir J. Laing & Sons, Sunderland). 1942 War Loss.

SS Kirkpool

LACKENBY (1), 2,120grt, built 1894 (Ropner & Son, Stockton) for R. Ropner & Co. 1927 sold to P. Danneberg, Latvia renamed BALVA. 1931

SS Lackenby

wrecked in Baltic Sea.

LACKENBY (2), 5,112grt, built 1928 (Wm. Gray & Co., West Hartlepool). 1943 War Loss.

LACKENBY (3), 64,640grt, built 1977 (Harland & Wolff, Belfast). Launched as OTTERPOOL for the Norwegian Bulk Carrier Consortium but

M V Lackenby

completed as LACKENBY and chartered by British Steel Corporation, managed by Ropner's. 1999 arrived at Alang for scrapping.

LADY ESME, 114grt, built 1961 (Philip & Son, Dartmouth). 1966 sold to the Government of Seychelles and used for Seychelles Island ferry service. Since early 1980's the ferry had been the property of Island Development Company (IDC) and was still known to be in service in 2005 when the boat was put out to tender in October 2005.

LAKE ATLIN, 7,835grt, built 1954 (William Doxford & Sons Ltd, Sunderland) as JERSEY MIST for Morel Ltd, London. 1956 sold renamed LAKE ATLIN and managed by Sir R. Ropner Co. Ltd for the Lake Atlin Shipping Co. 1960 sold not renamed. 1963 sold not renamed. 1965 sold to Greece renamed IRENE XILAS. On the 19th January 1970 sustained a major engine failure on voyage from Tamateve, Madagascar to Japan and was towed to Singapore. 1974 due to be renamed IRENE'S CHARITY but never came about and ship was laid up at Shimonoseki, Japan. 1978 left Japan after being sold to Chinese shipbreaker and scrapped at Shanghai.

LAKE BURNABY, 6,140grt, built 1952 (Bartram & Sons Ltd, Sunderland) as LLANTRISTANT for A. Radcliffe SS Co. Ltd & E. Radcliffe SS Co. Ltd. 1957 renamed LAKE BURNABY and managed by Sir R. Ropner Co. Ltd for the Western Canada SS Co. Ltd. November 1958 wrecked on the Bancoran Reef in the Sulu Sea on voyage from the Philippines to Antwerp with a cargo of dried coconut.

LAKE KOOTENAY, 7,167grt, built 1943 (North Van Shipyard Repairs, Vancouver) as FORT COLVILLE for the Dominion of Canada for bareboat charter to the British MOWT and used by the Admiralty as an Air Stores Issuing Ship. 1945 placed under the management of Blue Star Line. 1947 management took over by Common Bros. Ltd. 1950 returned to the Canadian government and sold to Western Canada SS Co. Ltd and renamed LAKE KOOTENAY. 1954 transferred to the British register at West Hartlepool and put under Ropner management. 1957 sold to Liberia and renamed ANDROS CYGNET. Resold the same year and renamed THEOSKEPASTI. 1960 transferred under the Greek flag same name. 1965 renamed MARIETTA T. 1966 scrapped at Hong Kong.

LEVEN, 2,381grt, built 1889 (Wm. Gray & Co., West Hartlepool) for R.

SS Levenpool

Ropner & Co. 1905 wrecked near Peniche, Portugal on voyage from Cardiff to Malta with a cargo of coal.

LEVENPOOL (1), 4,844grt, built 1911 (Ropner & Son, Stockton) for the Pool Shipping Co. Ltd. On the 16th December 1915 the ship was seriously damaged by a German mine off the Kentish Knock on voyage from New York to Rotterdam and beached without loss of life. Later Refloated she was temporarily repaired and made her own way to the Tyne where permanent repairs were made. 1934 she was eventually scrapped in Scotland.

LEVENPOOL (2), 7,030grt, built 1942 (Wm. Gray & Co., West Hartlepool) as EMPIRE LIONEL for MOWT. 1945 purchased from Ministry of War transport and renamed LEVENPOOL. 1962 sold to Trafalgar S.S. Co., London renamed NEWLANE. 1969 scrapped at Chittagong, Pakistan.

LUFRA (1), 1,366grt, built 1872 (Denton, Gray & Co., Hartlepool). Completed for Appleby, Ropner & Co., 1874 transferred to R. Ropner & Co., 1879 abandoned and lost in Bay of Biscay.

LUFRA (2), 1,765grt, built 1880 (Wm. Gray & Co., West Hartlepool) for R. Ropner & Co. 1887 disappeared after sailing from Cardiff to Genoa with cargo of coal.

MAGDALA, 703grt, built 1870 (Withy, Alexander & Co., West Hartlepool). Completed for Appleby, Ropner & Co., 1872 wrecked on Ameland, Frisian Islands off the Dutch coast on voyage from St. Petersburg to London.

MAGDEBURG, 950grt, built 1871 (Denton, Gray & Co., Hartlepool).

SS Maltby

Completed for Appleby, Ropner & Co., 1874 transferred to R. Ropner & Co. 1877 sold to T. Appleby not renamed. 1879 wrecked on Doganosler Shoal, Gallipoli on voyage from Cardiff to Sulina, Romania.

MALTBY (1), 2,752grt, built1889 (Ropner & Son, Stockton) for R. Ropner & Co. 1899 wrecked on River Tyne on voyage to Cape Town with a cargo of coal.

MALTBY (2), 3,977grt, built1906 (Ropner & Son, Stockton) for R. Ropner & Co. 1916 registered under the Sir R. Ropner & Co. Ltd. 1918 War Loss.

SS Mansepool

MANSEPOOL, 4,894grt, built 1928 (Wm. Gray & Co., West Hartlepool) for the Pool Shipping Co. Ltd. 1941 War Loss.

SS Millpool

MARTIN, 1,904grt, built 1895 (Wm. Gray & Co., West Hartlepool) as MARTIN. 1909 purchased from Leask, Clark & Co. for R. Ropner & Co., not renamed 1917 War Loss.

MILLPOOL, 4,218grt, built 1906 (Ropner & Son, Stockton) for the Pool Shipping Co. Ltd. Sunk without trace in a severe storm in the North Atlantic on the 3rd October 1934 on voyage from Danzig to Montreal with a cargo of Rye. The ships distress message sent from position 53' 30N 37' 10W and was picked up by the Ropner ship SS AINDERBY caught in the same storm, with the MILLPOOL stating her "aft hatch stove in and her topmast gone". One of the last messages received telling how her engine room was flooding, then no more was heard. When rescue vessels reached her last known position there was no trace of her to be found.

MOORBY (1), 2,606grt, built 1896 (Ropner & Son, Stockton) for R. Ropner & Co. 1916 registered under Sir R. Ropner Co. Ltd. 1919 registered under Ropner Shipping Co. Ltd. 1926 sold to Italy renamed ORESTA. 1942 mined and sunk in the Adriatic Sea.

MOORBY (2), 4,992grt, built 1936 (Wm. Doxford & Sons, Sunderland) for the Ropner Shipping Co. Ltd. 1948 sold to Power S.S.Co. London renamed MOORCOT. 1951 renamed HUNTSFIELD. 1955 sold to Bermuda renamed ELBOW RIVER. 1966 scrapped at Hong Kong.

MOSSEL BAY, 7,161grt, built 1944 (Prince Rupert Drydock & Shipyard, British Columbia) as the EARLSCOURT PARK for the Canadian Government. Launched as FORT CONTI. 1946 sold to the Western Canada SS Co. Ltd and renamed LAKE CHILLIWACK. 1950 renamed MOSSEL BAY and transferred to the West Hartlepool register and put under Ropner management. 1954 sold to Liberia and renamed NOUTIS. March 1965 ran aground off Constantza in the Black Sea and was declared a total loss.

SS Newby

MOUNTBY, 3,263grt, built1898 (Ropner & Son, Stockton) for the R. Ropner & Co. 1916 registered under the Sir R. Ropner & Co. Ltd. 1918 War Loss.

NEWBY, 2,168grt, built 1890 (Ropner & Son, Stockton) for R. Ropner & Co. 1915 sold to Temple Thomson & Clark, London not renamed. 1916 sunk by gunfire from German submarine U-35 near Barcelona, sailing from San Rafael to Larne.

NORSE VIKING, 14,833grt, built 1970 (Uddevallavarvet, Uddevalla, Sweden) for the Cardigan Shipping Co. Ltd and placed under management of the Ropner Co. 1981 sold to Greymouth Shipping Co, Bahamas renamed NORSE CAPTAIN. 1985 sold to Greece renamed LYDI. 1997 scrapped at Alang.

OAKBY (1), 1,976grt, built 1897 (Ropner & Son, Stockton) for R. Ropner & Co. 1915 War Loss.

OAKBY (2), 7,173grt, built 1942 (Todd Bath Iron S.B. Corp., Portland) as OCEAN PRIDE for MOWT. 1947 purchased from Ministry of War Transport and renamed OAKBY. 1959 sold to Lebanon renamed ERINIO. 1963 sold to Liberia renamed SUSANA K.L. 1966 abandoned at sea after engine room fire. Towed into Keelung, Taiwan and considered a total loss. Wreck scrapped same year.

OAKBY (3), 35,603grt, built 1983 (Hyundai Heavy Industries Co. Ltd., Ulsan, South Korea) as CONTINENTAL RELIANCE. 1992 purchased renamed OAKBY. 1997 sold to Tsakos Shipping and Trading Co. renamed GLOBAL VIGOUR. 2003 sold to Selero Shipping Co, Cyprus renamed IRENES VIGOR - no later info.

ONAWAY, 3,283grt, built 1912 (Earle's Shipbuilding & Engineering Co. Ltd, Hull) as PORTSEA for the Sea SS Co. Ltd. 1923 sold to Web & Kenward Ltd, Hull, renamed ONAWAY. Management taken over by Sir R. Ropner & Co. Ltd. Sold to Greece the following year renamed AGHIOS GEORGIOS. 1941 mined and sunk in the Suez Canal.

ORMESBY, 2,205grt, built 1890 (Ropner & Son, Stockton) for R. Ropner & Co. 1914 sold to Wilson & Reid, Belfast not renamed. 1914 resold to Russian Government renamed ORMEDIA. 1914 wrecked on Orlov Bank in the White Sea on voyage from Barry to Archangel with a cargo of coal.

SS Otterpool

OTTERPOOL (1), 4,867grt, built 1926 (Wm. Gray & Co., West Hartlepool) for the Pool Shipping Co. ltd. 1940 War Loss.

OTTERPOOL (2), 35,750grt, built 1982 (Hitachi Shipbuilding) as PACER. 1988 renamed UNITED ACE. 1991 purchased from World Wide Shipping renamed OTTERPOOL. 1997 sold and scrapped.

PARKLANDS, 1,758grt, built 1880 (Wm. Gray & Co., West Hartlepool) for R. Ropner & Co. 1891 stranded and sold to Sweden renamed THYRA. 1910 sold same name. 1915 sold same name. 1923 sold to Germany renamed MARIE FERDINAND. 1927 sold renamed CONSUL HINTZ. On the 6th June 1941 the ship collided with the quay at Wilhelmshaven suffering structural damage made worse by the ships age and 61 years in service and was later condemned.

PICTON, 2,371grt, built 1887 (E. Withy & Co., West Hartlepool) for R. Ropner & Co. Disappeared after sailing from Newport News on 20th January 1899 for Sligo, Ireland.

PIKEPOOL (1), 3,683grt, built 1909 (Ropner & Son, Stockton) for the Pool Shipping Co. Ltd. February 1918 damaged by U-boat on voyage from Rouen to Wales. Arrived safely under tow in Portland and repaired. 1940 War Loss.

PIKEPOOL (2), 7,178grt, built 1942 (Todd Bath Iron S.B. Corp., Portland) as OCEAN PILGRIM. 1947 purchased by Ropner from Ministry of War Transport and renamed PIKEPOOL. 1959 sold to Greece renamed MARIGO. 1966 sold to Cyprus renamed AMFITRITI. 1967 scrapped at Taiwan.

PRESTON (1), 2,539grt, built 1882 (Wm. Gray & Co., West Hartlepool) for R. Ropner & Co. Disappeared after sailing from New York on 31ˢᵗ January 1885 for Avonmouth with a cargo of wheat.

PRESTON (2), 2,157 built 1885 (M. Pearse & Co., Stockton) for R. Ropner & Co.1899 sold to General Steam Nav. Co., London not renamed, 1906 wrecked at Point Bay, near the fishing port of Camarinas on voyage from London to Genoa.

PRESTON (3), 3,275grt, built 1921 (Hanlon Dry Dock & Shipbuilding Co., Oakland) as MEMNON for United States Shipping Board. 1940 sold to British Ministry of Shipping renamed EMPIRE MOUFLON. 1946 purchased by Ropner from Ministry of War Transport and renamed PRESTON. 1951 sold to Panama renamed AVANCE. 1957 renamed AVLIS. 1962 scrapped in Greece.

MV Ravenscraig

RAISBY, 2,205grt, built 1889 (Ropner & Son, Stockton) for R. Ropner & Co. 1901 wrecked off the Cape Verde Islands on voyage from Rosario to Las Palmas with a cargo of maize.

RAVENSCRAIG, 64,651grt, built 1979 (Harland & Wolff, Belfast) for Orion Leasing Ltd. Placed on long term charter to British Steel and managed by Ropner Shipping Co. Ltd. Sold 1997 to Ore Carriers Ltd, Bahamas. 1999 scrapped at Alang.

SS Reedpool

REEDPOOL, 4,845grt, built 1924 (Ropner Shipbuilding & Repairing Co., Stockton) for the Pool Shipping Co. Ltd. 1942 War Loss.

RENPOR (1), 1,323grt, built 1874 (Short Bros., Sunderland) for R. Ropner & Co. 1882 sunk by pack ice in North Atlantic on voyage to Boston from Hartlepool with a cargo of potatoes and iron.

RENPOR (2), 1,917grt, built 1883 (E. Withy & Co., West Hartlepool) for R. Ropner & Co. 1897 abandoned 300 miles off the Azores and sank after crankshaft broke on voyage from Porman, Spain to Philadelphia with a cargo

SS Rockpool

of iron ore.

ROCKPOOL (1), 4,502grt, built 1912 (Ropner & Son, Stockton) for the Pool Shipping Co. Ltd. 1918 War Loss.

ROCKPOOL (2), 4,889grt, built 1927 (Wm. Gray & Co., West Hartlepool) for the Ropner Shipping Co. Ltd. 1941 ran aground on the Clyde and abandoned. Salvaged by British MOWT renamed EMPIRE TRENT. 1946

SS Romanby

sold to South Africa renamed GENERAL GEORGE BRINK. 1947 sold to Panama renamed AFRICANA. 1959 scrapped at Osaka, Japan.

ROLLESBY, 3,955grt, built 1906 (Ropner & Son, Stockton) for R. Ropner & Co. 1916 registered under the Sir R. Ropner & Co. Ltd. 1917 War Loss.

ROMANBY (1), 1,745grt, built 1882 (Wm. Gray & Co., West Hartlepool). 1887 purchased from Middleton & Co. by R. Ropner & Co., not renamed. 1899 sold to T.H. Skogland, Norway renamed HEIM. 1917 sunk by submarine on voyage from Hull to Rouen with a cargo of coal.

ROMANBY (2), 3,835grt, built 1908 (Ropner & Son, Stockton) for R. Ropner & Co. 1916 registered under the Sir R. Ropner & Co. Ltd. December 1917 lost after a collision with the S.S. ROMERA in the North Atlantic after sailing from Cardiff.

ROMANBY (3), 4,887grt, built 1927 (Wm. Gray & Co., West Hartlepool) for the Ropner Shipping Co. Ltd. 1940 War Loss.

MV Romanby

ROMANBY (4), 10,488grt, built 1957 (Sir J. Laing & Sons, Sunderland) for the Ropner Shipping Co. Ltd. 1969 sold to Greece renamed SALLY. 1971 renamed SANDRA N. 1973 renamed CANTON. 1973 sold same name. 1974 sold renamed TOMABI. 1976 sold renamed SWEDE SURPRISE. 1983 scrapped at Chittagong.

ROXBY (1), 3,043grt, built 1893 (Ropner & Son, Stockton) for R. Ropner & Co. September 1904 lost in collision with S.S. GLASGOW near Hook of Holland on voyage from Taganrog, Russia to Hamburg with a cargo of grain.

ROXBY (2), 4,252grt, built 1923 (Ropner & Son, Stockton) for the Ropner Shipping Co. Ltd. 1942 War Loss.

RUDBY (1), 4,846grt, built 1924 (Wm. Gray & Co., West Hartlepool) for the Ropner Shipping Co. Ltd. 1943 sold to Cassar Co., Malta not renamed. 1946 renamed KNIGHT TEMPLAR. 1947 sold to Panama renamed VANMIL. 1950 sold to Finland renamed LAILA NURMINEN. 1955 sold to Italy renamed AMANITA. 1958 scrapped at Savonna, Italy.

RUDBY (2), 7,219grt, built1944 (Bethlehem Fairfield Shipyard Inc., Baltimore) as SAMTAY for United States War Shipping Administration. 1947 purchased by Ropner and renamed RUDBY. 1952 sold to Panama renamed THEKLA. 1954 sold renamed ADAMAS. 1968 scrapped at Sakaide, Japan.

RUDBY (3), 57,255grt, built 1971(Harland & Wolff, Belfast) for the Ropner Shipping Co. Ltd. 1980 sold to Liberia renamed ORIENT PIONEER. 8th January 1990 damaged in heavy seas and abandoned in the Indian Ocean on voyage from Tubarao, Brazil to Kaohsiung, Taiwan with cargo of iron ore. Finally sank 21st January.

SS Rushpool

RUSHPOOL (1), 5,125grt, built 1928 (Cowpen Dry Docks & Shipbuilding Co., Blyth) for the Pool Shipping Co. Ltd. 1941 War Loss.

RUSHPOOL (2), 10,488grt, built 1957 (Sir J. Laing & Sons, Sunderland) for

SS Salmonpool

the Pool Shipping Co. Ltd. 1970 sold to Greece renamed EUTHALIA. 1974 sold renamed ELEFTHEROES. 1979 sold renamed FORUM SPIRIT. August 1982 damaged by fire off Piraeus and laid up. 1984 scrapped at Split, Croatia.

SALMONPOOL (1), 4,905 built 1913 (Ropner & Son, Stockton) for the Pool Shipping Co. Ltd. 1916 War Loss.

SALMONPOOL (2), 4,803grt, built 1924 (Irvine's Shipbuilding & Drydock Co. Ltd, West Hartlepool) for the Pool Shipping Co. Ltd. 1940 seized by the

M V Salmonpool

Germans during invasion of Norway and renamed PUTZIG. 1945 retaken at Bremerhaven for MOWT renamed EMPIRE SALMONPOOL and put under Ropner management. 1947 sold renamed IRENE K. 1955 sold renamed WHITE LODGE. 1955 sold to Costa Rica renamed PUNTARENAS. 1958 scrapped at Aviles, Spain.

SALMONPOOL (3), 24,785grt, built 1982 (Eleusis Shipyard). Purchased on the stocks by Ropner Shipping Co Ltd and named SALMONPOOL. 1990 sold to Egon Oldendorff renamed YEOMAN BANK. 1991 converted into self-unloader. January 2006 still known to be in service under Liberian flag.

SAMSUVA, 7,219grt, built 1944 (New England Shipbuilding Corp., Portland, Maine) for the United States War Shipping Administration for bareboat charter to the British MOWT and managed by Ropner. 1944 War Loss.

SAMSYLARNA, 7,210grt, built 1944 (Bethlehem Fairfield Shipyard Inc., Baltimore) for the United States War Shipping Administration for bareboat charter to the British MOWT and managed by Ropner. On the 4th August 1944 in the Mediterranean off Benghazi on voyage from New York to Bombay & Colombo via Suez with a general cargo & explosives, the ship was hit by an aerial torpedo, blowing the ships stern completely off. Abandoned

88

SS Saxilby

then re-boarded, the ship was beached near Benghazi and eventually towed to Alexandria where she was taken out of commission and laid up for the duration of the war. 1951 sold to Italy renamed TITO CAMPANELLA. 1961 sold to Poland renamed HUTA SOSNOWIEC. 1971 scrapped Bilbao.

SAXILBY, 3,630grt, built 1914 (Ropner & Son, Stockton) for R. Ropner & Co. 1916 registered under the Sir R. Ropner & Co. Ltd. 1919 registered with under Ropner Shipping Co. Ltd. for R. Ropner & Co. 1916 registered under the Sir R. Ropner & Co. Ltd. 1919 registered with under Ropner Shipping Co.

SS Seapool

Ltd. On the 15th November 1933 the ship foundered in the North Atlantic 400 miles West of Newfoundland on voyage from Wabana, Canada to Port Talbot with cargo of iron ore. A distress signal was picked up in position 51' 50N 19' 15W and several ships went to her assistance, but nothing more was seen of the ship and her entire crew.

SCAWBY, 3,658grt built 1911 (Ropner & Son, Stockton) for R. Ropner Co. 1915 War Loss

SEAPOOL (1), 4,502grt, built 1913 (Ropner & Son, Stockton) for the Pool Shipping Co. Ltd. 1936 sold to McCowen & Gross, London renamed PILCOT. 1939 sold to Estonia renamed VAPPER. 1940 torpedoed and sunk by German U-34 off Lands End.

SEAPOOL (2), 4,820grt, built1940 (Burntisland Shipbuilding Co., Burntisland) for the Pool Shipping Co. Ltd 1951 sold to Hamburg Amerika Line renamed GRUNEWALD. 1953 sold to Schulte & Bruns renamed ESTHER SCHULTE. 1962 scrapped at Hamburg.

SEATON, 891grt, built 1871 (Denton, Gray & Co., Hartlepool). Completed for Appleby, Ropner & Co. 1874 transferred to R. Ropner & Co. 1888 sold to O. Thoresen, Norway not renamed. 1898 sold to Sweden same name. 1916 sold same name. 1918 sold renamed RUSKEN. 1919 sold not renamed. 1920

renamed PAN. 1922 sold same name. 1922 sold to Danzig not renamed. 1925 sold to Sweden not renamed. 1934 scrapped at Copenhagen.

SEDGEPOOL (1), 6,530grt, built 1918 (Ropner & Son, Stockton) for the Pool Shipping Co. Ltd. 1940 War Loss.

SEDGEPOOL (2), 7,279grt, built 1944 (South-eastern S.B. Corp., Savannah) as SAMDART for United States War Shipping Administration on bareboat charter for British MOWT, managed by Mungo Campbell & Co. Ltd. 1947 purchased by Ropner renamed SEDGEPOOL. 1954 sold to Nassau renamed BOBARA. 1956 sold renamed FLEVARIOTISSA. 1958 sold to

SS Selby

Costa Rica renamed KAPETAN ANDREAS. 1965 sold to Greece renamed KITSA. 1967 scrapped at Kaohsiung, Taiwan.

M V Silver Comet

SELBY, 2,137grt, built 1895 (Ropner & Son, Stockton) for R. Ropner & Co. 1914 War Loss.

SHOTTON, 754grt, built 1870 (Withy, Alexander & Co., West Hartlepool). Completed for Appleby, Ropner & Co. 1874 transferred to R. Ropner & Co. 1877 sold to T. Appleby not renamed. 1887 sold to J.A. Waller, Sweden renamed APOLLO. 1889 abandoned and sank in North Atlantic.

SILVER COMET, 1,279grt, built 1961 (Arnhemsche Schps. Maats. Arnhem) for the Bonny Shipping Co. Ltd and placed under Ropner. 1968 sold to the Netherlands, Antilles renamed SILVER STAR. 1969 sold to the Netherlands renamed GERDA and managed by Irish & Continental Shipping Co. Ltd. 1973 sold renamed MEGREZ. 1977 sold to Greece renamed FRIGO KING. 1982 sold to International Food Stuff Co, United Arab Emirates renamed IFFCO 1. Still on Lloyds Register 1984-1985, but disappeared from records thereafter.

SKIDBY, 3,703grt, built 1892 (Ropner & Son, Stockton) for R. Ropner & Co. January 1905 wrecked on Sable Island off Nova Scotia's old No. 2 Life Station on a voyage from South Shields to Baltimore in ballast. Her crew were able to safely walk ashore during the low tide.

SLINGSBY, 3,231grt, built 1892 (Ropner & Son, Stockton) for R. Ropner & Co. 1915 sold to the Lowlands Steam Shipping Co., Newcastle renamed

SS Somersby

LOWTYNE. June 1918 torpedoed and sunk without warning by submarine about three miles East South-East of Whitby killing 3 crew.

SOMERSBY (1), 3,347grt, built 1913 (Ropner & Son, Stockton) for R. Ropner & Co. 1916 registered under the Sir R. Ropner & Co. Ltd. 1919

MV Somersby

registered with under Ropner Shipping Co. Ltd. December 1923 wrecked near Corunna on voyage from Cardiff to Civitavecchia, Italy with a cargo of coal.

SOMERSBY (2), 5,168grt, built 1930 (Wm. Gray & Co., West Hartlepool) for the Ropner Shipping Co. Ltd. 1941 War Loss.

SOMERSBY (3), 5,893grt, built 1954 (Sir J. Laing & Sons, Sunderland) for the Ropner Shipping Co. Ltd. 1958 sold to the Admiralty and converted into a Air Store Support Ship renamed RELIANT. 1977 scrapped at Inverkeithing.

SOMERSBY (4), See IRON SOMERSBY.

SOWERBY, 1,254grt, built 1878 (Wm. Gray & Co., West Hartlepool) for Middleton & Co. 1887 purchased by R. Ropner & Co., not renamed. 1897 wrecked on Understen Rock, Gulf of Bothnia.

SPILSBY, 3,661grt, built 1910 (Ropner & Son, Stockton) for R. Ropner & Co. 1916 registered under the Sir R. Ropner & Co. Ltd. 1919 registered under the Ropner Shipping Co. Ltd. 1935 sold to Italy for scrap, sale later cancelled. 1936 scrapped at Blyth.

STAGPOOL (1), 4,621grt, built 1905 (Ropner & Son, Stockton) for the Pool Shipping Co. Ltd. 1935 scrapped at Rosyth.

STAGPOOL (2), 4,560grt, built (Wm. Doxford & Sons, Sunderland) as IRON CHIEF for Interstate Steamships. 1935 purchased by Ropner from

SS Stonepool

Essex Oak and renamed STAGPOOL. 1950 sold to Heron S.S. Co, London renamed GRANNY SUZANNE. 1954 sold to Costa Rica renamed CARMEN. 1956 sold same name. 1963 sunk in collision with SADIKZADE, with the loss of 2 lives.

M V Stonepool

STONEPOOL (1), 4,803grt, built 1928 (Smiths Dock Co., Middlesbrough) for the Pool Shipping Co. Ltd. 1941 War Loss

STONEPOOL (2), 27,049grt, built 1966 (Charles Connell & Co., Glasgow) for the Pool Shipping Co. Ltd. 1982 sold to Liberia not renamed. 1986 scrapped at Kaohsiung.

SWAINBY (1), 2,680grt, built 1888 (Wm. Gray & Co., West Hartlepool) for R. Ropner & Co. 1900 sold to A.G. Vassiliade & Co., Greece renamed CLEMENTINE. 1904 foundered near Ushant.

SWAINBY (2), 3,653grt, built 1904 (Ropner & Son, Stockton) for R. Ropner & Co. November 1906 lost in collision with HILLBROOK off Hartland Point, Devon on voyage from Cardiff to Mauritius.

SS Swainby (4)

SWAINBY (3), 5,811grt, built 1917 (Ropner & Son, Stockton) for Sir R. Ropner & Co. Ltd. 1919 registered under Ropner Shipping Co. Ltd. 1940 War Loss.

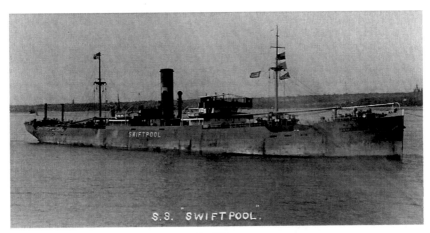

S.S. "SWIFTPOOL".

SWAINBY (4), 6,711grt, built 1941 (Wm. Gray & Co., West Hartlepool) as EMPIRE SUNBEAM. 1945 purchased by Ropner from Ministry of War Transport and renamed SWAINBY. 1962 sold to Trafalgar S.S. Co., London

MV Swiftpool

renamed NEWGATE. 1971 scrapped a Istanbul.

SWIFTPOOL (1), 5,205grt, built 1929 (Wm. Gray & Co., West Hartlepool) for the Pool Shipping Co. Ltd. 1941 War Loss.

SWIFTPOOL (2), 6,611grt, built 1954 (Caledon Shipbuilding & Engineering Co., Dundee) for the Pool Shipping Co. Ltd. 1964 sold to British India Steam Nav. Co. renamed CHAKLA. 1972 sold to Guan Guan Shipping, Singapore renamed GOLDEN BEAR. 1975 scrapped.

SS Teesdale

TARPEIA, 1,644grt, built 1877 (E. Withy & Co., West Hartlepool) as TARPEIA for R.C. Denton Co. 1888 purchased by R. Ropner & Co., not renamed. 1895 wrecked at Sandhammaren, Sweden.

TEESDALE, 2,470grt, built 1904 (Ropner & Son, Stockton) as TEESDALE for J.A. Wood & Co. 1908 purchased by Ropner not renamed. August 1917 foundered three miles off Saltburn Pier on voyage to the River Tees for repairs after earlier being damaged by torpedo in June on voyage from the Tyne to Gibraltar.

SS Teespool

TEESPOOL (1), 4,577grt, built 1905 (Ropner & Son, Stockton) for the Pool Shipping Co. Ltd. 1935 scrapped at Rosyth.

TEESPOOL (2), 7,174grt, built 1942 (Todd California Iron S.B. Corp., Richmond) as OCEAN VANITY. 1947 purchased from Ministry of War Transport and renamed TEESPOOL. 1960 sold to Wheelock, Marden & Co., Hong Kong renamed WYNN. 1964 renamed GOLDON PHOENIX. 1966 sold to Nassau same name 1968 scrapped at Onomichi, Japan.

TENBY, 3,969grt, built 1898 (Ropner & Son, Stockton) for R. Ropner & Co. 1904 wrecked off Sumatra on voyage from Java to Port Said.

THERESE HEYMANN, 2,393grt, built 1903 (Ropner & Son, Stockton) for Therese Heymann SS Co. Ltd. Same year taken over and managed by R. Ropner & Co. 1914 considered War Loss.

THIRLBY (1), 2,009grt, built 1898 (Ropner & Son, Stockton) for the R. Ropner & Co. 1916 registered under the Sir R. Ropner & Co. Ltd. On the 24th April 1917 SS THIRLBY fought a running battle for four and a half hours with a German U-boat. THIRLBY was damaged after sustaining a hit in one of her cargo holds but also managed to hit the U-boats conning tower causing the U-boat to break off the action. Later in 1917 she became a War Loss.

THIRLBY (2), 4,888grt, built 1928 (Wm. Gray & Co., West Hartlepool) for the Ropner Shipping Co. Ltd. 1942 War Loss.

MV Thirlby (4)

THIRLBY (3), 6,978grt, built 1941 (Lithgows Ltd, Port Glasgow) as EMPIRE TIDE. 1945 purchased by Ropner from Ministry of War Transport and renamed THIRLBY. 1956 sold to Panama renamed GURI. 1963 sold renamed ANTO. 1966 scrapped at Ikeda, Japan.

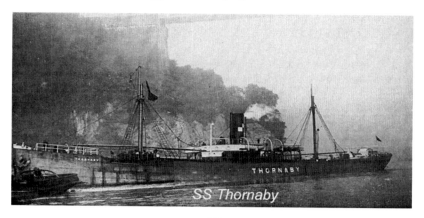

SS Thornaby

THIRLBY (4), 13,105grt, built 1958 (Sir J. Laing & Sons, Sunderland) for the Ropner Shipping Co. Ltd. 1982 sold to Greece renamed DIAMANDO. 1985 scrapped at Aliaga, Turkey.

MV Thornaby

THORNABY (1) 1,730 built 1889 (Ropner & Son, Stockton) for R. Ropner & Co. 1916 War Loss

THORNABY (2), 12,146grt, built 1955 (Sir J. Laing & Sons, Sunderland) for the Ropner Shipping Co. Ltd. 1966 sold to Greece renamed D.G. PAPALIOS. 1969 laid up. 1970 scrapped at Gandia, Spain.

TOLESBY, 3,967grt, built 1901(Ropner & Son, Stockton) for the R. Ropner & Co. 1908 wrecked in Trepassey Bay, Newfoundland on voyage from Galveston, Texas to Havre, Quebec with a cargo of cotton.

TROUTPOOL (1), 3,281grt, built 1903 (Ropner & Son, Stockton) for the Pool Shipping Co. Ltd. September 1923 wrecked near St. Pierre, Miquelon, Newfoundland on voyage from Las Palmas to St. John's, Newfoundland in ballast.

TROUTPOOL (2), 4,886grt, built 1927 (Wm. Gray & Co., West Hartlepool) for the Pool Shipping Co. Ltd. 1940 War Loss.

TROUTPOOL (3), 7,989grt, built 1956 (J.L. Thompson & Sons, Sunderland) for the Pool Shipping Co. Ltd. 1963 sold to Peru renamed PERENE. 1969

SS Trunkby

sold to Greece renamed AGIS ASTERIADIS. 1974 renamed POLA. 1979
scrapped.

SS Ullapool

TRUNKBY, 2,635grt, built 1896 (Ropner & Son, Stockton) for R. Ropner &
Co. 1916 War Loss

ULLAPOOL, 4,891grt, built 1927 (Wm. Gray & Co., West Hartlepool) for
the Pool Shipping Co. Ltd. 1941 War Loss.

WALVIS BAY, 7,147grt, built 1944 (West Coast Shipbuilders, Vancouver)
as WINONA PARK for the Canadian Government. 1946 sold to the Western
Canada SS Co. Ltd and later renamed LAKE TATLA. 1950 renamed
WALVIS BAY and transferred to the West Hartlepool register and put under
Ropner management. 1957 sold to Liberia renamed ANDROS HALCYON.

Sold to Italy same year renamed MAS PRIMO. 1959 sold to Turkey renamed KIRLANGICLAR. 1960 sold not renamed. 1972 arrived Rangoon and taken over by Burmese Government. 1973 sold and scrapped at Kaohsiung, Taiwan.

WANDBY (1), 3,981grt, built 1899 (Ropner & Son, Stockton) for the R.

M V Wandby

Ropner & Co. 1916 registered under the Sir R. Ropner & Co. Ltd. On the 2nd April 1917 SS WANDBY had an encounter with a German U-boat and after an exchange of gunfire managed to hit and sink the U-boat. March 1921 wrecked off Portland, Maine on voyage from Genoa in ballast.

WANDBY (2), 4,947grt, built 1940 (Sir J. Laing & Sons, Sunderland) for the Ropner Shipping Co. Ltd. 1940 War Loss.

WANDBY (3), 11,545grt, built 1959 (Bartram & Sons, Sunderland) for the Ropner Shipping Co. Ltd. 1972 sold to Greece renamed SEA RANGER. 1984 sold renamed LEDRA. 1984 sold to Pakistan ship breakers at Gadani Beach.

WAR DEER, 5,324grt, built 1918 (William Doxford & Sons Ltd, Sunderland) for the WWI Shipping Controller and put under Ropner management. On the 30th August 1918 torpedoed and damaged on voyage from Sunderland to Blyth. Towed into the Tyne for repairs. 1919 sold to France, renamed FORT DE DOUAUMONT. 1951 sold to Italy and renamed SANGIULIANO. 1958 scrapped at Antwerp.

WAR HIND, 5,263grt, built 1918 (Short Bros., Sunderland) for the WWI Shipping Controller and put under Ropner management. 1919 sold to Prince Line Ltd, renamed GRECIAN PRINCE. 1924 transferred to Warren Line Ltd, renamed SAVANNAH. 1927 sold to Yugoslavia, renamed NEVESINJE.

SS Warlaby

September 1928 ran aground off Chile and re-floated two month later, beached and declared a total loss. 1929 again re-floated and sold to Chile, renamed COQUIMBO. 1932 sold, renamed VALPARAISO. 1935 sold back to Yugoslavia, renamed PRINCE PAVLE. 1942 renamed FRANKA. 1946 sold under the same name. 1959 scrapped at Hong Kong.

WARLABY, 4,876grt, built 1927 (Wm. Gray & Co., West Hartlepool) for the Ropner Shipping Co. Ltd. 1941 War Loss.

WATLINGTON, 1,814grt, built 1882 (Wm. Gray & Co., West Hartlepool) for R. Ropner & Co. 1899 sold to N. Dubuisson, France renamed LUCIEN. March 1905 wrecked on Labanche Rocks, St Nazaire.

WAVE (1), 957grt, built 1871 (Denton, Gray & Co., Hartlepool). Completed for Appleby, Ropner & Co. 1874 transferred to R. Ropner & Co. 1890 sold to J.C. Twaites, Hartlepool same name. 1881 repurchased by R. Ropner & Co. 1886 wrecked near Romso Light.

WAVE (2), 2,264grt, built 1887 (Wm. Gray & Co., West Hartlepool) for R. Ropner & Co. 1900 sold to D.G. Moiratis & Co., Greece renamed ANTONIOS. 1905 wrecked on Andros Island, Greece.

WEARPOOL (1), 4,929grt, built 1913 (Ropner & Son, Stockton) for the Pool Shipping Co. Ltd. 1935 sold to Greece renamed AIKATERINI. 29th January 1941 torpedoed and sunk by U-93 on voyage from Sydney, Cape Breton to Liverpool in Convoy SC-19.

WEARPOOL (2), 4,982grt, built 1936 (Wm. Doxford & Sons, Sunderland) for the Pool Shipping Co. Ltd. 1954 sold to Sweden renamed ADELSO. 1964 sold to Greece renamed LEFKIPOS. 1971 sold renamed DIMITROS. 1979 scrapped at La Spezia, Italy.

WELLFIELD, 1,907grt, built 1882 (E. Withy & Co., West Hartlepool) for R. Ropner & Co. 1899 sold to Netherlands renamed BESTEVAER. 1901 sold to Sweden renamed MERKUR. 1903 stranded, Refloated, sold renamed RESERV. 1920 sold and again 1929 same name, 1932 sold renamed HOLMIA. 1935 scrapped in Italy.

WESTERN BRIDGE, 55,695grt, built 1991 (Hashihama Zosen, Tadotsu, Japan) under Ropner supervision for British Steel, Western Bridge Shipping Ltd, Bahamas. Placed on British Steel charter under Ropner management. 1994 registered owner Nat. West, (GB). 2003 sold renamed YEOMAN BONTRUP for Foster Yeoman/Beheersmaatschapij FR. Bontrup B.V. of Holland partnership. 2006 still in service.

WESTONBY, 3,795grt, built 1901 (Ropner & Son, Stockton) for the R. Ropner & Co. 1916 registered under the Sir R. Ropner & Co. Ltd. 1917 War Loss.

WILLERBY, 3,630grt, built 1912 (Ropner & Son, Stockton) for R. Ropner & Co. 1915 War Loss

MV Willowpool

WILLOWPOOL (1), 4,815grt, built 1925 (Ropner Shipbuilding & Repairing Co., Stockton) for the Pool Shipping Co. Ltd. 1939 War Loss.

WILLOWPOOL (2), 8,972grt, built 1960 (A/B Finnboda Varf, Stockholm) for the Pool Shipping Co. Ltd. 1967 sold to Liberia renamed EMMANUEL MARCOU. 1983 scrapped.

WRAGBY 3,641grt built 1901 (Ropner & Son, Stockton) for the R. Ropner & Co. 1916 registered under the Sir R. Ropner & Co. Ltd. 1917 War Loss.

YEARBY (1), 2,639grt, built 1896 (Ropner & Son, Stockton) for R. Ropner & Co. 1916 registered under the Sir R. Ropner & Co Ltd. 1919 sold to M.H. Bland, Gibraltar renamed GIBEL YEDID. 1925 sold to Greece renamed INDIA 1930 sold to the Netherlands for demolition. 1931 broken up.

YEARBY (2), 5,666grt, built 1929 (Wm. Gray & Co., West Hartlepool) for the Ropner Shipping Co. Ltd. 1950 sold to Italy renamed BONITAS. On the 19th February 1958 the ship foundered off Cape Lookout after developing a leak on voyage from Macapa, Brazil to Baltimore with a cargo of ore.

Appendix

The following list is of Dutch, Norwegian & Yugoslav Merchant ships belonging to owners from the German occupied countries, which escaped the occupation and were taken over by the MOS/MOWT during WWII and placed under Ropner management.

Netherlands 1940

FLENSBURG, 6,429grt, built 1922. Owned by Halcyon-Lijn NV, Rotterdam. 1942 War Loss

ROZENBURG, 2,068grt, built 1918. Owned by NV Stoomboot Rederij. Sunk after a collison with the Dutch tanker MURENA off Halifax, Nova Scotia on the 2nd August 1941.

SAWAHLOENTO, 3,085grt, built 1921. Owned by Koninklijke Paketvaart Mij NV, Amsterdam. 1942 War Loss.

STAD ALKMAAR, 5,750grt, built 1940. Owned by Halcyon Lijn NV, Rotterdam. 1940 War Loss.

STAD AMSTERDAM, 3,780grt, built 1920. Owned by Halcyon Lijn NV, Rotterdam. 1942 War Loss.

STAD ARNHELM, 3,819grt, built 1919. Owned by Halcyon Lijn NV, Rotterdam. Returned to owners in 1945.

STAD HAARLEM, 4,518grt, built 1929. Owned by Halcyon Lijn NV, Rotterdam. Returned to owners in 1945.

STAD MAASLUIS, 6,541grt, built 1918. Owned by Halcyon Lijn NV, Rotterdam. Returned to owners in 1945.

STAD MAASTRICHT, 6,552grt, built 1924. Owned by Halcyon Lijn NV, Rotterdam. 1940 War Loss.

STAD SCHIEDAM, 5,918grt, built 1911. Owned by Halcyon Lijn NV, Rotterdam. After loading a cargo of Sulphur in Port Sulphur, Louisiana for the UK the ship had made a stop off in Bermuda and was then ordered to Halifax, Nova Scotia to join a homeward bound convoy. On the 16th September 1940, two days out of Bermuda the ship was suddenly rocked by two huge explosions followed by several smaller ones, breaking in two and sinking within five minutes taking twenty men with her. Twelve survivors were picked up after five days by the British Merchant ship WHITE CREST and landed at Baltimore. No U-boat ever claimed this ship and rumours started that the ship had been sabotaged by placing a bomb in her cargo. This theory was later discounted and it is believed the explosion was probably caused by a mixture of the sulhur gas and dust being ignited by an internal spark caused by friction in the ships steel plating.

STAD VLAARDINGEN, 8,501grt, built 1925. Owned by Halcyon Lijn NV, Rotterdam. Returned to owners in 1945.

Norway 1940

AUST, 5,630grt, built 1920. Owned by Lundegaard & Sønner, Farsund. 1942 War Loss.

CORNEVILLE, 4,544grt, built 1930. Owned by A. F. Klaveness & Co., Oslo. 1943 War Loss.

MARIE BAKKE, 4,307grt, built 1926. Owned by Knut Knutsen O. A. S., Haugesund. Returned to owners 1945.

STIRLINGVILLE, 4,995grt, built 1935. Owned by A. F. Klaveness & Co. A/S, Oslo. Returned to owners 1945.

VELOX, 3,831grt, built 1922. Owned by C. H. Sørensen & Sønner, Arendal. Returned to owners 1945.

VEST, 5,074grt, built 1920. Owned by Lundegaard & Sønner, Farsund. Returned to owners 1945.

VILLANGAR, 4,884grt, built 1929. Owned by Westfal-Larsen & Co. A/S, Bergen. Returned to owners 1945.

Yugoslavia 1941

BOSILJKA, 3,009grt, built 1896. Owned by 'Alcusu' Parobrodarsko Drustvo S.O.J. of Susak. 1942 War Loss.

DRAVA, 3,508grt, built 1919. Owned by Jugslavenska Oceansaka Plovidba DD of Susak. Returned to owners 1945.

DUBRAVKA, 3,798grt, built 1905. Owned by Dubrovaka Plovidba Ackionarsko Drustvo of Dubrovnik. Returned to owners 1945.

DUNAV, 4,369grt, built 1912. Owned by Oceania, Brodarsko Ackionarsko Drustvo of Susak. Returned to owners 1945.

IVAN, 1,275grt, built 1914. Owned by Barbaravoic of Susak, managers: Levant DD. Returned to owners 1945.

IVAN TOPIC, 4,943grt, built 1920. Owned by Slobodna Plovidba Topic DD of Susak. Returned to owners 1945.

KARMEN, 2,541grt, built 1896. Owned by 'Alcusu' Parobrodarsko Drustvo S.O.J. of Susak. Returned to owners 1945.

KUPA, 4,382grt, built 1917. Owned by Prekomorska Plovidba DD of Zagreb. 1942 War Loss.

LJUBICA MATKOVIC, 3,289grt, built 1919. Owned by Matkovic, Brodarsko Poduzece Eugen of Split. 1942 War Loss

NIKOLINA MATKOVIC, 3,898grt, built 1918. Owned by Matkovic, Brodarsko Poduzece Eugen of Split. 1942 War Loss.

OLGA TOPIC, 4,375grt, built 1918. Owned by Slobodna Plovidba Topic DD of Susak. Returned to owners 1945.

TREPCA, 5,042grt, built 1930. Owned by Jugoslavenski Lloyd Ackionarsko Drustvo of Zagreb. 1942 War Loss.

VIS, 1,772grt, built 1921. Owned by Oceania, Brodarsko Ackionarsko Drustvo of Susak. Returned to owners 1945.

Ropner's Merchant Shipping Losses 1914-1918

Not including ships partially damaged/salvaged or lost through the forces of nature. The 1905 built SS TEESPOOL survived the war but was seriously damaged by a torpedo in 1917 resulting in the death of some of her crew, so the ship is added to the list.

Alongside the ships names are the Official No. from the Lloyds Register which will help trace any surviving Log Books & Crew Agreements held at The National Archives at Kew for more in depth research. Unfortunately the information is fairly limited. All surviving Logbooks for WW1 are supposedly in BT165 but the facts are there are also a couple of thousand in BT99. For BT165 these run from BT165/614 to BT165/1898 search by official number. There is also some kind of alphabetical index for every year which is the last or thereabouts entry for the year concerned. The same applies to BT99, these files run from BT99/2982 to BT99/3472.

SS BALDERSBY, 3,613grt, built 1913, (ON. 135888). Torpedoed and sunk by German submarine UB-91 on the 28th September 1918 sailing from Montreal with a cargo of grain. 2 crew killed. Captain Eves was removed from his lifeboat and was expecting to be taken prisoner. After being questioned onboard UB-91 he was returned to his crew.

SS BROOKBY, 3,679grt, built 1905, (ON. 119870). Sunk by German submarine U-60 near Fastnet on the 19th June 1917 sailing from Sagunto for Middlesbrough with iron ore. U-60 attacked the ship on the surface using her deck gun eventually hitting BROOKBY who had been returning fire with her stern mounted gun. Captain B. Maughan and all crew picked up by a passing patrol boat and landed at Falmouth.

BURNBY, 3,665grt, built 1905, (ON. 119867) Torpedoed and sunk by German submarine U-39 near Cape Falcon on the 26th February 1917 sailing from Barry Roads to Algiers with coal. Captain J.C. Wilson was taken prisoner and interned for the duration of the war in Austria. All remaining crew managed to get away in lifeboats.

SS COLEBY, 3,824grt, built 1907, (ON. 124274). Captured by German auxiliary cruiser Kronprinz Wilhelm and sunk by gunfire on the 27th March 1915 460 miles North-East by North of Pernambuco. After forcing the ship to heave to the COLEBY's Captain William Crighton was given a hand written note declaring his ship was to be sunk and the crew given time to collect their personal belongings. They were eventually landed in America.

SS DALEBY (1), 3,628grt, built 1900, (ON. 112419). Torpedoed and sunk by U-70, 150 miles South-East of Cape Clear on the 29th April 1917 sailing from Huelva to Garston with copper & silver ore. Sinking almost immediately, Captain Charles Hord and 24 crew went down with their ship. 1 crewmember and 1 naval DEMS gunner floating amongst the wreckage made it to a lifeboat and were eventually picked up by a passing steamer and landed at Avonmouth.

SS DROMONBY, 3,628grt, built 1900, (ON. 112424). Captured by German auxiliary cruiser Moewe 220 miles West of Lisbon and sunk by bombs on the 13th January 1916 sailing from Cardiff to St Vincent with coal. Captain J. Brockett and his crew were taken onboard the raider, later transferred to the captured steamer SS APPAM and landed in America.

SS GADSBY, 3,497grt, built 1899, (ON. 112411). Torpedoed and sunk by U-39 33 miles South, South –West of Wolf Rock, Cornwall on the 1st July 1915 sailing from Sydney, Cape Breton to London with a cargo of wheat. Captain and all crew landed off the Irish coast.

SS GLENBY, 2,196grt, built 1900, (ON. 112417). Sunk by gunfire from U-38 in the St. George's Channel on the 17th August 1915 sailing from Cardiff to Archangel with a cargo of coal. 2 crew killed as the U-boat continued to shell them as they abandoned ship.

SS KIRKBY, 3,034grt, built 1891, (ON. 98517). Torpedoed and sunk by U-38 23 miles West by South of Bardsey Island, Llyn Peninsular, North Wales on the 17th August 1915 sailing from Cardiff with a cargo of coal.

SS MALTBY (2), 3,977grt, built 1906, (ON. 119898). Torpedoed and sunk by UC-27 10 miles South-West by West of the Mediterranean Island of Pantellaria on the 26th February 1918 sailing from Cardiff to Malta with a cargo of coal for the Royal Navy. 4 crew killed.

SS MARTIN, 1,904grt, built 1895, (ON. 99495). Sunk by gunfire from UC-18 8 miles off Ushant on the 14th January 1917 sailing from Bayonne to Barry with pit props. Captain John White and all crew picked up by a French patrol boat.

SS MOUNTBY, 3,263grt, built 1898, (ON. 106994). Torpedoed and sunk by UC-49 off the Lizard on the 10th June 1918 sailing from Swansea with Admiralty stores.

SS OAKBY (1), 1,976grt, built 1897, (ON. 106960). Torpedoed and sunk by U-8, 4 miles East of the Royal Sovereign Light Vessel near Folkestone Pier on the 23rd February 1915 sailing from London to Cardiff in ballast. The ship was hit in number one hold and sank almost as her lifeboats touched the water. Captain F.J. Bartley and all crew saved.

SS ROCKPOOL (1), 4,502grt, built 1912, (ON. 132819). Torpedoed and sunk by U-94, off Eagle Island on the 2nd March 1918 sailing from New Orleans to Dublin with a cargo of wheat & steel. The ships Master, John White was taken prisoner. He was repatriated after the war on 14th December 1918.

SS ROLLESBY, 3,955grt, built 1906, (ON. 119894). Sunk by U-48 off Muckle Flugga on the 15th September 1917 sailing from Cardiff to the White Sea with a cargo of coal. U-48 first attacked by shelling the ROLLESBY and was eventually abandoned by Captain Donald McKenzie and his crew after shrapnel round began homing in. Shortly afterwards a British destroyer was sighted and as the ship was not in danger of sinking, Captain McKenzie and crew re-boarded her only to be torpedoed by the U-boat and forced to abandon ship again.

SS SALMONPOOL (1), 4,905grt, built 1913, (ON. 132834). Torpedoed and sunk by U-39, 30 miles from Cape Carbon, Algeria on the 1st June 1916 sailing from Naples to Baltimore in ballast.

SS SCAWBY, 3,658grt, built 1911, (ON. 124278). Captured by U-33, 220 miles East of Malta and sunk by bombs on the 2nd October 1915 while sailing from Mudros to Malta with a cargo of coal.

SS SELBY, 2,137grt, built 1895, (ON. 99726). Sunk by a mine 34 miles South-East by South of the Newarp Light Vessel on the 30th September 1914.

SS TEESDALE, 2,470grt, built 1904, (ON. 115169). After being damaged by a torpedo in the English Channel sailing from Hartlepool to Gibraltar with a cargo of coal on the 15th June 1917. The ship had been temporarily repaired and was making her way to the Tees when the ship broke up and sank 3 miles off Saltburn Pier on the 2nd August 1917. 2 crew killed. Captain T.C. Hill and remaining crew abandoned ship.

SS TEESPOOL, 4,577grt, built 1905, (ON. 119888). Torpedoed and severely damaged on the 19th October 1917 sailing from the Tyne to Falmouth with a cargo of coal & coke. Captain J.N. Chard and a skeleton crew remained onboard the sinking ship and managed to beach the ship off Dartmouth. 4 crew killed.

SS THERESE HEYMANN, 2,393grt, built 1903. (ON. 98097). Sailed from the Tyne 25th December 1914 on voyage to Savona, Italy and disappeared. The ship was not officially classed as missing/untraced until 3rd March 1915, though it is believed she was one of several ships mined off Filey around Christmas time. No wreckage or any bodies from her 21 crew were ever found.

SS THIRLBY (1), 2,009grt, 1898, (ON. 106990). Torpedoed and sunk by UC -31 near Fastnet on the 2nd July 1917 sailing from Seville to Garston with a cargo of copper & copper ore. 2 crew killed. Captain T.C. Hill and remaining crew took to the lifeboats and were eventually picked up by a passing patrol boat and landed on the Irish Coast

SS THORNABY (1), 1,730grt, built 1889, (ON. 95897). Sank after hitting a mine laid by UC-3, 4 miles North-East of the Shipwash Light Vessel on the 28th February 1916 sailing from Marbella to Hartlepool with a cargo of iron ore. 19 crew killed. 2 crew and the River Pilot were picked up by a passing ship.

SS TRUNKBY, 2,635grt, built 1896, (ON. 106955). Sunk by gunfire from U-34 near Port Mahon, Minorca on the 28th May 1916 sailing from Newport News to Leghorn with a cargo of oats & steel rails. Captain William Owens and all crew saved.

SS WESTONBY, 3,795grt, built 1901, (ON. 112445). Torpedoed and sunk by U-82 195 miles off Fastnet on the 15th June 1917 sailing from Huelva to London with a cargo of lead & pyrites.

SS WILLERBY, 3,630grt, built 1912, (ON. 124279). Captured by German auxiliary cruiser Prinz Eitel Friedrich 400 miles off Pernambuco, and sunk by bombs on the 20th February 1915 while sailing from Huelva to Garston with a cargo of copper & sunflower oil. The SS WILLERBY made a failed attempt to ram the cruiser. Captain Wedgewood and his crew were later landed in America.

SS WRAGBY, 3,641grt, built 1901, (ON. 112432). Sunk by gunfire from UC -37 near Cape Spartel on the 4th January 1917 sailing from Newport to Gibraltar with a cargo of coal. Captain J.C. White and all crew saved.

Ropners Merchant Shipping Losses 1939-1945

This list also includes Merchant ships built/owned by the MOS/MOWT (Ministry of Shipping/Ministry of War Transport) and managed by Ropners in WWII with the prefix Empire, plus 1 SAM boat, 1Fort boat and 1 captured Vichy French ship under their management. Not included are ships slightly damaged/salvaged or lost through forces of nature. SS CLEARPOOL (2) although not lost due to a war cause after being wrecked on Skitter Sands, River Humber on the 4th June 1944. She has been added to the list as she sustained loss of life after being seriously damaged during an air attack in 1941.

All surviving WWII Log Books & Crew Agreements 1939-1946 are held at The National Archive in Kew under the ships ON. (Official Number) in file BT381. Where possible the exact BT file number for each ship is listed for their war service period up to, and including the time each ship was lost. Each file runs from January 1st to December 31st of any given year.

SS AINDERBY, 4,860grt, built 1925, (ON139237). Torpedoed and sunk by U-552 130 miles off Bloody Foreland on the 10th June 1941 while sailing independently from Santos to the Tyne with a cargo of iron ore. 11 crew and 1 DEMS gunner killed. The Captain, 27 crew and 1 gunner were rescued by the destroyer HMS VETERAN and landed at Greenock. (1939-BT 381/114, 1940 -BT 381/672, 1941-BT 381/1335).

SS ALDERPOOL, 4,313grt, built 1930, (ON. 161994). Torpedoed and damaged by U-46 South-West of Reykjavik on the 3rd April 1941 in Convoy

SC-26 sailing from New York to Hull via Sydney, Cape Breton with a cargo of wheat. Torpedoed and sunk by U-73 later the same day after being abandoned. All crew rescued by another Ropner ship SS THIRLBY and landed at Loch Ewe. (1939-BT 381/425, 1940-BT 381/1057).

SS ASHBY (2), 4,871grt, built 1927, (ON. 139249). Torpedoed and sunk by U-43 on the 30th November 1941, a straggler from Convoy OS-12 sailing from Middlesbrough to Pepel via Liverpool in ballast. On the 29th November during the crossing, the ship became detached from the main Convoy after developing engine trouble and was forced to stop for repairs 170 miles off Flores, Azores. One of the Convoy escorts stayed with the Ashby for several hours, but eventually had to depart to catch the rest of the Convoy up. With the repairs finished by the 30th November the Ashby was underway once again, when she was suddenly torpedoed off the Azores and sank in two minutes. Captain, 11crew and 5 DEMS gunners lost. 37 survivors landed at Fayal in the Azores and eventually returned home on the Polish ship SS BATORI. SS ASHBY was damaged earlier in the war after being attacked by German aircraft on the 3rd September 1940 off Rattary Head without loss of life. (1939-BT 381/116, 1940-BT 381/674, 1941-BT 381/1336).

SS BOULDERPOOL, 4,805grt, built 1928, (ON. 160758). Sunk by German E-boat S-61, 10 miles South of the Sheringham Buoy in position 52' 58N 1' 28E on the 7th March 1941 sailing in the coastal Convoy FN-26 from London to the Tyne in ballast. All crew saved. (1939-BT 381/382, 1940-BT 381/1005, 1941-BT 381/1538).

SS CARPERBY (2), 4,890grt, built 1928, (ON. 139257). Torpedoed and sunk by U-588 420 miles South off Newfoundland on the 1st March 1942 sailing independently to Buenos Aries from the Tyne via St. Vincent with a cargo of coal & coke, after dispersing from Convoy ON-66. Captain, all 40 crew and 6 DEMS gunners lost. (1939-BT 381/116, 1940-BT 381/675, 1941-BT 381/1337, 1942-BT 381/1836).

SS CLEARPOOL (2), 5,404grt, built 1935, (ON. 162107). Attacked by German aircraft off Scarborough sailing from London to the Tyne in ballast on 10th June 1941. Raked with machine gunfire and hit by a bomb setting fire to the ships bunkers and bursting the pipes on her boilers. Filling with seawater the ship began to heel over and was ordered abandoned while retaining a skeleton crew to bring the fire under control. The following day she was taken in tow to the River Tees and arrived at Hartlepool for permanent repairs. 2 crew killed.

SS CRITON, 4,564grt, built 1927 (No. Official No.). Attacked and sunk on the 21st June 1941 by the Vichy French sloop AIR FRANCE IV off the West coast of Africa sailing independently from Pepel to Belfast with a cargo of iron ore after becoming detached from Convoy SL-78. 4 crew died in prison of war camps. The ship had originally been under the flag of the Vichy French and was arrested by the Royal Navy for carrying contraband. The ship was taken over by a scratch British crew of DBS (Distressed British Seamen) returning home from previous sinkings and local African engine room Firemen & Trimmers.

SS DALEBY (2), 4,640grt, built 1929, (ON. 161316). Torpedoed and sunk by U-89 South-East of Cape Farewell on the 4th November 1942 in Convoy SC-107 sailing from Halifax, Nova Scotia to London with a cargo of grain, tanks & motor parts. Captain, 39 crew and 7 DEMS gunners picked up by the Icelandic ship BRUARFOSS and landed at Reykjavik. (1939-BT 381/401, 1940-BT 381/1028, 1941-BT 381/1552, 1942-BT 381/2037).

SS EMPIRE ARNOLD, 7,045grt, built 1942, (ON. 168939). Torpedoed and sunk by U-155 500 miles North-East of Trinidad on the 4th August 1942 sailing independently after dispersing from Convoy E-6 from New York to Cape Town & Alexandria via Trinidad with a cargo of government stores and 2 passengers. Captain Frederick Tate was taken prisoner. 8 crew and 1 DEMS gunner killed. 51 survived. A number of survivors were rescued after 8 days by the Norwegian ship DALVANGER and landed at George Town, British Guinea. The Chief Officer, R.W. Thompson's lifeboat with 24 survivors in navigated the boat 500 miles to safety. Captain Tate was removed from one of the lifeboats suffering from wounds. In September 1942 he was landed in Lorient and eventually interned at the Merchant Navy PoW camp Milag Nord where he spent the remainder of the war until the camp was liberated 28th April 1945. (1942-BT 381/2200).

SS EMPIRE BISON, 5,612grt, built 1919, (ON. 167628). Torpedoed and sunk by U-124 400 miles West of Rockall on the 1st November 1940 sailing independently from Baltimore to the Clyde via Halifax, Nova Scotia with a cargo of scrap steel and a number of passengers. Captain, 29 crew and 1 DEMS gunner killed. 3 crew and passenger were rescued after 8 and half days adrift on a liferaft by the Danish ship OLGA and landed at Gourock. (1940-BT 381/1220).

SS EMPIRE DRYDEN, 7,164grt, built 1942, (ON 169010). Torpedoed and sunk by U-572 East of Cape Hatteras on the 20th April 1942 sailing independently from New York to Alexandria via Table Bay with a cargo of general & government stores. Captain, 22 crew and 3 gunners killed. 25 survivors picked up by the MONARCH of BERMUDA and landed in Bermuda. (1942-BT 381/2204).

SS EMPIRE MERLIN, 5,763grt, built 1919, (ON. 167595). Torpedoed and sunk by U-48 90 miles off the Flannan Isles on the 25th August 1940 in Convoy HX-65 sailing from Port Sulphur to Hull with a cargo of sulphur. The ship broke in two and sank in 35 seconds taking the Captain, 31 crew with her. The corvette HMS GODETIA rescued the sole survivor, an Ordinary Seaman named John Lee. (Captain, David W. Simpson MBE had been Master of the SS Wandy who had attacked and sunk a German U-boat in WWI). (1940-BT 381/1220).

SS EMPIRE MOONBEAM, 6,849grt, built 1941, (ON. 172784) Torpedoed and damaged by U-211, later sunk by U-608 on the 11th September 1942 in Convoy ON-127 sailing from Glasgow to New York in ballast, carrying 1 passenger. 3 crew killed. Captain, 44 crew, 6 DEMS gunners and passenger were picked up by the corvette RCN ARVIDA and landed at St. John's, Newfoundland on the 15th September. (1941-BT 381/1733, 1942-BT 381/2210).

SS EMPIRE RAINBOW, 6,942grt, built 1941, (ON. 166999). Torpedoed and sunk by U-607 & U-704 on the 26th July 1942 in Convoy ON-113 sailing from Avonmouth to Halifax, Nova Scotia via the Belfast Lough in ballast. Captain and all 46 crew rescued by the destroyer HMS BURNHAM & RCN corvette DAUPHIN and landed at St. John's, Newfoundland. (1941-BT 381/1673, 1942-BT 381/2136).

SS EMPIRE STARLIGHT, 6,850grt, built 1941, (ON. 172787). Repeatedly bombed by German aircraft while discharging in Murmansk on the 3rd April 1942. Continued to be bombed over several weeks eventually sinking in the dock on the 1st June 1942. 1 crew killed. (1941-BT 381/1734, 1942-BT 381/2211).

SS FIRBY, 4,868grt, built 1926, (ON. 139238). Damaged by gunfire from U-48, abandoned, then torpedoed and sunk the 11th September 1939 270 miles West of the Hebrides while sailing independently from the River Tyne to Hudson Bay in ballast. The whole crew were rescued after the U-boat Commander transmitted in an open message stating "Transmit to Mr. Churchill. I have sunk British steamer FIRBY, position 59. 40N 13. 50W. Save the crew if you will please." The message was picked up by the US Merchant ship SCANPENN and received by the Admiralty a few hours after the sinking. Captain and all 33 crew picked up by the destroyer HMS

FEARLESS 15 hours later and landed at Scapa Flow the following day. (1939 -BT 381/114).

SS FISHPOOL (2), 4,950grt, built 1940, (ON. 160785) Sunk in an air raid at Syracuse on the 26th July 1943 while discharging ammunition and aviation spirit brought from Alexandria killing 23 crew and 5 DEMS gunners. 18 survived. Earlier in the war on the 14th November 1940 the Fishpool had been sailing from the Tyne to Vancouver in ballast when she was hit by seven incendiary bombs South-West of Rockall killing several crew. The ship was abandoned and one lifeboat with 15 crew was never seen again. The ship was taken in tow and repaired. Also on the 9th May 1941 while loading stores at Barrow-in-Furness the ship was again damaged by a parachute mine, which detonated next to the ship killing 2 crew. (1940-BT 381/1008, 1941-no longer exist. 1942-BT 381/2026, 1943-BT 381/2461).

FORT PELLY, 7,131grt, built 1942, (ON. 168346). Sunk in an air raid on the 20th July 1943. On the 6th July 1943 the Fort Pelly sailed from Alexandria with a cargo of cased petrol, ammunition, vehicles and stores for the invasion of Sicily, arriving in Port Augusta on the 18th to discharge her vital cargo. Two days later on the 20th a dive-bomber attacked Fort Pelly while lying at anchor and the ship sustained two direct hits and one near miss. One bomb exploded in the ships engine room killing all the Engineers and the other in number 5 hold destroying everything aft including the crew accommodation. Out of a crew of 60, 32 crew and 6 DEMS gunners were lost in the attack. (1942-BT 381/2181, 1943- BT 381/2633).

SS HAWNBY (2), 5,380grt, built 1936, (ON. 162111) Sunk by a mine on the 20th April 1940 laid by German aircraft from the 9th Fliegerdivision in the Thames Estuary while sailing from the Tyne to Gibraltar with a cargo of coal. Captain Harland MBE and all 38 crew saved. (Captain Harland MBE had been the Master of the SS ROCKPOOL in 1939, which severely damaged a German U-boat in a surface engagement. The U-boat was lost the same day. (1939-BT 381/426, 1940-BT 381/1059).

SS HAXBY (2), 5,207grt, Built 1929, (ON. 160760). Sunk by the commerce raider Orion on the 24th April 1940 sailing independently from Glasgow to Corpus Christie in ballast. 17 crew killed. Remaining 40 crew taken prisoner and transferred to the German prize ship SS TROPIC SEA which had been captured from the Norwegian's. The HAXBY's crew were later freed after the TROPIC SEA was intercepted by the British submarine HMS TRUANT in the Bay of Biscay on the 3rd September 1940 and the German's were forced to scuttle their war prize. (1939-BT 381/382, 1940-BT 381/1005).

SS HERONSPOOL (2), 5,202grt, built 1929, (ON. 160759) Attacked by gunfire from U-48 on the 12th October 1939 after becoming a straggler from Convoy OB-17 sailing from Newport to Montreal with a cargo of coal. The HERONSPOOL fought a running battle for 4 and a half hours, returning fire with her 4-inch deck gun, forcing the U-boat to submerge. A torpedo exploded prematurely 10 yards before hitting the ship. The U-boat surfaced once again and began shelling the ship only to be forced to dive again. A second torpedo found its mark and broke the back of the HERONSPOOL. Captain Batson ordered the ship abandoned which was achieved without loss and all hands were picked up soon after by the US passenger ship PRESIDENT HARDING. Captain Batson was later awarded the OBE and the gunner, Able Seaman George Pearson the BEM. (1939-BT 381/382).

SS HINDPOOL, 4,897grt, built 1928, (ON. 139256). Torpedoed and sunk by U-124 North of the Cape Verde Islands on the 8th March 1941 in Convoy SL-67 sailing from Pepel to Middlesbrough via Freetown with a cargo of iron ore. Captain and 27crew killed. 6 survivors were picked up by the destroyer HMS FAULKNOR and landed at Gibraltar, a further 6 picked up by British SS GUIDO. (1939-BT 381/116, 1940-BT 381/675, 1941-BT 381/1337).

SS KIRKPOOL, 4,842grt, built 1928, (ON. 139258). The Kirkpool had been sailing independently from Durban to the River Plate with a cargo of coal. On the 10th April 1942 the ship was making about 8 knots in a Westerly direction about 200 miles North of Tristan da Cunha when she was sighted by the German commerce raider THOR. At a distance of about two miles the THOR opened up with a salvo of shrapnel rounds, bursting just above the foremast. THOR turning on her powerful searchlight then continued shelling the KIRKPOOL sending a series of shells into the engine room. A torpedo was then believed to of been fired which exploded in number 1 hold. The ship now down by the head and developing a heavy list was ordered to be abandoned by her Captain. As the boats were being lowered, the raider raked the boat deck with gunfire destroying the boats, killing and wounding a number of crew. The survivors now made their way to the liferafts as the raider continued using shrapnel rounds and several more crew were killed. Eventually those still alive got away from the burning ship on the remaining liferafts, some clinging onto hatch-boards. Half an hour later the THOR approached those in the water and picked up a number of survivors over a period of three and a half hours. The nightmare was far from over for the survivors as they were landed in Japan while the THOR was in dry-dock. Along with PoW's from other sunken Merchant ships, the KIRKPOOL survivors were transferred to the supply ship REGENBURG and landed in Yokohama and taken to the

Kawasaki PoW camp where they remained for the next three years. The KIRKPOOL'S Captain Kennington would die in captivity on the 14th March 1944 and is now buried in the Yokohama War Cemetery. (1939-BT 381/116, 1940-BT 381/675, 1941-BT 381/1337, 1942-BT 381/1836).

SS LACKENBY (2), 5,112grt, built 1928, (ON. 139260). Torpedoed and sunk by U-624 South of Cape Farewell on the 25th January 1943, a straggler from Convoy SC-117 sailing from Tampa to London via New York & Loch Ewe with a cargo of phosphate. Captain, all 38 crew and 6 DEMS gunners lost. (1939-BT 381/116, 1940-BT 381/675, 1941-BT 381/1337, 1942-BT 381/1837, 1943-BT 381/2305).

SS MANESPOOL, 4,894grt, built 1928, (ON. 139250) Torpedoed and sunk by U-97 South-West of the Faroe Islands on the 24th February 1941 in Convoy OB-289 sailing in ballast from Cardiff to Halifax, Nova Scotia. 2 crew killed. Captain and 19 crew picked up by the British Merchant ship THOMAS HOLT and transferred over to the corvette HMS PETUNIA who had already rescued another 19 members of MANSEPOOL's crew, landing them all at Stornaway. (1939-BT 381/116, 1940-BT 381/674, 1941-BT 381/1336).

SS OTTERPOOL, 4,867grt, built 1926, (ON. 139239) Torpedoed and sunk by U-30 130 miles West of Ushant on the 20th June 1940 in Convoy HGF-34 sailing from Bona to Middlesbrough with a cargo of iron ore. Captain, 21 crew and 1 DEMS gunner killed. 16 crew rescued by the naval sloop HMS SCARBOROUGH and landed at Liverpool. (1939-BT 381/114, 1940-BT 381/672).

SS PIKEPOOL, 3,683grt, built 1909, (ON. 127453). Sunk by a mine 25 miles off the Smalls Light on the 22nd November 1940 sailing from Glasgow to Barry in ballast. 17 crew and 1 DEMS gunner killed. 15 crew survived. 5 men were picked up from a liferaft 3 and a half days later by a Norwegian Merchant ship and landed at Swansea. (1939-BT 381/45, 1940-BT 381/599).

SS REEDPOOL, 4,838grt, built 1924, (ON. 135609). Torpedoed and sunk by U-515 240 miles South-East of Trinidad on the 20th September 1942 while sailing independently from Massowah, Ethiopia to Florida via Cape Town in ballast. A week before she was sunk she had picked up 16 survivors from the SS MEDON, which had been sunk in the Gulf of Mexico. REEDPOOL's Captain William J. Downs was taken prisoner. 6 crew Killed. The British schooner MILLIE M. MASHER picked up 32 crew, 4 DEMS gunners and the 16 survivors from the MEDON and landed them at Georgetown, British Guinea. (Captain Downs was landed at Lorient on the 14th October 1942 and

117

spent the remainder of the war interned at the Merchant Navy PoW camp Milag Nord until the camp was liberated 28th April 1945). (1939-BT 381/84, 1940-BT 381/640, 1941-BT 381/1310, 1942-BT 381/1814).

SS ROMANBY (3), 4,487grt, built 1927, (ON. 139244). Captured at Narvik on the 9th April 1940 during the German invasion of Norway. Sunk by an explosion between 22/23rd April 1940 while loading iron ore alongside in Narvik. Captain Nicholson and 38 crew taken prisoner but later forced to march to the neutral Swedish border and interned in Sweden. Before the forced march to Sweden, 3 crew made their escape onboard a Norwegian Merchant ship. ROMANBY's Captain and 12 crew volunteered to help crew another two Norwegian ships escape through the German blockade in Sweden in June 1942. Both ships sunk, resulting in them all being made prisoners of war again. (1939-BT 381/115, 1940-BT 381/673).

SS ROXBY (2), 4,252grt, built 1923, (ON. 139228). Torpedoed and sunk South-West of Cape Clear by U-613 on the 7th November 1942, a straggler from Convoy ON-142 sailing from Cardiff & Gourock to Halifax, Nova Scotia with a cargo of coal. 30 crew and 5 DEMS gunners killed. 13 survivors rescued by the Irish Merchant ship IRISH BEECH and landed at St. John's, Newfoundland. (1939-BT 381/113, 1940-BT 381/671, 1941-BT 381/1335, 1942-BT 381/1834).

SS RUSHPOOL, 5,125grt, built 1928, (ON.160757). Torpedoed and sunk by U-94 South-East of Rockall on the 29th January 1941, a straggler from Convoy SC-19 sailing from St. John, New Brunswick to Belfast via Halifax, Nova Scotia with a cargo of grain. Captain and all 39 crew rescued by the destroyer HMS ANTELOPE and landed at Greenock. The ship had been missed earlier that day by two torpedoes before finally being hit. (1939-BT 381/382, 1940-BT 381/1005, 1941-BT 381/1538).

SS SALMONPOOL (2), 4,803grt, built 1924, (ON. 139231). Seized by German troops at Sandafjord on the 15th April 1940. 27 crew sent to Germany and interned for duration of the war. (1939-BT 381/113, 1940 BT 381/671).

SS SAMSUVA, 7,219grt, built 1944, (ON. 169894). Torpedoed and sunk by U-310 in the Barent Sea North of North Cape on the 29th September 1944 sailing in Convoy RA-60 from Archangel to Loch Ewe with a cargo of pit props. 3 crew killed. Captain and 56 survivors picked up by the Convoy Rescue Ship RATHLIN and landed at Clyde on the 5th October. (1944-BT 381/3178).

SS SEDGEPOOL, 6,530grt, built 1918, (ON. 139224). Torpedoed and sunk by U-123 80 miles West by South of St. Kilda on the 19th October 1940 in Convoy SC-7 sailing from Montreal to Manchester via Sydney, Cape Breton with a cargo of wheat. Captain and 2 crew killed. 35 crew and 1 DEMS gunner rescued by the naval tug HMS SALVONIA and landed at Gourock. (1939-BT 381/113, 1940-BT 381/670).

SS SOMERSBY (2), 5,168grt, built 1930, (ON. 160769). Torpedoed and sunk by U-111 South-West of Reykjavik on the 13th May 1941, a straggler from Convoy SC-30 sailing from Halifax, Nova Scotia to Hull via Loch Ewe with a cargo of grain. After being hit amidships by one torpedo, the ship lay dead in the water until a second torpedo hit an hour later on the bow capsized the ship. Captain, 38 crew and 4 DEMS gunners picked up by the Greek Merchant ship MARIKA PROTOPAPA and landed at Loch Ewe. (1939-BT 381/383, 1940-BT 381/1007, 1941-BT 381/1539).

SS STONEPOOL, 4,803grt, built 1928, (ON. 139259). Torpedoed and sunk by U-207 East of Cape Farewell on the 11th September 1941 in Convoy SC-42 sailing from Montreal to Avonmouth via Sydney, Cape Breton with a cargo of oats, grain & trucks. Captain, 33 crew and 8 DEMS gunners killed. 12 survivors were originally picked up including the ships Captain by the Canadian corvette RCN KENOGAMI, but 7 died from the effects of exposure the same day and were buried at sea two days later. (1939-BT 381/116, 1940-BT 381/675, 1941-BT 381/1337).

SS SWAINBY (3), 5,811grt, built 1917, (ON. 135603). Torpedoed and sunk by U-13 25 miles North of Mukkle Flugga, Shetland Islands during the German invasion of Norway on the 17th April 1940 while sailing independently from Kirkwall to Norway in ballast. Captain and 37 crew landed safely at Nor Wick Bay, Shetland Islands. (1939-BT 381/84, 1940-BT 381/639).

SS SWIFTPOOL, 5,205grt, built 1929, (ON. 160761) Torpedoed and sunk by U-372 West of Ireland on the 5th August 1941 in Convoy SL-81 sailing from Pepel to Middlesbrough via Freetown with a cargo of iron ore. Captain, 36 crew and 5 DEMS gunners killed. 2 survivors picked up by the corvette HMS BLUEBELL and landed at Greenock. (1939-BT 381/383, 1940-BT 381/1006, 1941-BT 381/1006).

SS THIRLBY (2), 4,888grt, built 1928, (ON. 139251). Torpedoed and sunk by U-109 12 miles from Seal Island, Cape Sable on the 23rd January 1942 sailing independently after dispersing from Convoy SC-66 from New York to

Loch Ewe with a cargo of maize. 3 crew killed. Captain, 30 crew, 9 DEMS gunners and the American River Pilot were rescued by the American ship BELLE ISLE and landed at Halifax, Nova Scotia. SS THIRLBY was damaged earlier in the war after being torpedoed by U-69 on 3rd April 1941. She was then attacked again by German aircraft on 10th April 1941 killing 2 crew, eventually arriving at Loch Ewe for temporary repairs. (1939-BT 381/116, 1940-BT 381/674, 1941-BT 381/1336, 1942-BT 381/1836).

SS TROUTPOOL (2), 4,886grt, built 1927, (ON. 139243). Sunk by an aerial magnetic mine in the Belfast Lough 8 cables from Bangor Pier Light on the 20th July 1940 after sailing from Rosario for Glasgow via Belfast with a cargo of grain. 11 crew killed. (1939-BT 381/115, 1940-BT 381/673).

SS ULLAPOOL, 4,891grt, built 1927, (ON. 139248). Sunk after suffering a direct hit by a German parachute mine in the Mersey on the 13th March 1941during an air raid while berthing at the Princes Landing Stage with a cargo of wheat. 16 crew killed. (1939-BT 381/115, 1940-BT 381/673, 1941-BT 381/1336).

SS WANDBY (2), 4,947grt, built 1940, (ON. 160784) Torpedoed and damaged by U-47, 135 miles North-West of Rockall on the 19th October 1940 in Convoy HX-79 sailing on her maiden voyage from Victoria, British Columbia to Middlesbrough via Panama & Halifax, Nova Scotia with a cargo of lead, zinc & timber. Abandoned by her crew she sank two days later. Captain, 33 crew rescued by the naval trawler HMS ANGLE and landed at Belfast a week later. (1940-BT 381/1008).

SS WARLABY, 4,876grt, built 1927, (ON. 139241). Sunk East of the Azores by the German heavy cruiser Admiral Hipper on the 12th February 1941 while sailing in the unescorted Convoy SL-64S sailing from Alexandria to Oban via Freetown with a cargo of cottonseed & oil cake. Captain, 35 crew and 2 naval signalman killed. 2 crew survived and were picked up. (1939-BT 381/115, 1940-BT 381/673, 1941-BT 381/1335).

SS WILLOWPOOL, 4,815grt, built 1925, (ON. 139236). Sunk by a mine laid by U-20, 3 miles East of the Newarp Light Vessel off the Norfolk coast on the 10th December 1939 whilst sailing independently from Bona to Middlesbrough with a cargo of iron ore. All crew survived. (1939-BT 381/114).

Appendix

The following foreign Merchant vessels were lost to enemy action during WWII while under Ropner management on behalf of the MOS/MOWT.

Netherlands

FLENSBURG, 6,429grt, built 1922. Torpedoed and sunk by U-202 500 miles of Surinam (former Dutch Guiana) while sailing independently in ballast from Alexandria to New York via Durban & Trinidad on the 9th October 1942. All crew picked up four days later by a Yugoslavian ship heading the opposite direction to Durban. FLENSBURGS Master decided to proceed in his own lifeboats for the coast of Surinam and three days later were taken in tow by a Dutch landing craft at the mouth of the Marowijne River and landed at the village of Albina, Surinam.

SAWAHLOENTO, 3,085grt, built 1921. Torpedoed and sunk by U-177 off the coast of Durban while sailing independently in ballast from Port Sudan to Durban via Beira, Mozambique on the 14th December 1942. 53 crew killed. 19 survivors set course in one of the lifeboats for South Africa and were picked up two days later by a local fishing boat and landed at Durban.

STAD ALKMAAR, 5,750grt, built 1940. Torpedoed and sunk by German E-boat in the North Sea on the 7th September 1940, sailing in the coastal Convoy FS-273 from Methil to London with a cargo of sugar loaded in Cuba. 13 crew killed. 14 survivors

STAD AMSTERDAM, 3,780grt, built 1920. Torpedoed and sunk by U-164 on the 25th August 1942 on voyage from Key West to Trinidad & Demerara with a cargo of general stores and 300 bags of mail. The ship had become a straggler due to engine trouble while sailing in Convoy WAT-15 when the ship was hit by a dud torpedo, holing the ship. The ships Master first thought they had struck a small mine and as the ship developed a list he ordered the crew into their lifeboats. The ship was eventually sunk by a coupe de grace. 3 crew killed. 35 survivors.

STAD MAASTRICHT, 6,552grt, built 1924. Torpedoed and by German E-boat S-59 on the 23rd December 1940 in the North Sea sailing in ballast from London to the USA. The ship was taken in tow back towards London but finally sank on Christmas day, just over two and a half miles from the Barrow Deep Light Vessel. All crew survived.

Norway

AUST, 5,630grt, built 1920. Captured by the German commerce raider THOR on the 3rd April 1942 on voyage from New York to Bombay via Cape Town with a cargo of war stores. The whole crew were taken onboard the raider before the AUST was sunk by scuttling charges. A number of her crew were later handed over to the Japanese and interned at Yokohama, which included a number of British Crew serving on AUST. One of these men ROBERT OWEN would die in captivity on the 23rd December 1943 from acute bronchitis and was later buried in the Yokohama War Cemetery.

CORNEVILLE, 4,544grt, built 1930. Torpedoed and sunk off the coast of Takoradi, Ghana by U-515 on the 9th May 1943 on voyage from Cacutta to Liverpool via Trincomalee & Cape Town with a cargo of tea, pig iron and general stores. After being hit by two torpedoes the ship sank in eleven minutes without loss of life. The following day the fourty-one survivors including one British seaman and four British gunners landed at Anamabu, sixty miles East of Takoradi.

Yugoslavia

BOSILJKA, 3,009grt, built 1896. Sunk on the 19th June 1942 twenty-five miles North North-West of the Smith Shoal Light on voyage from New Orleans to Key West, Florida with a general cargo including pharmaceutical bottles. At first it was claimed by the ships Captain they had been torpedoed by a German U-boat, though no claim was ever made by the Germans for attacking this ship. It was later considered by the Admiralty that the ship had struck an American laid mine. All thirty-one crew survived.

KUPA, 4,382grt, built 1917. Torpedoed and sunk by U-156 on the 15th May 1942 about 500 miles North-East of Trinidad on voyage from New York to Alexandria via Table Bay with a cargo of military trucks aeroplane parts and drums of oil. Earlier that day the KUPA had picked up the survivors from the Norwegian ship Merchant ship SILJESTAD sunk by the same U-boat. Two crew from each ship were killed. After ten days the survivors eventually landed in Venezuela and Barbados.

LJUBICA MATKOVIC, 3,289grt, built 1919. Torpedoed and sunk by U-404 on the 24th June 1942 off the Frying Pan Shoals, Cape Fear, North Carolina sailing independently from Ciudad Trujillo, Dominican Republic to the UK via New York with a cargo of sugar, fuel oil and wood. The ship had earlier been missed by two torpedoes fired from U-404. Captain and all 29 crew saved.

NIKOLINA MATKOVIC, 3,898grt, built 1918. Torpedoed and sunk by U-661 on the 13th October 1942 in the North Atlantic in Convoy SC-104 sailing from Ciudad Trujillo, Dominican Republic to Liverpool via New York with a cargo of sugar and lumber. Fourteen crew killed including six British DEMS gunners. Twenty-one survivors rescued.

TREPCA, 5,042, built 1930. Torpedoed and sunk by U-332 on the 13th March 1942 off the Virginia coast on voyage from Demerara to Portland, Maine with a cargo of Bauxite. Four of the thirty-seven crew killed.

Names of casualties registered with the CWGC lost from Ropner ships

Whilst every effort has been made to ensure that the information contained within these pages are accurate, there may be a small percentage of errors contained therein. This will be mainly restricted to the military/service information and is due either to the fact that there were inaccuracies present in the original information compiled by the relevant authorities prior to their handing over to the Commission, or they occurred during the recent computerisation process, whereby the scanning of the original texts induced a small percentage error rate. The list includes Merchant Seamen, Royal Navy and Royal Artillery (Maritime Regt.) DEMS gunners as well as Commodore Naval Staff lost. Due to the fact that although the number of gunners lost can be verified, the CWGC records do not always state the name of the ship they were lost from. Records of Maritime Regt. gunners lost do not state the ships name at all. However the names of these gunners can be found by accessing the ships Log Books & Crew Agreements held at the TNA at Kew as all gunners signed crew articles. The majority of men named here have no known grave but the sea and are commemorated on the Tower Hill Memorial in London. Those who are buried ashore are marked accordingly. Also included are Lascar Merchant Seamen commemorated on the Bombay War Memorial, 28 Canadian's lost from Ropner ships of which 27 are named on the Halifax (Nova Scotia) Memorial at Point Pleasant Park, the other being buried in the UK. DEMS gunners are commemorated on the various Naval Memorials at Portsmouth, Plymouth & Chatham. One casualty commemorated on the Liverpool Naval Memorial who served under the T124 agreements, while a further 4 non-war dead graves from Ropner ships are looked after by the CWGC.

SS Ainderby

BRINCAT, Greaser, CARMEL, S.S. Ainderby (West Hartlepool). Merchant Navy. 10th June 1941. Age 40. Son of Salvatore and Concetta Brincat; husband of Teresa Brincat, of Hamrun, Malta, G.C.

CHESNEY, Greaser, JOHN, S.S. Ainderby (West Hartlepool). Merchant Navy. 10th June 1941. Age 42.

DEGUARA, Fireman and Trimmer, CARMEL, S.S. Ainderby (West Hartlepool). Merchant Navy. 10th June 1941. Age 36.

EVANS, Fireman and Trimmer, GORDON JAMES, S.S. Ainderby (West Hartlepool). Merchant Navy. 10th June 1941. Age 21. Son of James and Annie Evans of Treforest, Pontypridd, Glamorgan.

FEENEY, Able Seaman, THOMAS, S.S. Ainderby (West Hartlepool). Merchant Navy. 10th June 1941. Age 57.

MOGEN, Fireman and Trimmer, SIMON, S.S. Ainderby (West Hartlepool). Merchant Navy. 10th June 1941. Age 45.

LECOURT, Able Seaman, JAMES, D/MD/X 3042. H.M.S. President III. Royal Naval Volunteer Reserve. Lost in S.S. Ainderby. 10th June 1941.

MURRAY, Fireman and Trimmer, PATRICK JAMES, S.S. Ainderby (West Hartlepool). Merchant Navy. 10th June 1941. Age 55. Son of Patrick James Murray and Elizabeth Murray.

RUSSELL, Able Seaman, PATRICK, S.S. Ainderby (West Hartlepool). Merchant Navy. 10th June 1941. Age 50.

SCICLUNA, Fireman and Trimmer, JOSEPH, S.S. Ainderby (West Hartlepool). Merchant Navy. 10th June 1941. Age 31. Husband of H. Scicluna, of Liverpool.

SCOTT, Fireman and Trimmer, THOMAS, S.S. Ainderby (West Hartlepool). Merchant Navy. 10th June 1941. Age 58.

TYLDESLEY, Ordinary Seaman, DOUGLAS RONALD, S.S. Ainderby (West Hartlepool). Merchant Navy. 10th June 1941. Age 18.

SS Ashby WWI

GREEN, Captain, SAMUEL JOHN, S.S. Ashby. Mercantile Marine. Drowned whilst attempting reach shore from stranded steamer 15th February 1916. Age 45. Son of Samuel and Jane Green, Billingham, Stockton-on-Tees; husband of Emma Green, of Norwood, St. Dogmael's, Pembrokeshire. Buried Lampaul Churchyard Ile D' Ouessant.

SS Ashby

ANDERSON, Greaser, WILLIAM, S.S. Ashby (West Hartlepool). Merchant Navy. 30th November 1941.

BANNISTER, Fireman and Trimmer, FREDERICK WILLIAM, S.S. Ashby (West Hartlepool). Merchant Navy. 30th November 1941. Age 49.

BECK, Fireman and Trimmer, JULIUS CHRISTIAN, S.S. Ashby (West Hartlepool). Merchant Navy. 30th November 1941. Age 58.

BLAXILL, Lance Bombardier, BRUCE EDGAR, 1482064, 7/4 Maritime Regt., Royal Artillery. 30 November 1941. Age 27. Son of Reginald Arthur and Sarah Gladys Blaxill, of Enfield, Middlesex.

COOPER, Fireman and Trimmer, THOMAS, S.S. Ashby (West Hartlepool). Merchant Navy. 30th November 1941. Age 42.

DIACK, Chief Engineer Officer, JAMES, S.S. Ashby (West Hartlepool). Merchant Navy. 30th November 1941. Age 60. Son of James and Jamima Diack; husband of Margaret Diack, of Gosforth, Newcastle-on-Tyne.

EARLY, Able Seaman, JAMES CLIFFORD WALTER, P/JX 261348. H.M.S. President III. Royal Navy. (Lost in S.S. Ashby). 30th November 1941. Husband of Doris May Early, of Rochester, Kent.

FORREST, Fireman and Trimmer, ANTHONY THOMAS, S.S. Ashby (West Hartlepool). Merchant Navy. 30th November 1941. Age 36. Son of Joseph T. and Annie Forrest, of Sunderland, Co. Durham.

FRANK, Master, TOM VALENTINE, O B E, S.S. Ashby (West Hartlepool). Merchant Navy. 30th November 1941. Age 43.

HAGGERTY, Greaser, DENIS, S.S. Ashby (West Hartlepool). Merchant Navy. 30th November 1941. Age 49.

HASLOCK, Third Engineer Officer, GEORGE, S.S. Ashby (West Hartlepool). Merchant Navy. 30th November 1941. Age 36. Son of Joseph and Margaret Haslock; husband of Agnes Haslock.

INGLIS, Second Engineer Officer, JOHN ROBERTSON, S.S. Ashby (West Hartlepool). Merchant Navy. 30th November 1941. Age 60.

KEMP, Lance Bombardier, KENNETH HAMILTON, 1485606, 7/4 Maritime Regt., Royal Artillery. 30 November 1941. Age 32. Son of Arthur Locke Kemp, and of Belle Kemp, of St. John's Wood, London.

PELL, Gunner, JACK, 1463830, 7/4 Maritime Regt., Royal Artillery. 30 November 1941. Age 30.

SARGINSON, Fourth Engineer Officer, WILLIAM, S.S. Ashby (West Hartlepool). Merchant Navy. 30th November 1941. Age 19. Son of Joseph William and Olive Freda Sarginson, of Norton, Stockton-on-Tees, Co. Durham.

WESTBROOK, Gunner, HENRY CHARLES, 2100499, 7/4 Maritime Regt., Royal Artillery. 30 November 1941. Age 22.

WIGHT, Second Officer, JAMES EDWARD, S.S. Ashby (West Hartlepool). Merchant Navy. 30th November 1941. Age 23. Son of Edward Richardson Wight and Genevieve Wight, of Harton, South Shields. Co. Durham.

SS Aust

OWEN, Fireman, ROBERT, S.S. Aust (Norway). Merchant Navy. 23rd December 1943. Age 47. Father to D. Owen of St. Johns, Newfoundland, Canada. Died in Japanese PoW camp. Buried Yokohama War Cemetery.

SS Baldersby

DERBY, Fireman and Trimmer, JOHN JAMES, S.S. Baldersby (West Hartlepool). Mercantile Marine. Killed, as a result of an attack by an enemy submarine, 28th September 1918. Age 39. Son of the late Thomas and Ann Derby; husband of Rose Ann Derby (nee Ahern), of 58, Arlington St., Liverpool. Born at Liverpool.

FAGAN, Fireman and Trimmer, ARTHUR PATRICK, S.S. Baldersby (West Hartlepool). Mercantile Marine. Killed, as a result of an attack by an enemy submarine, 28th September 1918. Age 39. Son of Hugh and Elizabeth Fagan; husband of Margaret Fagan (nee Tennant), of 5 Back, Grafton St., Liverpool. Born at Liverpool.

SS Carperby

BARKER, Steward, ROBERT COULSON, S.S. Carperby (West Hartlepool). Merchant Navy. 1st March 1942. Age 37. Husband of Clarice Barker, of West Hartlepool, Co. Durham.

BENNETT, Ordinary Seaman, JOHN ALFRED, S.S. Carperby (West Hartlepool). Merchant Navy. 1st March 1942. Age 18. Son of Albert Alfred and Rose May Bennett; husband of Ethel May Bennett, of Bethnal Green, London.

BLACK, Able Seaman, JAMES, S.S. Carperby (West Hartlepool). Merchant Navy. 1st March 1942. Age 22. Son of Alexander E. and Elizabeth Black, of Jarrow, Co. Durham.

BRADLEY, Third Engineer Officer, JOHN, S.S. Carperby (West Hartlepool). Merchant Navy. 1st March 1942. Age 26. Son of William and Ellen Bradley, of Hebburn, Co. Durham.

BROWN, Fireman and Trimmer, JOSEPH, S.S. Carperby (West Hartlepool). Merchant Navy. 1st March 1942. Age 43.

BULL, Fireman and Trimmer, JOHN, S.S. Carperby (West Hartlepool). Merchant Navy. 1st March 1942. Age 39. Son of John B. Amara, of Freetown, Sierra Leone; husband of Gbandi Bull, of Freetown.

BURNETT, Second Radio Officer, HARRY, S.S. Carperby (West Hartlepool). Merchant Navy. 1st March 1942. Age 29. Son of Mr. and Mrs. Joseph Burnett, of Stonehaven, Kincardineshire.

COLE, Headman, SONNY MICHAEL, S.S. Carperby (West Hartlepool). Merchant Navy. 1st March 1942. Age 37.

COPELAND, Able Seaman, ROBERT, D/JX 268213. H.M.S. President III. Royal Navy. lost in S.S. Carperby. 1st March 1942. Age 38. Son of Robert and Bella Copeland, of Clydebank, Dunbartonshire.

FAIRLEY, Cook, ISAAC, S.S. Carperby (West Hartlepool). Merchant Navy. 1st March 1942. Age 22. Son of Isaac and Annie Fairley.

FARMER, Fireman and Trimmer, JOSEPH, S.S. Carperby (West Hartlepool). Merchant Navy. 1st March 1942. Age 40.

FREEMAN, Fireman and Trimmer, WILLIAM, S.S. Carperby (West Hartlepool). Merchant Navy. 1st March 1942. Age 32.

GARDINER, Master, FREDERICK, S.S. Carperby (West Hartlepool). Merchant Navy. 1st March 1942. Age 31. Son of Thomas Humphrey Gardiner and Emma Gardiner, of Orrell Park, Lancashire; husband of Dorothy L. Gardiner, of Crosby, Lancashire.

GIBBONS, Galley Boy, ALBERT MATTHEW JAMES, S.S. Carperby (West Hartlepool). Merchant Navy. 1st March 1942. Age 16. Son of Mr. and Mrs. A. M. J. Gibbons, of Southall, Middlesex.

GORDON, Able Seaman, PHILIP RALPH, S.S. Carperby (West Hartlepool). Merchant Navy. 1st March 1942. Age 18.

HARDING, Able Seaman, CHARLES, S.S. Carperby (West Hartlepool). Merchant Navy. 1st March 1942. Age 31. Son of Henry William and Louisa Caroline Harding.

HENDERSON, Third Radio Officer, JOHN, S.S. Carperby (West Hartlepool). Merchant Navy. 1st March 1942. Age 17. Son of John and Laura Henderson, of Cleadon, Co. Durham.

HICKLIN, Able Seaman, GEORGE THOMAS, D/JX 187560. H.M.S. President III. Royal Navy. 1st March 1942.

HULME, Gunner, GEORGE HARRY, 4459000, 3/2 Maritime Regt., Royal Artillery. 1 March 1942. Age 23.

JOHNSON, Fireman and Trimmer, WILLIAM, S.S. Carperby (West Hartlepool). Merchant Navy. 1st March 1942. Age 35. Husband of Amy Massaquoi Johnson, of Freetown, Sierra Leone.

KENWORTHY, Chief Officer, JOSEPH, S.S. Carperby (West Hartlepool). Merchant Navy. 1st March 1942. Age 55. Son of Herbert Wyndham Kenworthy and Annie Katherine Kenworthy.

KNOWLES, Carpenter, BRYAN, S.S. Carperby (West Hartkpool). Merchant Navy. 1st March 1942. Age 32.

LARSEN, Sailor, NIELS HENRY, S.S. Carperby (West Hartlepool). Merchant Navy. 1st March 1942. Age 28.

LLOYD, Fourth Engineer Officer, WILLIAM, S.S. Carperby (West Hartlepool). Merchant Navy. 1st March 1942. Age 30. Son of George and Annie Lloyd; husband of Doris Lloyd, of South Shields, Co. Durham.

LOGAN, Cabin Boy, PATRICK, S.S. Carperby (West Hartlepool). Merchant Navy. 1st March 1942. Age 19. Son of Patrick and Margaret Logan, of South Shields, Co. Durham.

McKEEVER, Able Seaman, JAMES, C/JX 311683. H.M.S. President III. Royal Navy. lost in S.S. Carperby. 1st March 1942. Age 19. Son of James and Mary Ann McKeever, of Springburn, Glasgow.

MAIDMENT, Mess Room Boy, HAROLD, S.S. Carperby (West Hartlepool). Merchant Navy. 1st March 1942. Age 17. Son of Mr. and Mrs. H. Maidment, of Carshalton, Surrey.

MAKIN, Lance Bombardier, HERBERT, 4458917, 3/2 Maritime Regt., Royal Artillery. 1st March 1942. Age 24.

MANNEY, Fireman and Trimmer, JAMES, S.S. Carperby (West Hartlepool). Merchant Navy. 1st March 1942. Age 44.

MASSALLEY, Fireman and Trimmer, JOE, S.S. Carperby (West Hartlepool). Merchant Navy. 1st March 1942. Age 37.

MENDI, Fireman and Trimmer, JOE, S.S. Carperby (West Hartlepool). Merchant Navy. 1st March 1942. Age 45. Husband of Dora Mendi, of South Shields, Co. Durham.

MENDI ABU, Fireman and Trimmer, S.S. Carperby (West Hartlepool). Merchant Navy. 1st March 1942. Age 44.

MUGERIDGE, Sailor, VICTOR, S.S. Carperby (West Hartlepool). Merchant Navy. 1st March 1942. Age 22.

MUIRHEAD, Second Engineer Officer, JAMES, S.S. Carperby (West Hartlepool). Merchant Navy. 1st March 1942. Age 51.

McNALLY, Donkeyman, MICHAEL, S.S. Carperby (West Hartlepool). Merchant Navy. 1st March 1942. Age 27. Son of Daniel and Mary E. McNally; husband of Mary McNally, of Primrose, Jarrow, Co. Durham.

POOK, Deck Boy, WALTER, S.S. Carperby (West Hartlepool). Merchant Navy. 1st March 1942. Age 17. Son of Henry Albert and Susan Florence Pook, of Carshalton, Surrey.

QUARTERLY, Able Seaman, NORMAN WILLIAM, P/JX 311033. H.M.S. President III. Royal Navy. (lost in S.S. Carperby). 1st March 1942. Age 40. Son of John and Louisa Ellen Quarterly; husband of Violet Emily Quarterly, of Barnehurst, Kent.

RYCE, Able Seaman, LEONARD, S.S. Carperby (West Hartlepool). Merchant Navy. 1st March 1942. Age 24. Son of Mrs. S. E. Robson, of Chesham, Buckinghamshire,

SCARTH, Second Officer, WILLIAM, S.S. Carperby (West Hartlepool). Merchant Navy. 1st March 1942. Age 26. Son of William and Mary Scarth, of Darlington, Co. Durham; husband of E. Scarth, of Hetton-le-Hole, Co. Durham.

SMITH, Assistant Cook, JAMES, S.S. Carperby (West Hartlepool). Merchant Navy. 1st March 1942. Age 18.

STRANG, Chief Radio Officer, ALEX DOUGAL, S.S. Carperby (West Hartlepool). Merchant Navy. 1st March 1942. Age 23. (Canadian)

TAYLOR, Donkeyman, GEORGE, S.S. Carperby (West Hartlepool). Merchant Navy. 1st March 1942. Age 34. Son of Henry and Margaret Ann Taylor; husband of M. Taylor, of Raynes Park, Surrey.

TERRELL, Third Officer, HERBERT EDWARD, S.S. Carperby (West Hartlepool). Merchant Navy. 1st March 1942. Age 26.

THOMPSON, Deck Boy, ROBERT HENRY, S.S. Carperby (West Hartlepool). Merchant Navy. 1st March 1942. Age 16. Son of Ada Cadwallader; grandson and ward of Mr. W. W. Cadwallader, of Tottenham, Middlesex.

VILENSKIS, Donkeyman, JOSEPH, S.S. Carperby (West Hartlepool). Merchant Navy. 1st March 1942. Age 49. Of Lithuania.

WEISBERG, Boatswain, ROMAN, S.S. Carperby (West Hartlepool). Merchant Navy. 1st March 1942. Age 39.

WILLIAMS, Chief Engineer Officer, RICHARD EDWARD, S.S. Carperby (West Hartlepool). Merchant Navy. 1st March 1942. Age 57.

SS Clearpool

ALI AHMED, Fireman, S.S. Clearpool (Cardiff). Merchant Navy. 11th June 1941.

ABDO, Fireman, NAIF, S.S. Clearpool (Cardiff). Merchant Navy. 10th June 1941. Buried Hartlepool (Hart Road) Cemetery.

SS Criton.
(Died in captivity)

FREEMAN, Fireman and Trimmer, WILLIAM, S.S. Criton. Merchant Navy. 19th November 1942. Age 28. Buried Dakar (Bel-Air) Cemetery.

SAVAGE, Greaser, JOHN, S.S. Criton. Merchant Navy. 10th September 1941. Age 29. Buried Dakar (Bel-Air) Cemetery.

STRIKER, Donkeyman, WILLIAM THEOPHILUS, S.S. Criton. Merchant Navy. 20th August 1942. Age 43. (Served as WILLIAMS, George). Son of William and Albertina Belvina Striker, of Freetown Sierra Leone; husband of Jestina Striker, of Freetown. Buried Dakar (Bel-Air) Cemetery.

HYLAND, Mess Room Boy, DOUGLAS IRVINE. S.S. Criton. Merchant Navy. 16th January 1943. Son of Sidney George and Jessie Violet Hyland, of Ringwood, Victoria, Australia. Buried Freetown (King Tom) Cemetery.

SS Daleby WWI

ANDERSON, Able Seaman, J, S.S. Daleby (West Hartlepool). Mercantile Marine. Drowned, as a result of an attack by an enemy submarine, 29th April 1917. Age 55. Born in Sweden.

ANDRE, Fireman, G, S.S. Daleby (West Hartlepool). Mercantile Marine. Drowned, as a result of an attack by an enemy submarine, 29th April 1917. Age 30. Born in Malta.

ARPOUDIS, Sailor, T, S.S. Daleby (West Hartlepool). Mercantile Marine. Drowned, as a result of an attack by an enemy submarine, 29th April 1917. Age 24. Born at Athens.

BALBY, Sailor, E M, S.S. Daleby (West Hartlepool). Mercantile Marine. Drowned, as a result of an attack by an enemy submarine, 29th April 1917. Age 20. Born in Danish West Indies.

BUNN, Steward, FRED, S.S. Daleby (West Hartlepool). Mercantile Marine. Drowned, as a result of an attack by an enemy submarine, 29th April 1917. Age 26. Son of Walter Bunn of 14, Duke St., West Hartlepool, and the late Rachael Hannah Bunn.

CAMERON, Sailor, NEIL, S.S. Daleby (West Hartlepool). Mercantile Marine. Drowned, as a result of an attack by an enemy submarine, 29th April 1917. Age 28. Son of Dugeld Cameron, and the late Barbara Cameron; husband of Catherine Cameron (nee. Doran), of 64, Abbotsford Place, Glasgow. Born at Glasgow.

COX, Third Engineer, HORACE JAMES LEONARD, S.S. Daleby (West Hartlepool). Mercantile Marine. Drowned, as a result of an attack by an enemy submarine, 29th April 1917. Age 31. Son of Ada Eliza Gale (formerly Cox), of The Bryn, Redwick, Magor, Mon., and the late James Leonard Cox. Born at Redwick, Mon.

DAVISON, First Engineer, JOSEPH, S.S. Daleby (West Hartlepool). Mercantile Marine. Drowned, as a result of an attack by an enemy submarine, 29th April 1917. Age 46. Son of Elizabeth and the late Joseph Davison; husband of Mary Davison, of 17, Beechwood Rd., Eaglescliffe, Durham. Born at Darlington.

DICK, Boatswain (Bosun), WILLIAM, S.S. Daleby (West Hartlepool). Mercantile Marine. Drowned, as a result of an attack by an enemy submarine, 29th April 1917. Age 31. Son of the late Thomas and Elizabeth Dick. Born at Islandmagee, Co. Antrim.

DORAI, Pantryman, A, S.S. Daleby (West Hartlepool). Mercantile Marine. Drowned, as a result of an attack by an enemy submarine, 29th April 1917. Age 29. Born in Italy.

GARCIA, Fireman, FELIPE, Daleby (West Hartlepool). Mercantile Marine. Drowned, as a result of an attack by an enemy submarine, 28th April 1917. Age 41. Husband of Dona Maria Bua, viuda de Garcia, of Muros, Spain. Born in Spain.

HORD, Master, CHARLES, S.S. Daleby (West Hartlepool). Mercantile Marine. Drowned, as a result of an attack by an enemy submarine, 29th April 1917. Age 50. Husband of Emily Hord, of 45, Arncliffe Gardens, West Hartlepool.

JOHNSON, Fireman, A, S.S. Daleby (West Hartlepool). Mercantile Marine. Drowned, as a result of an attack by an enemy submarine, 29th April 1917. Age 43. Born at Sierra Leone.

KANIDA, Donkeyman, T, S.S. Daleby (West Hartlepool). Mercantile Marine. Drowned, as a result of an attack by an enemy submarine, 29th April 1917.

LORD, Second Engineer, HUGH HIRST, S.S. Daleby (West Hartlepool). Mercantile Marine. Drowned, as a result of an attack by an enemy submarine, 29th April 1917. Age 34. Son of the late Robert and Eliza Ann Lord; husband of Jane Smith Lord (nee Rimer), of 20, Laburnum Avenue, Wallsend, Northumberland. Born at West Hartlepool.

MACRI, Able Seaman, J C, S.S. Daleby (West Hartlepool). Mercantile Marine. Drowned, as a result of an attack by an enemy submarine, 29th April 1917. Age 39. Born in Greece.

MARLES-THOMAS, Second Mate, LEWIS WILLIAM, S.S. Daleby (West Hartlepool). Mercantile Marine. Drowned, as a result of an attack by an enemy submarine, 29th April 1917. Age 40. Son of the late Rev. William Marles-Thomas, and Mary (Gwilym Marles) Marles-Thomas (nee Williams). Born at Llandyssul, Cardiganshire.

MARTIN, Chief Officer, WILLIAM JAMES, S.S. Daleby (West Hartlepool). Mercantile Marine. Drowned, as a result of an attack by an enemy submarine, 29th April 1917. Age 48. Son of Mary Martin and the late James Wm. Martin; husband of Elizabeth Ann Martin (nee Leffaze), of 4, Mulgrave Rd., West Hartlepool. Born at North Wells.

MILSOM, Cook, VALENTINE, S.S. Daleby (West Hartlepool). Mercantile Marine. Drowned, as a result of an attack by an enemy submarine, 29th April 1917. Age 32. Son of Sarah Ann Milson, of 216, Cathey's Terrace, Cardiff, and the late George Milson.

NOLAN, Greaser, T, S.S. Daleby (West Hartlepool). Mercantile Marine. Drowned, as a result of an attack by an enemy submarine, 29th April 1917. Age 35. Husband of Mrs. Nolan, of 28, Main St., Inniskillen. Born at Inniskillen.

OLSEN, Sailor, V, S.S. Daleby (West Hartlepool). Mercantile Marine. Drowned, as a result of an attack by an enemy submarine, 29th April 1917. Age 23. Born at Copenhagen.

PEARSON, Fireman, A, S.S. Daleby (West Hartlepool). Mercantile Marine. Drowned, as a result of an attack by an enemy submarine, 29th April 1917. Age 21. Son of Mary Pearson, of 19, Patrick St., Cardiff, and the late Charles Pearson.

PETERS, Sailor, WILLIAM ANDREW GEORGE, S.S. Daleby (West Hartlepool). Mercantile Marine. Drowned, as a result of an attack by an enemy submarine, 29th April 1917. Age 26. Son of Mary Logan (formerly Peters, nee Sisk), of 19, Walker Rd., Cardiff, and the late William Andrew Peters. Born at Bristol.

WESTLAKE, Mess Room Steward, RICHARD HERMAN, S.S. Daleby (West Hartlepool). Mercantile Marine. Drowned, as a result of an attack by an enemy submarine, 29th April 1917. Age 17. Son of Rosina Westlake, of Lamoma House, Beer, Devon, and the late William John Westlake.

SS Daleby

HAWKE, Fireman and Trimmer, EDWIN KEMP, S.S. Daleby. Merchant Navy. 15th February 1942. Buried Newcastle-Upon–Tyne (St. Nicholas) Cemetery. (Canadian)

SS Drakepool
(Non-war dead looked after by the CWGC)

AITMAN, Boatswain (Bosun), ROBERT, SS Drakepool. Merchant Navy. 21st March 1945. Buried Morocco Ben M'Sik European Cemetery.

SS Empire Arnold

BURKE, Fireman and Trimmer, JAMES, S.S. Empire Arnold (West Hartlepool). Merchant Navy. 4th August 1942. Age 26. Husband of Harriet Burke, of Liverpool.

CASSIE, Chief Engineer Officer, GEORGE, S.S. Empire Arnold (West Hartlepool). Merchant Navy. 4th August 1942. Age 37.

CUNNINGHAM, Fireman and Trimmer, JAMES JOSEPH, S.S. Empire Arnold (West Hartlepool). Merchant Navy. 4th August 1942. Age 37. Son of Patrick and Bridget Cunningham; husband of Elizabeth Cunningham, of Liverpool.

DAVIS, Fireman and Trimmer, JOSEPH, S.S. Empire Arnold (West Hartlepool). Merchant Navy. 4th August 1942. Age 42.

HAND, Donkeyman, JOHN ALEXANDER, S.S. Empire Arnold (West Hartlepool). Merchant Navy. 4th August 1942. Age 50. Son of William Hand, and of Elizabeth Hand, of West Hartlepool, Co. Durham.

HULL, Second Engineer Officer, REYNOLD NICHOLSON, S.S. Empire Arnold (West Hartlepool). Merchant Navy. 4th August 1942. Age 34. Son of George and Ida Hull; husband of Dorothy Hull, of South Shields, Co. Durham.

LAIGHT, Able Seaman, CHARLES HENRY, D/JX 333739. H.M.S. President III. Royal Navy. Lost in S.S. Empire Arnold. 4th August 1942. Age 27. Son of Frank and Ethel Kate Laight, of Cotteridge, Birmingham.

REED, Fourth Engineer Officer, JOHN, S.S. Empire Arnold (West Hartlepool). Merchant Navy. 4th August 1942. Age 21. Son of John Reed, and of Charlotte Reed, of West Hartlepool, Co. Durham.

SYMONDS, Ordinary Seaman, JAMES MARK, S.S. Empire Arnold (West Hartlepool). Merchant Navy. 4th August 1942. Age 21.

SS Empire Bison

ALLISON, Cabin Boy, JOSEPH, S.S. Empire Bison (London). Merchant Navy. 1st November 1940. Age 16. Son of John Thomas Allison and Agnes Allison, of Fulwell, Sunderland, Co. Durham.

BISSETT, Mess Room Boy, JOHN, S.S. Empire Bison (London). Merchant Navy. 1st November 1940. Age 19.

BRYANT, Able Seaman, SAMUEL, S.S. Empire Bison (London). Merchant Navy. 1st November 1940. Age 55. (Canadian)

COOK, Fireman, FREDERICK, S.S. Empire Bison (London). Merchant Navy. 1st November 1940. Age 45. Son of William W. and Mary J. Cook.

COSWAY, Able Seaman, MAURICE ROY, D/JX 204755. H.M.S. President III. Royal Navy. Lost in S.S. Empire Bison. 1st November 1940. Age 30. Son of Frederick Thomas Cosway and Emma Cosway; husband of V. K. Cosway, of Countess Wear, Devon.

CURTIS, Able Seaman, GEORGE, S.S. Empire Bison(London). Merchant Navy. 1st November 1940. Age 39. (Canadian)

FISHER, Steward, CHARLES JOYCE MEYNELL, H.M.S. Ranpura, Naval Auxiliary Personnel (Merchant Navy). Lost in Empire Bison 1 November 1940. Age 24.

GEORGE, Petty Officer, STANLEY ALAN, D/J 108479 H.M.S. Drake, Royal Navy. Lost in Empire Bison 1 November 1940. Age 32. Son of Rithchard and Olive George; husband of Florence Ruby George, of St. Budeaux, Devon.

HALL, Cook, JOHN WILLIAM, S.S. Empire Bison (London). Merchant Navy. 1st November 1940. Age 25. Husband of D. Hall, of West Hartlepool, Co. Durham.

HARLAND, Master, WILLIAM HERBERT, O B E, S.S. Empire Bison (London). Merchant Navy. 1st November 1940. Age 46. Son of Alfred Charles and Frances Jane Harland; husband of Gwyneth Harland, of West Hartlepool, Co. Durham.

HATCHETT, Carpenter, WILLIAM ALBERT SYDNEY, 1010228, H.M.S. Rajputana, Naval Auxiliary Personnel (Merchant Navy). Lost in Empire Bison 6 November 1940.

HODGSON, Galley Boy, JOHN FREDERICK, S.S. Empire Bison (London). Merchant Navy. 1st November 1940. Age 15. Son of Frederick H. and Marion Hodgson, of Seaton Carew, West Hartlepool, Co. Durham.

ISAACS, First Radio Officer, MARCUS, S.S. Empire Bison (London). Merchant Navy. 1st November 1940. Age 39. Husband of Blanche A. R. Isaacs, of Flixton, Lancashire.

KING, Able Seaman, RICHARD, S.S. Empire Bison (London). Merchant Navy. 1st November 1940. Age 29 (Canadian)

LIDDELL, Greaser, THOMAS, S.S. Empire Bison (London). Merchant Navy. 1st November 1940. Age 49.

MAYFIELD, Second Radio Officer, PHILIP LEETHAM, S.S. Empire Bison (London). Merchant Navy. 1st November 1940. Age 17.

McLAUGHLIN, Carpenter's Mate, JOHN, 8126, H.M.S. Ascania, Naval Auxiliary Personnel (Merchant Navy). Lost in Empire Bison 6 November 1940. Age 21. Son of James Hamilton McLaughlin and Elizabeth McLaughlin, of Bebington, Cheshire.

NECY, Donkeyman, PETER, S.S. Empire Bison (London). Merchant Navy. 1st November 1940. Age 63. Son of James and Helen Necy; husband of Agnes Necy, of West Hartlepool, Co. Durham.

PARSONS, Chief Engineer Officer, RICHARD, S.S. Empire Bison (London). Merchant Navy. 1st November 1940. Age 44. Son of Tom and Hannah Jane Parsons; husband of Ethel Parsons, of Whitby, Yorkshire.

PEARCE, Greaser, JOHN, 925345, H.M.S. Rajputana, Naval Auxiliary Personnel (Merchant Navy). 1st November 1940. Lost in Empire Bison. Age 52.

PICO, Able Seaman, RALPH, S.S. Empire Bison (London). Merchant Navy. 1st November 1940. Age 46. (Canadian)

PLOWMAN, Able Seaman, ISRAEL, S.S. Empire Bison (London). Merchant Navy. 1st November 1940. Age 39. (Canadian)

POTTS, Fireman, JOHN JACKSON, 17774, H.M.S. Rajputana, Naval Auxiliary Personnel (Merchant Navy). 1 November 1940. Lost in Empire Bison. Age 32. Son of Arthur Jackson Potts and Sarah Wetherall Potts, of Southsea, Hampshire.

REED, Fireman, JOHN THOMAS, 292, H.M.S. Rajputana, Naval Auxiliary Personnel (Merchant Navy). 6 November 1940. Lost in Empire Bison. Age 46. Son of John William and Margaret Ellen Reed, of Sunderland, Co. Durham; husband of Mrs. M. Reed.

REDMOND, Third Officer, GEORGE EDWARD, S.S. Empire Bison (London). Merchant Navy. 1st November 1940. Age 64. Son of Philip Redmond, and of Elizabeth Redmond, of Anfield, Liverpool. Formerly Lieut., R.N.V.R.

ROBINSON, Chief Officer, ALBERT EDWARD, S.S. Empire Bison (London). Merchant Navy. 1st November 1940. Age 52.

SHAW, Greaser, HENRY, S.S. Empire Bison (London). Merchant Navy. 1st November 1940. Age 23.

SMITH, Able Seaman, MICHAEL, S.S. Empire Bison (London). Merchant Navy. 1st November 1940. (Canadian)

SPRAKLIN, Able Seaman, RALPH, S.S. Empire Bison (London). Merchant Navy. 1st November 1940. Age 36. (Canadian)

SQUIRES, Able Seaman, RICHARD, S.S. Empire Bison (London). Merchant Navy. 1st November 1940. (Canadian)

THOMAS, Fireman, IVOR, S.S. Empire Bison (London). Merchant Navy. 1st November 1940. Age 23. Son of Albert Henry Thomas, and of Maud Thomas, of West Hartlepool, Co. Durham.

WHYTE, Second Engineer Officer, ALFRED WILLIAM, S.S. Empire Bison (London). Merchant Navy. 1st November 1940. Age 60. Son of George and Mary Anna Whyte.

WILKINSON, Fireman, WILLIAM CHARD, S.S. Empire Bison (London). Merchant Navy. 1st November 1940. Age 50. Husband of M. E. Wilkinson, of West Hartlepool, Co. Durham.

WILSON, Steward, GEORGE, S.S. Empire Bison (London). Merchant Navy. 1st November 1940. Age 28. Son of George Edward and Nellie Wilson; husband of Selina Wilson, of West Hartlepool, Co. Durham.

WILYMAN, Carpenter, ROBERT, S.S. Empire Bison (London). Merchant Navy. 1st November 1940. Age 61. Husband of Mahala Maud Wilyman, of West Hartlepool, Co. Durham.

WOOD, Fourth Engineer Officer, ADAM ANTHONY, S.S. Empire Bison (London). Merchant Navy. 1st November 1940. Age 30. Son of Adam Wood. and of Sarah Wood, of Meliden, Flintshire.

WOOD, Third Engineer Officer, FREDERICK HENRY, S.S. Empire Bison (London). Merchant Navy. 1st November 1940. Age 52. Son of George and Annie Wood, of Thornaby-on-Tees, Yorkshire.

YARD, Able Seaman, STEPHEN, S.S. Empire Bison (London). Merchant Navy. 1st November 1940. (Canadian).

SS Empire Cabot

THOMAS, Fireman, WILLIAM VENTON, S.S. Empire Cabot (West Hartlepool). Merchant Navy. 6th July 1943. Age 45. Husband of Janet Thomas, of Liverpool. Buried Liverpool (Allerton) Cemetery.

SS Empire Dryden

ANDERSON, Cook, ANGUS, S.S. Empire Dryden (Sunderland). Merchant Navy. 23rd April 1942. Age 41. Son of Mr. and Mrs. William Anderson.

ARMSTRONG, Fireman and Trimmer, JOSEPH, S.S. Empire Dryden (Sunderland). Merchant Navy. 23rd April 1942. Age 22. Son of Joseph Armstrong, and of Mary Jane Armstrong, of Hendon, Sunderland, Co. Durham.

BARNES, Third Engineer Officer, JAMES, S.S. Empire Dryden (Sunderland). Merchant Navy. 23rd April 1942. Age 25. Son of Arthur and Maria Barnes.

BEDDELL, Fireman and Trimmer, NORMAN, S.S. Empire Dryden (Sunderland). Merchant Navy. 23rd April 1942. Age 27. Son of William and Ann Beddell.

BROOKS, Able Seaman, DENNIS, C/JX 311162, S.S. Empire Dryden, Royal Navy. 20 April 1942. Age 20. Son of Henry Samuel and Catherine Brooks, of Hackney, London.

BROWN, Able Seaman, JOHN RAYMOND, C/JX 312382, S.S. Empire Dryden, Royal Navy. 20 April 1942. Age 19. Son of John and Ivy Ella Brown, of Consett, Co. Durham.

CONNOR, Boy, PATRICK, S.S. Empire Dryden (Sunderland). Merchant Navy. 23rd April 1942. Age 18.

FARRER, Fireman and Trimmer, WALTER, S.S. Empire Dryden (Sunderland). Merchant Navy. 23rd April 1942. Age 23.

GARRIGAN, Galley Boy, JOHN COLIN, S.S. Empire Dryden (Sunderland). Merchant Navy. 23rd April 1942. Age 19. Son of Robert and Isabella Garrigan, of Houghton-le-Spring, Co. Durham.

GIBSON, Able Seaman, ERNEST, S.S. Empire Dryden (Sunderland). Merchant Navy. 23rd April 1942. Age 35. Son of David and Margaret Gibson; husband of Emma Gibson, of Sunderland, Co. Durham.

HANLON, Sailor, THOMAS, S.S. Empire Dryden (Sunderland). Merchant Navy. 23rd April 1942. Age 19.

JOHNSON, Donkeyman, WILLIAM GEORGE, S.S. Empire Dryden (Sunderland). Merchant Navy. 23rd April 1942. Age 41. Husband of Ada Isabela Johnson, of Sunderland, Co. Durham.

LOADER, Fireman and Trimmer, GEORGE RICHARD, S.S. Empire Dryden (Sunderland). Merchant Navy. 23rd April 1942. Age 22. Son of George Richard and Alice Loader, of Jarrow, Co. Durham.

LONGLEY, Third Radio Officer, VICTOR LEONARD, S.S. Empire Dryden (Sunderland). Merchant Navy. 23rd April 1942. Age 19. Son of Arthur T. and Sarah Ann Longley, of Edgware, Middlesex.

MASON, Sailor, JOHN, S.S. Empire Dryden (Sunderland). Merchant Navy. 23rd April 1942. Age 19.

MONEY, Third Officer, THOMAS WILLIAM, S.S. Empire Dryden (Sunderland). Merchant Navy. 23rd April 1942. Age 26. Son of Jason William and Maria Money, of Heaton, Newcastle-on-Tyne.

McCUTCHEON, Fireman and Trimmer, PATRICK, S.S. Empire Dryden (Sunderland). Merchant Navy. 23rd April 1942. Age 50.

PAINTER, Able Seaman, THOMAS, S.S. Empire Dryden (Sunderland). Merchant Navy. 23rd April 1942. Age 32. Son of Duke Robertshaw Painter and Catherine Painter, of Coxhoe, Co. Durham.

POWLEY, Master, ROBERT, S.S. Empire Dryden (Sunderland). Merchant Navy. 23rd April 1942. Age 35. Son of Wilfred and Mary Powley; husband of Mary Powley, of Sunderland, Co. Durham.

SELLARS, Able Seaman, GEORGE WAITE STEEL, S.S. Empire Dryden (Sunderland). Merchant Navy. 23rd April 1942. Age 52. Son of George Waite Steel Sellars and Mary Jane Sellars; husband of Elizabeth Ann Sellars, of Sunderland, Co. Durham.

SMITH, Fireman and Trimmer, RALPH FREDERICK, S.S. Empire Dryden (Sunderland). Merchant Navy. 23rd April 1942. Age 24. Son of Robert James Smith and Sara Nesbit Smith, of Tynemouth, North Shields, Northumberland.

SNARY, Gunner, JOHN EDWARD, 4462871, 3/2 Maritime Regt., Royal Artillery. 20 April 1942. Age 30. Son of John Robert and Louise Snary; husband of Ivy Florence Snary, of Tottenham, Middlesex.

STABLER, Second Engineer Officer, RALPH HUGGUP, S.S. Empire Dryden (Sunderland). Merchant Navy. 23rd April 1942. Age 26.

WRATHMALL, Sailor, JOHN THOMAS, S.S. Empire Dryden (Sunderland). Merchant Navy. 23rd April 1942. Age 21.

WRIGHT, Fireman and Trimmer, CHARLES WILLIAM, S.S. Empire Dryden (Sunderland). Merchant Navy. 23rd April 1942. Age 25. Son of Charles William and Hannah Wright; husband of Frances Irene Wright, of West Hartlepool, Co. Durham.

ZAMMIT, Chief Steward, RAYMOND, S.S. Empire Dryden (Sunderland). Merchant Navy. 23rd April 1942. Age 44. Son of Paul and Elizabeth Zammitt; husband of Mary Victoria Zammit, of Sunderland, Co. Durham.

SS Empire Merlin

BARNFATHER, Chief Officer, THOMAS, S.S. Empire Merlin (London). Merchant Navy. 25th August 1940. Age 38. Son of Thomas and Mary Alice Barnfather; husband of Ellen Barnfather, of Newcastle-on-Tyne.

BUCKLEY, Able Seaman, WILLIAM ALBERT, S.S. Empire Merlin (London). Merchant Navy. 25th August 1940. Age 60. Husband of Catherine Buckley, of Rochdale, Lancashire.

CAKE, Able Seaman, EDWIN CHARLES, S.S.Empire Merlin (London). Merchant Navy. 25th August 1940. Age 30. (Canadian).

CHERRY, Fireman, JOHN ROBERT HENRY, S.S. Empire Merlin (London). Merchant Navy. 25th August 1940. Age 23. Son of James and Elizabeth Jane Cherry, of Hartlepool, Co. Durham.

CLARK, Fourth Engineer Officer, RAYMOND STANLEY, S.S. Empire Merlin (London). Merchant Navy. 25th August 1940. Age 26. Son of Stanley Gilbert Clark and Lillian Gertrude Clark, of Grosvenor, Bath, Somerset.

COLLINGE, Able Seaman, JOHN, S.S. Empire Merlin (London). Merchant Navy. 25th August 1940. Age 21.

DICK, Donkeyman, JOHN, S.S. Empire Merlin (London). Merchant Navy. 25th August 1940. Age 64.

DOYLE, Fireman, OWEN, S.S. Empire Merlin (London). Merchant Navy. 25th August 1940. Age 63.

EVANS, Deck Hand, V, S.S. Empire Merlin (London). Merchant Navy. 25th August 1940. Age 25. Son of Vincent and Bridget Grimes Evans; husband of Jean Evans, of Glasgow.

GOSSE, Able Seaman, DAVID JOSEPH, S.S. Empire Merlin (London). Merchant Navy. 25th August 1940. Age 27. (Canadian).

HART, Able Seaman, JOHN FRANCIS, S.S. Empire Merlin (London). Merchant Navy. 25th August 1940. (Canadian).

HATCH, Fireman, SYDNEY, S.S. Empire Merlin (London). Merchant Navy. 25th August 1940. Age 28. Son of Frank and Amelia Jane Hatch.

HUDSON, Third Engineer Officer, WILLIAM, S.S. Empire Merlin (London). Merchant Navy. 25th August 1940. Age 26.

HUTCHISON, Greaser, DAVID, S.S. Empire Merlin (London). Merchant Navy. 25th August 1940. Age 55. Son of William and Janet Hutchison; husband of Elizabeth A. Hutchison, of Openshaw, Manchester.

JOHNSON, Cabin Boy, LESLIE, S.S. Empire Merlin (London). Merchant Navy. 25th August 1940. Age 20.

LITHERLAND, Galley Boy, EDWARD, S.S. Empire Merlin (London). Merchant Navy. 25th August 1940. Age 20. Son of Edward Charles and Julia Litherland, of Chorlton-upon-Medlock, Manchester.

McGRILL, Second Officer, ALFRED, S.S. Empire Merlin (London). Merchant Navy. 25th August 1940. Age 24. Son of Austin and Jane Rutherford McGrill, of North Shields, Northumberland.

MILLS, Bosun, GEORGE, S.S. Empire Merlin (London). Merchant Navy. 25th August 1940. (Canadian)

MOORES, Able Seaman, CHARLES, S.S. Empire Merlin (London). Merchant Navy. 25th August 1940. (Canadian)

PARKES, Fireman, ISAAC JAMES, S.S. Empire Merlin (London). Merchant Navy. 25th August 1940. Age 23. Son of William James Parkes and Susan Parkes; husband of Margaret Parkes, of West Hartlepool, Co. Durham.

PARSONS, Radio Officer, ENOS, S.S. Empire Merlin (London). Merchant Navy. 25th August 1940. Age 41. Son of Enos and Lily Parsons; husband of Lily May Parsons, of Stourbridge, Worcestershire.

PATERSON, Second Engineer Officer, ALEXANDER, S.S. Empire Merlin (London). Merchant Navy. 25th August 1940. Age 59. Son of James and Elizabeth Paterson; husband of Barbara Paterson, of Culduthel, Inverness-shire.

PEPPER, Greaser, JOHN, S.S. Empire Merlin (London). Merchant Navy. 25th August 1940. Age 43. Husband of Mary Jane Pepper, of Middlesbrough, Yorkshire.

PRODHAM, Third Officer, HENRY, S.S. Empire Merlin (London). Merchant Navy. 25th August 1940. Age 27. Son of Herbert and Caroline Prodham.

RALPH, Ordinary Seaman, FREDERICK, S.S. Empire Merlin (London). Merchant Navy. 25th August 1940. Age 19. Son of Joseph and Jane A. Ralph, of Denton, Lancashire.

ROBERTS, Boy, JOHN, S.S. Empire Merlin (London). Merchant Navy. 25th August 1940. Age 17.

ROWELL, Cook, ROBERT, S.S. Empire Merlin (London). Merchant Navy. 25th August 1940. Age 49.

RUSSELL, Able Seaman, JAMES, S.S. Empire Merlin (London). Merchant Navy. 25th August 1940. Age 25. Son of William and Mary Russell, of Tollcross, Glasgow.

SHEPPARD, Ordinary Seaman, JAMES, S.S. Empire Merlin (London). Merchant Navy. 25th August 1940. (Canadian)

SIMPSON, Master, DAVID WILLIAM, M B E, S.S. Empire Merlin (London). Merchant Navy. 25th August 1940. Age 69. Son of David and Harriet Simpson; husband of Margaret Taylor Simpson, of Beccles, Suffolk. Awarded Lloyd's Medal.

STANSFIELD, Steward, GEORGE S., S.S. Empire Merlin (London). Merchant Navy. 25th August 1940. Age 50. Husband of Flora Stansfield, of Muckhart, Clackmannanshire.

WESLEY, Carpenter, JOHN WILLIAM, S.S. Empire Merlin (London). Merchant Navy. 25th August 1940. Age 23. Son of William and Anne Wesley; husband of Christine Wesley, of Sale, Cheshire.

SS Empire Moonbeam

ATKINS, Chief Cook, WILLIAM JOHN THOMPSON, S.S. Empire Moonbeam (Hong Kong). Merchant Navy. 8th August 1942. Age 36. Son of George and Elizebeth Atkins; husband of Ida Atkins, of North Shields, Northumberland.

BRICE, Fireman and Trimmer, JOHN HENRY, S.S. Empire Moonbeam (Hong Kong). Merchant Navy. 8th August 1942. Age 39. Son of John and Ellen Phoebe Brice.

CUSHNAHAN, Able Seaman, THOMAS, S.S. Empire Moonbeam (Hong Kong). Merchant Navy. 8th August 1942. Age 28. Son of Joseph and Elizabeth Cushnahan, of Portglenone, Co. Antrim, Northern Ireland; husband of Annie Cushnahan, of Lurgan, Co. Armagh, Northern Ireland.

DWYER, Fireman and Trimmer, T, S.S. Empire Moonbeam (Hong Kong). Merchant Navy. 8th August 1942. Age 27.

ELSON, Carpenter, WILFRED JOHN, S.S. Empire Moonbeam (Hong Kong). Merchant Navy. 8th August 1942. Age 20. Husband of Frances Elizabeth Elson, of Chester.

GRAHAM, Fireman and Trimmer, ROBERT SLOAN, S.S. Empire Moonbeam (Hong Kong). Merchant Navy. 11th September 1942. Age 20. Son of Elizabeth Robertson, of Stevenston, Ayrshire.

HUGHES, Fireman and Trimmer, THOMAS, S.S. Empire Moonbeam (Hong Kong). Merchant Navy. 8th August 1942. Age 40.

JENKINS, Fourth Engineer Officer, EDWARD B., S.S. Empire Moonbeam (Hong Kong). Merchant Navy. 8th August 1942. Age 21. Son of Winifred Jenkins, of Porth, Glamorgan.

MacLEOD, Fireman and Trimmer, ALEXANDER MURDO, S.S. Empire Moonbeam (Hong Kong). Merchant Navy. 11th September 1942. Age 42. Son of Murdo and Christina Murray MacLeod.

RUTHERFORD, Fireman and Trimmer, JAMES, S.S. Empire Moonbeam (Hong Kong). Merchant Navy. 11th September 1942. Age 34.

SS Empire Moonrise

BUTCHER, Chief Engineer Officer, JAMES ALBERT, D S C, S.S. Empire Moonrise (Hong Kong). Merchant Navy. 6th March 1945. Age 43. Son of William Noble Butcher and Hanah Butcher; husband of Doris Butcher. Buried Marley Hill (St Cuthbert) Churchyard.

SS Empire Starlight

NG KING, Assistant Steward, S.S. Empire Starlight (Hong Kong). Merchant Navy. 15th April 1942. Age 34. Buried Murmansk Russian Cemetery.

SS Empire Trent

BYRNE, Carpenter, WILLIAM, S.S. Empire Trent (West Hartlepool). Merchant Navy. 31st July 1943. Age 45. (At the time of writing, Mr Byrne has no official commemoration with the Commonwealth War Graves Commission and his name does not appear on Tower Hill. I am working on having this rectified)

GATES, Chief Engineer Officer, WILLIAM ALEXANDER, S.S. Empire Trent (West Hartlepool). Merchant Navy. 9th August 1943. Age 51. Son of Walter and Margaret Gates, of South Shields, husband of Adelaide O. Gates, of South Shields. Buried South Shields (Harton) Cemetery.

REYNOLDS, Fireman and Trimmer, STANLEY, S.S. Empire Trent (West Hartlepool). Merchant Navy. 6th August 1943. Age 41. (Served as SMITH, Stanley). Buried Inverness (Tomnahurich) Cemetery.

SS Fishpool

ADDERLEY, Junior Engineer Officer, THOMAS JAMES, M.V. Fishpool (West Hartlepool). Merchant Navy. 26th July 1943. Age 22.

ALLEN, Sailor, LEONARD SPENCER, M.V. Fishpool (West Hartlepool). Merchant Navy. 14th November 1940. Age 20. Son of William H. G. and Mary E. R. Allen.

ATKINSON, Galley Boy, GEORGE WILLIAM, M.V. Fishpool (West Hartlepool). Merchant Navy. 14th November 1940. Age 17. Son of Christopher Byers Atkinson and Agnes Atkinson, of Hendon, Sunderland, Co. Durham. His brother Stanley also died on service. Buried Rothesay Cemetery.

ATKINSON, Cabin Boy, STANLEY, M.V. Fishpool (West Hartlepool). Merchant Navy. 14th November 1940. Age 18. Son of Christopher Byers Atkinson, and of Agnes Atkinson, of Hendon, Sunderland, Co. Durham. His brother George William also died on service. Buried Rothesay Cemetery.

BENNETT, Sailor, EDGAR, M.V. Fishpool (West Hartlepool). Merchant Navy. 14th November 1940. Age 41.

BONAR, Junior Engineer Officer, JAMES, M.V. Fishpool (West Hartlepool). Merchant Navy. 14th November 1940. Age 20. Son of John and Sarah Bonar.

BROWN, Able Seaman, JAMES ALEXANDER, M.V. Fishpool (West Hartlepool). Merchant Navy. 9th May 1941. Age 23. Son of Thomas and Catherine Brown, of Greenock. Buried Greenock Cemetery.

BYRNE, Junior Engineer Officer, JOHN JOSEPH CHARLES, M.V. Fishpool (West Hartlepool). Merchant Navy. 26th July 1943. Age 22. Son of Alexander and Cathrine Byrne, of Glasgow.

CHRISTIE, Junior Engineer Officer, JOHN, M.V. Fishpool (West Hartlepool). Merchant Navy. 14th November 1940. Age 20.

COLE, Master, RALPH, M.V. Fishpool (West Hartlepool). Merchant Navy. 26th July 1943. Age 28. Son of Ralph and Margaret Constance Cole.

COLLIE, Gunner, THOMAS PRIEST, 2875823, 2 Maritime Regt., Royal Artillery. 25 July 1943. Age 33. Husband of Dora R. Collie, of Hatfield, Hertfordshire. Buried Syracuse War Cemetery.

COOPER, Able Seaman, GEORGE ARTHUR, M.V. Fishpool (West Hartlepool). Merchant Navy. 26th July 1943. Age 23. Son of James Arthur and Elizabeth Cooper, of West Hartlepool, Co. Durham.

CROMBIE, Donkeyman, DANIEL, M.V. Fishpool (West Hartlepool). Merchant Navy. 14th November 1940. Age 43.

CROPLEY, Third Officer, HAROLD ERNEST, M.V. Fishpool (West Hartlepool). Merchant Navy. 14th November 1940. Age 22. Son of George and Jane Cropley, of West Hartlepool, Co. Durham. Buried Rothesay Cemetery.

CUMMINGS, Gunner, JOSEPH PETER, 1809118, 1 Maritime Regt., Royal Artillery. 25 July 1943. Age 32. Son of Robert and Margaret Cummings, of West Withington, Manchester. Buried Syracuse War Cemetery.

EDMONDSON, Chief Engineer Officer, ERNEST, M.V. Fishpool (West Hartlepool). Merchant Navy. 21st November 1940. Age 42. Son of Thomas and Jessie Edmondson; husband of Elizabeth Lewis Edmondson, of Barry. Buried Barry (Merthyr Dyfan) Burial Ground.

FLINT, Fourth Engineer Officer, EDWIN MOSS, M.V. Fishpool (West Hartlepool). Merchant Navy. 14th November 1940. Age 25. Son of E. Flint, and of Ada Flint, of Newcastle-on-Tyne. His brother Leonard also fell.

FORSYTH, Third Engineer Officer, ROBERT MARTIN, M.V. Fishpool (West Hartlepool). Merchant Navy. 26th July 1943. Age 31. Son of Thomas Harvey Forsyth, and of Janet Forsyth, of Glasgow.

FRANCKE, Junior Engineer Officer, CARLTON LANCELOT, M.V. Fishpool (West Hartlepool). Merchant Navy. 26th July 1943. Age 23. Son of Kenneth Charles Francke, and of Maude Francke, of Felling, Co. Durham.

GRANT, Donkeyman, JOHN, M.V. Fishpool (West Hartlepool). Merchant Navy. 14th November 1940. Age 43. Son of Kieran and Margaret Grant, of Waterford, Irish Republic.

GURNEY, Chief Officer, CHARLES HENRY, M.V. Fishpool (West Hartlepool). Merchant Navy. 26th July 1943. Age 27. Son of Alfred and Elizabeth Gurney, of Glenluce, Wigtownshire.

HAMMOND, Third Officer, JOHN, M.V. Fishpool (West Hartlepool). Merchant Navy. 26th July 1943. Age 37. Son of Charles Frewin Hammond and Edith Hammond; husband of Edith Emily Hammond, of Chessington, Surrey.

HARDY, Cook, THOMAS WEARS, M.V. Fishpool (West Hartlepool). Merchant Navy. 26th July 1943. Age 26. Buried Syracuse War Cemetery.

HARKER, Mess Room Boy, CHARLES, M.V. Fishpool (West Hartlepool). Merchant Navy. 14th November 1940. Age 17. Buried Rothesay Cemetery.

HENDERSON, Second Officer, GEORGE, M.V. Fishpool (West Hartlepool). Merchant Navy. 14th November 1940. Age 33. Son of Thomas and Mary Elizabeth Henderson, of Hartlepool, Co. Durham. Buried Rothesay Cemetery.

HILL, Master, THOMAS MORGAN, M.V. Fishpool (West Hartlepool). Merchant Navy. 14th November 1940. Age 61. King's Commendation for Brave Conduct. Husband of Mary Hill, of West Hartlepool, Co. Durham.

HOOD, Mess Room Boy, JOHN HENDERSON, M.V. Fishpool (West Hartlepool). Merchant Navy. 14th November 1940. Age 18. Son of John and Ruth Hood, of Maryport, Cumberland.

HUGHES, Second Radio Officer, RONALD BERTRAM, M.V. Fishpool (West Hartlepool). Merchant Navy. 14th November 1940. Age 20. Son of Thomas and Winifred Louisa Fanny Hughes, of Victoria Park, Manchester. Buried Rothesay Cemetery.

HUGILL, First Officer, JOSEPH, M.V. Fishpool (West Hartlepool). Merchant Navy. 14th November 1940. Age 30. Buried Rothesay Cemetery.

IRVING, Third Engineer Officer, JOHN HENRY, S.S. Fishpool (West Hartlepool). Merchant Navy. 1st December 1940. Age 24. Son of Albert Frederick and Florence May Irving, of Tooting, Surrey. Buried Cardiff (Cathys) Cemetery.

JONES, Gunner, ROBERT JOHN, 1564978, 1 Maritime Regt., Royal Artillery. 25 July 1943. Age 28. Son of Henry and Bessie Jones, of Dymock, Gloucestershire. Buried Syracuse War Cemetery.

KIRKPATRICK, Second Radio Officer, JOHN, M.V. Fishpool (West Hartlepool). Merchant Navy. 26th July 1943. Age 22. Son of John and Helen Kirkpatrick, of Closeburn, Dumfriesshire.

KNIGHT, Mess Room Boy, GEOFFREY JAMES PETER, M.V. Fishpool (West Hartlepool). Merchant Navy. 26th July 1943. Age 19. Son of Cicel James John and Mary Gertrude Knight, of Camberwell, London.

KNOX, Second Officer, DOUGLAS, M.V. Fishpool (West Hartlepool). Merchant Navy. 26th July 1943. Age 23. Son of Thomas and Elizabeth Morgan Knox, of Prestwick, Ayrshire.

LEACH, Gunner, LEONARD ALEXANDER, 6297100, 6 Maritime Regt., Royal Artillery. 26 July 1943. Age 34. Son of William Thomas Leach and Caroline Leach; husband of Florance Ruth Leach, of Plumstead, London

LOWN, Sailor, ALFRED JAMES, M.V. Fishpool (West Hartlepool). Merchant Navy. 14th November 1940. Age 23. Son of Benjamin and Ellen Lown.

MACLEAN, Sailor, MURDO, M.V. Fishpool (West Hartlepool). Merchant Navy. 26th July 1943. Age 21. Son of Kenneth and Mary Ann Maclean, of Stornoway, Isle of Lewis.

MACMILLAN, Able Seaman, EVANDER, M.V. Fishpool (West Hartlepool). Merchant Navy. 26th July 1943. Age 35. Son of Donald and Christina Macmillan.

MAWBY, Mess Room Boy, JOHN JAMES, M.V. Fishpool (West Hartlepool). Merchant Navy. 26th July 1943. Age 19. Son of John Edward and Esther Mawby, of South Shields, Co. Durham.

MORDEY, Carpenter, JOHN GEORGE, M.V. Fishpool (West Hartlepool). Merchant Navy. 14th November 1940. Age 21. Son of John George and Grace Mordey, of Hendon, Sunderland, Co. Durham.

McKENZIE, Junior Engineer Officer, MALCOLM, M.V. Fishpool (West Hartlepool). Merchant Navy. 14th November 1940. Age 21. Son of Henry and Marion McKenzie, of Greenock, Renfrewshire.

PFISTERER, Steward, PAUL ANTOINE, M.V. Fishpool (West Hartlepool). Merchant Navy. 26th July 1943. Age 34. Son of Paul Antoine and Isabella Pfisterer; husband of Lily Pfisterer, of Carshalton, Surrey.

PROCTER, Third Radio Officer, ERIC, M.V. Fishpool (West Hartlepool). Merchant Navy. 26th July 1943. Age 21. Son of Henry and Jane Alice Procter. of Blackburn, Lancashire.

REID, Junior Engineer Officer, WILLIAM JOHNSTONE, M.V. Fishpool (West Hartlepool). Merchant Navy. 26th July 1943. Age 48.

SCOTT, Fourth Engineer Officer, DAVID, M.V. Fishpool (West Hartlepool). Merchant Navy. 26th July 1943. Age 43. Husband of Mary Scott, of West Hartlepool, Co. Durham.

SLOAN, Apprentice, JAMES WALTER, M.V. Fishpool (West Hartlepool). Merchant Navy. 14th November 1940. Age 21. Son of James Hutchison Sloan and Annie Lena Sloan, of North Ferriby, Yorkshire. Buried Rothesay Cemetery.

SMITH, Second Engineer Officer, WILLIAM HENRY, M.V. Fishpool (West Hartlepool). Merchant Navy. 26th July 1943. Age 29.

TABLEY, Steward, THOMAS EDWARD, M.V. Fishpool (West Hartlepool). Merchant Navy. 26th July 1943. Age 31.

THOMPSON, Cook, WILLIAM JOHN MORRISON, M.V. Fishpool (West Hartlepool). Merchant Navy. 14th November 1940. Age 23. Buried Rothesay Cemetery.

THOW, First Radio Officer, ALEXANDER MORRISON, M.V. Fishpool (West Hartlepool). Merchant Navy. 26th July 1943. Age 27.

TODD, Chief Engineer Officer, LAWRENCE, M.V. Fishpool (West Hartlepool). Merchant Navy. 26th July 1943. Age 57.

TUCKNUTT, Ordinary Seaman, CHRISTOPHER HEDLEY HENDERSON, M.V. Fishpool (West Hartlepool). Merchant Navy. 14th November 1940. Age 23.

WATSON, Leading Seaman, MATTHEW, Mentioned in Despatches, D/JX 229934. H.M.S. President III. Royal Navy. Lost in M.V. Fishpool. 26th July 1943. Age 26. Son of Matthew and Elizabeth Ann Watson, of Cambois, Northumberland; husband of Helen Watson, of Cambois.

WHARTON, Steward, WILSON, M.V. Fishpool (West Hartlepool). Merchant Navy. 14th November 1940. Age 34. Son of William and Mary Ann Wharton; husband of Annie Wharton, of Grasslot, Cumberland.

SS Fort George

CANLAN, Boatswain (Bosun), EDWARD, B E M, S.S. Fort George (Liverpool). Merchant Navy. 25th December 1946. Age 33. Buried Durban (Stellawood) Cemetery.

WILDING, Fireman and Trimmer, JOHN, S.S. Fort George (Liverpool). Merchant Navy. 21st March 1944. Age 34. Husband of Eleanor Wilding, of Huyton, Lancashire. (Died from Malaria, buried at sea in position 29'49N 12'48W)

SS Fort Henley
(Non-war dead looked after by the CWGC)

ANDERSON, Chief Steward, AXEL A, SS FORT HENLEY. Merchant Navy. 19th February 1944. Age 33. Buried Morocco Ben M'Sik European Cemetery.

SS Fort Pelly

BALCHIN, Cabin Boy, EDMUND CHARLES, S.S. Fort Pelly (London). Merchant Navy. 20th July 1943. Age 18. Son of Edmund Balchin, and of Maud Elizabeth Balchin, of Hull.

BAYLEY, Able Seaman, ERIC, D/JX 253001. H.M.S. President III. Royal Navy. Lost in S.S. Fort Pelly. 20th July 1943. Age 28. Husband of Alice Bayley, of Elworth, Cheshire.

BENSON, Mess Room Boy, KENNETH, S.S. Fort Pelly (London). Merchant Navy. 20th July 1943. Age 19. Son of John Arthur and Gertrude Benson, of Hull.

BICKFORD, Carpenter, FREDERICK JAMES, S.S. Fort Pelly (London). Merchant Navy. 20th July 1943. Age 67. Husband of Agnes Mary Bickford, of Hull.

BRADBURY, Able Seaman, FREDERICK, D/JX 266991. H.M.S. President III. Royal Navy. Lost in S.S. Fort Pelly. 20th July 1943. Age 34. Son of Arthur and Sarah Elizabeth Bradbury; husband of Mabel Bradbury, of Wallasey, Cheshire.

BROWN, Able Seaman, SYDNEY HAROLD, Naval Auxiliary Personnel (Merchant Navy). Lost in S.S. Fort Pelly. 20th July 1943. Age 34. Commemorated Liverpool Naval Memorial.

BURTON, Assistant Cook, NORMAN WEETMAN, S.S. Fort Pelly (London). Merchant Navy. 20th July 1943. Age 18.

CAMPBELL, Sailor, GERALD, S.S. Fort Pelly (London). Merchant Navy. 20th July 1943. Age 22.

CHAMBERS, Second Engineer Officer, GEORGE HOLMES, S.S. Fort Pelly (London). Merchant Navy. 20th July 1943. Age 56. Husband of Lavinia Chambers of Whitley Bay.

COX, Chief Engineer Officer, JOHN THOMAS, S.S. Fort Pelly (London). Merchant Navy. 20th July 1943. Age 63. Husband of Alice Cox, of West Hartlepool, Co. Durham.

CROWTHER, Galley Boy, KENNETH, S.S. Fort Pelly (London). Merchant Navy. 20th July 1943. Age 18. Son of John Samuel and Lily Crowther, of Hull.

DAVIES, Fireman and Trimmer, DAVID, S.S. Fort Pelly (London). Merchant Navy. 20th July 1943.

DILLEY, Senior Ordinary Seaman, PETER JAMES, S.S. Fort Pelly (London). Merchant Navy. 20th July 1943. Age 19. Son of Gladys May Quintrell, of Crowan, Cornwall.

EIMAN, Donkeyman, OTTO, S.S. Fort Pelly (London). Merchant Navy. 20th July 1943. Age 59. Husband of Ivy May Eiman.

FEWSTER, Fireman and Trimmer, ROBERT, S.S. Fort Pelly (London). Merchant Navy. 20th July 1943. Age 33.

GEMMELL, Fireman and Trimmer, HUGH, S.S. Fort Pelly (London). Merchant Navy. 20th July 1943. Age 29.

GERAGHTY, Donkeyman, JOHN PATRICK, S.S. Fort Pelly (London). Merchant Navy. 20th July 1943. Age 21. Son of John and Emma Sturdy Geraghty of Hull; nephew of Mr. P. F. Gallagher, of Hull.

HAIRSINE, Fireman and Trimmer, JOSEPH, S.S. Fort Pelly (London). Merchant Navy. 20th July 1943. Age 21. Son of George Francis Hairsine and Maria Hairsine, of Hull.

HOPPER, Apprentice, CHARLES HENRY, S.S. Fort Pelly (London). Merchant Navy. 20th July 1943. Age 17. Son of W. G. and Nora Hopper, of Durham.

153

HUTCHEON, Able Seaman, THOMAS, P/JX 338770. H.M.S. President III. Royal Navy. (Lost in S.S. Fort Pelly). 20th July 1943. Age 19. Son of Robert and Janet Hutcheon, of Sunderland, Co. Durham.

HUTCHINSON, Able Seaman, JOHN HERBERT, P/JX 334353. H.M.S. President III. Royal Navy. (Lost in S.S. Fort Pelly). 20th July 1943. Age 20. Son of John Hutchinson, and of Phoebe Elizabeth Hutchinson, of Grays, Essex.

JOHNSON, Ordinary Seaman, ARTHUR LEONARD, S.S. Fort Pelly (London). Merchant Navy. 20th July 1943. Age 19. Son of Charles Johnson, and of Kate Johnson, of Hull.

KIRK, Donkeyman, WILLIAM IAN, S.S. Fort Pelly (London). Merchant Navy. 20th July 1943. Age 59. Brother of Mrs Edith Stevens of Anlaby Common, Hull.

LAMBERT, Third Engineer Officer, ROBERT, S.S. Fort Pelly (London). Merchant Navy. 20th July 1943. Age 30. Son of Robert and Margaret Lambert; husband of Doris Lambert, of Hebburn, Co. Durham.

LILLIE, Assistant Steward, JAMES PATRICK, S.S. Fort Pelly (London). Merchant Navy. 20th July 1943. Age 16.

MOODY, Seaman, ROBERT, S.S. Fort Pelly (London). Merchant Navy. 20th July 1943. (Canadian)

NYBORG, Cook, HUGO, S.S. Fort Pelly (London). Merchant Navy. 20th July 1943. Age 54. Husband of Florence Nyborg, of Hull.

PHILLIPS, Fireman and Trimmer, JAMES FREDERICK, S.S. Fort Pelly (London). Merchant Navy. 20th July 1943. Age 48. Son of James Frederick and Elizabeth Phillips; husband of M. L. Phillips, of Aldbrough, Yorkshire.

ROBINSON, Able Seaman, SIDNEY WOODCLIFEE, S.S. Fort Pelly (London). Merchant Navy. 20th July 1943. Age 27.

ROBINSON, Fireman and Trimmer, THOMAS HENRY, S.S. Fort Pelly (London). Merchant Navy. 20th July 1943. Age 24. Husband of Emma Gillyan Robinson, of Hull.

ROWNTREE, Ordinary Seaman, EDWARD, S.S. Fort Pelly (London). Merchant Navy. 20th July 1943. Age 20. Son of Alice Pretoria Rowntree, and stepson of Henry Thomas Eade, of Hull.

SWEENEY, Fireman and Trimmer, THOMAS, S.S. Fort Pelly (London). Merchant Navy. 20th July 1943. Age 43. Husband of Ellen Sweeney, of Kingston-upon-Hull, Yorkshire.

TREACY, Able Seaman, THOMAS JOSEPH, S.S. Fort Pelly (London). Merchant Navy. 20th July 1943. Age 61. Son of Mr. and Mrs. P. Treacy, of Arklow, Co. Wicklow, Irish Republic; husband of Annie Treacy, of Hull.

WALLGATE, Fireman and Trimmer, ALAN HALL, S.S. Fort Pelly (London). Merchant Navy. 20th July 1943. Age 31. Son of Robert Hall Wallgate and Kate Wallgate; husband of M. Wallgate, of Scunthorpe, Lincolnshire.

WALSBY, Fourth Engineer, GEORGE, S.S. Fort Pelly (London). Merchant Navy. 20th July 1943. Age 30. (Canadian)

WILLIAMS, Able Seaman, ERNEST ARTHUR, S.S. Fort Pelly (London). Merchant Navy. 20th July 1943. Age 40. Son of John William and Sarah Lilly Williams, of Hull.

WRIGHT, Able Seaman, CHARLES WILLIAM, P/JX 394141. H.M.S. President III. Royal Navy. (Lost in S.S. Fort Pelly). 20th July 1943. Age 19. Son of Charles and Elizabeth Wright, of Small Heath, Birmingham.

SS Fort Stager

LOVE, Master, PETER, S.S. Fort Stager (London). Merchant Navy. 30th December 1947. Age 53. King's Commendation for brave conduct. Son of Peter and Jane Love, of Birkenhead; husband of Elsie Love, of Birkenhead. Buried Bidston (St. Oswald) Churchyard.

SS Glenby

HALL, Donkeyman, ERNEST, S.S. Glenby (West Hartlepool). Mercantile Marine. Killed, as a result of an attack by an enemy submarine, 17th August 1915. Born at Constantinople.

NIELSON, Boatswain (Bosun), C, S.S. Glenby (West Hartlepool). Mercantile Marine. Killed, as a result of an attack by an enemy submarine, 17th August 1915. Age 21. Born at Boda, Norway.

SS Haxby

CANNELL, Deck Hand, WALTER, S.S. Haxby (West Hartlepool). Merchant Navy. 24th April 1940. Age 32. Husband of Margaret F. Cannell, of Settle, Yorkshire.

COLLINS, Third Engineer Officer, CYRIL, S.S. Haxby (West Hartlepool). Merchant Navy. 24th April 1940. Age 20.

ENNIS, Fireman and Trimmer, JOHN, S.S. Haxby (West Hartlepool). Merchant Navy. 24th April 1940. Age 44. Son of William and Mary Ennis; husband of Margaret Ennis, of Margate.

FLIGHT, Ordinary Seaman, HERBERT, S.S. Haxby (West Hartlepool). Merchant Navy. 24th April 1940. Age 33. Son of George and Cecilia Flight.

GALLAGHER, Fireman and Trimmer, RICHARD, S.S. Haxby (West Hartlepool). Merchant Navy. 24th April 1940. Age 36. Husband of Janet Gallagher, of Balornock, Glasgow.

HENDERSON, Carpenter, HUGH, S.S. Haxby (West Hartlepool). Merchant Navy. 24th April 1940. Age 26. Son of Daniel and Mary Henderson, of Kilchoan, Argyllshire.

KULVINSKAS, Galley Boy, PETER, S.S. Haxby (West Hartlepool). Merchant Navy. 24th April 1940. Age 19. Son of Peter and Agota Kulvinskas, of Glasgow.

MACARTHUR, Ordinary Seaman, DONALD JOHN, S.S. Haxby (West Hartlepool). Merchant Navy. 24th April 1940. Age 25. Son of Angus and Christina Macarthur. of Carloway. Isle of Lewis.

MACIVER, Ordinary Seaman, NORMAN, S.S. Haxby (West Hartlepool). Merchant Navy. 24th April 1940. Age 27. Son of John and Henrietta Maciver, of Carloway, Isle of Lewis.

MacLEAN, Able Seaman, ROBERT ALEXANDER, S.S. Haxby (West Hartlepool). Merchant Navy. 24th April 1940. Age 23. Son of Malcolm and Christina MacLean. of Dalaburgh, South Uist.

McCORMICK, Fourth Engineer Officer, MARTIN LEO, S.S. Haxby (West Hartlepool). Merchant Navy. 24th April 1940. Age 20. Son of Martin and Charlotte McCormick, of Norton, Stockton-on-Tees, Co. Durham.

McNEIL, Cabin Steward, THOMAS AUSTIN, S.S. Haxby (West Hartlepool). Merchant Navy. 24th April 1940. (Canadian)

ROBERTSON, Mess Room Boy, EDWARD GEORGE, S.S. Haxby (West Hartlepool). Merchant Navy. 24th April 1940. Age 15.

ROBERTSON, Boatswain, NEIL, S.S. Haxby (West Hartlepool). Merchant Navy. 24th April 1940. Age 54. Husband of Mary Ann Robertson, of Breakish, Isle of Skye.

STEENSOHN, Greaser, EDWARD, S.S. Haxby (West Hartlepool). Merchant Navy. 24th April 1940. Age 60. Son of Laurits and Marie Haun Steensohn; husband of Catherine McFarlane Steensohn.

STIDOLPH, Cook, DAVID NORMAN, S.S. Haxby (West Hartlepool). Merchant Navy. 24th April 1940. Age 31. Son of Edward and Mary Jane Stidolph; husband of Phyllis Stidolph, of South Shields, Co. Durham.

SS Hindpool

ASHTON, First Radio Officer, THOMAS DONALD, S.S. Hindpool (West Hartlepool). Merchant Navy. 8th March 1941. Age 39. Son of Joseph and Rebecca Ashton, of Hull; husband of Margaret D. Ashton, of Statfield, Lossiemouth, Morayshire.

DUNCAN, Greaser, WILLIAM, S.S. Hindpool (West Hartlepool). Merchant Navy. 8th March 1941. Age 47. Husband of Mary A. Duncan, of Winlaton, Co. Durham.

DUNN, Sailor, WILLIAM, S.S. Hindpool (West Hartlepool). Merchant Navy. 8th March 1941. Age 19. Son of Edward and J. H. Dunn, of North Shields, Northumberland.

FERGUSON, Third Engineer Officer, THOMAS RICHARDSON, S.S. Hindpool (West Hartlepool). Merchant Navy. 8th March 1941. Age 45. Son of John James Ferguson and Jane Ferguson; husband of Margaret Lizzie Ferguson, of West Hartlepool, Co. Durham.

FINLAY, Boy, GEORGE, S.S. Hindpool (West Hartlepool). Merchant Navy. 8th March 1941. Age 16.

GALE, Mess Room Boy, LEONARD HAROLD, S.S. Hindpool (West Hartlepool). Merchant Navy. 8th March 1941. Age 17.

GREEN, Boy, WILLIAM HALL, S.S. Hindpool (West Hartlepool). Merchant Navy. 8th March 1941. Age 20.

IRVIN, Chief Engineer Officer, GEORGE, S.S. Hindpool (West Hartlepool). Merchant Navy. 8th March 1941. Age 59.

JENSEN, Fireman and Trimmer, OLAF, S.S. Hindpool (West Hartlepool). Merchant Navy. 8th March 1941. Age 28.

LEWIS, Second Engineer Officer, WILLIAM DOUGLAS, S.S. Hindpool (West Hartlepool). Merchant Navy. 8th March 1941. Age 28. Son of Ernest and Hilda Mary Lewis, of West Hartlepool, Co. Durham; husband of Hilda Lewis, of West Hartlepool.

MALLEN, Greaser, EDWARD, S.S. Hindpool (West Hartlepool). Merchant Navy. 8th March 1941. Age 41. Son of Edward and Winifred Mallen, of Sunderland, Co. Durham.

MATTHEWS, Second Officer, HAROLD, S.S. Hindpool (West Hartlepool). Merchant Navy. 8th March 1941. Age 22. Son of Arthur and Jennie Matthews, of Winton, Lancashire.

MOONEY, Able Seaman, HENRY, S.S. Hindpool (West Hartlepool). Merchant Navy. 8th March 1941. Age 25. Son of Henry and Annie Mooney, of West Chirton, North Shields, Northumberland.

MacLEAN, Fireman and Trimmer, JOHN, S.S. Hindpool (West Hartlepool). Merchant Navy. 8th March 1941. Age 42. Son of Hector MacLean, and of Catherine MacLean (nee MacKinnon); husband of Hannah MacLean, of Oban, Argyllshire.

McDONALD, Fireman and Trimmer, JOSEPH GRAY, S.S. Hindpool (West Hartlepool). Merchant Navy. 8th March 1941. Age 25. Son of Richard and Jane McDonald; husband of Edna McDonald, of Preston, North Shields, Northumberland.

O'DONOVAN, Third Officer, JEREMIAH DAVID JOSEPH, S.S. Hindpool (West Hartlepool). Merchant Navy. 8th March 1941. Age 28.

POWER, Donkeyman, P. S.S. Hindpool (West Hartlepool). Merchant Navy. 8th March 1941. (Canadian)

REGNELL, Boatswain, JOHN EDWIN, S.S. Hindpool (West Hartlepool). Merchant Navy. 8th March 1941. Age 47.

RODGERS, Sailor, DAVID, S.S. Hindpool (West Hartlepool). Merchant Navy. 8th March 1941. Age 19.

RUTHERFORD, Able Seaman, GEORGE ALLEN HENRY, S.S. Hindpool (West Hartlepool). Merchant Navy. 8th March 1941. Age 24.

SLATER, Fireman and Trimmer, PERCIVAL, S.S. Hindpool (West Hartlepool). Merchant Navy. 8th March 1941. Age 23. Son of John Richard and Bessie Slater.

SMITH, Able Seaman, JOHN WILLIAM, S.S. Hindpool (West Hartlepool). Merchant Navy. 8th March 1941. Age 21.

SMITH, Carpenter, ROBERT WHALEN, S.S. Hindpool (West Hartlepool). Merchant Navy. 8th March 1941. Age 23. Son of Robert and Susan Smith; husband of Irene Smith, of North Shields, Northumberland.

SMITH, Fireman and Trimmer, WILLIAM, S.S. Hindpool (West Hartlepool). Merchant Navy. 8th March 1941. Age 26. Son of Mrs. E. Smith, of North Shields, Northumberland.

TINNOCK, Master, MALCOLM VERNON ALLT, S.S. Hindpool (West Hartlepool). Merchant Navy. 8th March 1941. Age 30. Son of Alexander Tinnock, and of Ada Elizabeth Tinnock, of Torquay, Devon.

TOZER, Fireman and Trimmer, CYRIL, S.S. Hindpool (West Hartlepool). Merchant Navy. 8th March 1941. Age 40. Son of Benjamin and Florence Tozer; husband of Elizabeth Tozer, of Mallaig, Inverness-shire.

WEBBER, Fireman and Trimmer, WALTER RICHARD, S.S. Hindpool (West Hartlepool). Merchant Navy. 8th March 1941. Age 40. Husband of E. Webber, of North Shields, Northumberland.

YELLAND, Ordinary Seaman, ENOCH, S.S. Hindpool (West Hartlepool). Merchant Navy. 8th March 1941. Age 19. Son of Mr. and Mrs. G. Yelland, of North Shields, Northumberland.

SS Kirkpool

ABDUL HUSAIN, Greaser, S.S. Kirkpool (West Hartlepool), Indian Merchant Navy. 10 April 1942.

ABIR ULLAH, Fireman and Trimmer, S.S. Kirkpool (West Hartlepool). Merchant Navy. 10th April 1942. Age 42.

AITCHISON, Cabin Boy, JOHN FREDERICK, S.S. Kirkpool (West Hartlepool). Merchant Navy. 10th April 1942. Age 17.

ALI KOTUB, Fireman and Trimmer, S.S. Kirkpool (West Hartlepool). Merchant Navy. 10th April 1942. Age 28.

BISHOP, Sailor, SYDNEY RAYMOND, S.S. Kirkpool (West Hartlepool). Merchant Navy. 10th April 1942. Age 22. Son of George William and Margaret Jane Bishop, of North Shields, Northumberland.

CARR, Carpenter, JOSEPH, S.S. Kirkpool (West Hartlepool). Merchant Navy. 10th April 1942. Age 39. Son of Thomas Carr, and of Margaret Carr, of North Shields, Northumberland.

DANISH ULLAH, Fireman, S.S. Kirkpool (West Hartlepool), Indian Merchant Navy. 10 April 1942.

EBOE ULLAH, Fireman & Trimmer, S.S. Kirkpool (West Hartlepool), Indian Merchant Navy. 21st April 1945. Husband of Kachina Bibi, of Dakshinbagh, Sylhet, Pakistan. Buried Yokohama War Cemetery, Indian section

ELLIOTT, Third Officer, MATTHEW HUNTER, S.S. Kirkpool (West Hartlepool). Merchant Navy. 10th April 1942. Age 31. Son of William Henry and Winifred Elliott; husband of Elsie May Elliott, of West Hartlepool, Co. Durham.

HAMPTON, Gunner, WILLIAM ALEXANDER, 3196731, 3/2 Maritime Regt., Royal Artillery. 12 April 1942. Age 31. Son of William Alexander and Mary Hampton; husband of Agnes Jane Hampton, of Montrose.

KENNINGTON, Master, ALBERT, S.S. Kirkpool (West Hartlepool). Merchant Navy. 14th March 1944. Age 32. Son of Samuel Charles and Martha Kennington; husband of Olive May Kennington, of Grimsby, Lincolnshire. Died in a Japanese PoW camp. Buried Yokohama War Cemetery.

LEONARD, Second Engineer Officer, FRANCIS, S.S. Kirkpool (West Hartlepool). Merchant Navy. 12th April 1942. Age 39.

MAKBOL ALI, Fireman and Trimmer, S.S. Kirkpool (West Hartlepool). Merchant Navy. 10th April 1942. Age 27.

MUHAMMAD SHAKUR, Fireman, S.S. Kirkpool (West Hartlepool), Indian Merchant Navy. 10 April 1942.

MUSIFAR ALI, Fireman and Trimmer, S.S. Kirkpool (West Hartlepool). Merchant Navy. 10th April 1942. Age 27.

McGEE, Galley Boy, JOHN, S.S. Kirkpool (West Hartlepool). Merchant Navy. 10th April 1942. Age 18. Son of Michael and Margaret McGee, of Tynemouth, Northumberland.

OWENS, Able Seaman, THOMAS ALFRED STEPHEN, D/JX 290578. H.M.S. President III. Royal Navy. Lost in S.S. Kirkpool. 12th April 1942.

SAYID ULLAH, Fireman, S.S. Kirkpool (West Hartlepool), Indian Merchant Navy. 10 April 1942.

WALKER, Fourth Engineer Officer, CYRIL, S.S. Kirkpool (West Hartlepool). Merchant Navy. 10th April 1942. Age 26. Son of Thomas Wilkinson Walker and Jane Bell Walker, of Grangetown, Sunderland, Co. Durham.

WATIR ULLAH, Donkeyman, S.S. Kirkpool (West Hartlepool). Merchant Navy. 10th April 1942. Age 26.

WILSON, Ordinary Seaman, GEORGE, S.S. Kirkpool (West Hartlepool). Merchant Navy. 10th April 1942. Age 18. Son of Alice Wilson, of Hull.

YOUNG, Steward, HARRY, S.S. Kirkpool (West Hartlepool). Merchant Navy. 10th April 1942. Age 34. Son of Tom and Ellen Young; husband of Isabella Young, of Sunderland, Co. Durham.

SS Lackenby

ADAMS, Greaser, PHILIP SCOTT, S.S. Lackenby (West Hartlepool). Merchant Navy. 25th January 1943. Age 30. Son of Mr. and Mrs. Frank Adams; husband of Susannah Miller Adams, of Dawdon, Seaham, Co. Durham.

ALLINSON, Chief Engineer Officer, GEORGE FRANK, S.S. Lackenby (West Hartlepool). Merchant Navy. 25th January 1943. Age 40. Husband of M. Allinson, of Sunderland, Co. Durham.

ALLON, Master, WILLIAM ARTHUR, M B E, S.S. Lackenby (West Hartlepool). Merchant Navy. 25th January 1943. Age 29. Son of J. J. and Clara Clark Allon; grandson of Mrs. H. Bolton, of South Shields. Co. Durham.

COWIE, Fireman and Trimmer, JAMES NATHANIEL, S.S. Lackenby (West Hartlepool). Merchant Navy. 25th January 1943. Age 23. (served as JOHNSON, ALBERT EDWARD) Son of Daniel and Ann Matilda Cowie.

DONNACHIE, Greaser, JAMES, S.S. Lackenby (West Hartlepool). Merchant Navy. 25th January 1943. Age 40. Son of Thomas and Isabella Donnachie; husband of Agnes Donnachie, of Paisley, Renfrewshire.

ELLIOTT, Assistant Cook, GEORGE, S.S. Lackenby (West Hartlepool). Merchant Navy. 25th January 1943. Age 23. Son of Mrs. M. Elliott, of South Shields, Co. Durham.

ELSWORTH, Fireman and Trimmer, JOSEPH WILLIAM SUTTON, S.S. Lackenby (West Hartlepool). Merchant Navy. 23rd January 1943. Age 22.

ERRINGTON, Fireman and Trimmer, JACOB, S.S. Lackenby (West Hartlepool). Merchant Navy. 25th January 1943. Age 37.

FLANAGAN, Sailor, DANIEL, S.S. Lackenby (West Hartlepool). Merchant Navy. 25th January 1943. Age 22. Son of Owen and Marion Flanagan, of Jarrow, Co. Durham.

FOWLIE, Donkeyman, THOMAS, S.S. Lackenby (West Hartlepool). Merchant Navy. 23rd January 1943. Age 44.

FOX, Able Seaman, ROBERT, S.S. Lackenby (West Hartlepool). Merchant Navy. 25th January 1943. Age 22.

FRASER, Fireman and Trimmer, PETER ALEXANDER, S.S. Lackenby (West Hartlepool). Merchant Navy. 25th January 1943. Age 44.

GASS, Able Seaman, LESLIE, C/JX 337528, S.S. Lackenby, Royal Navy. 23 January 1943. Age 35. Son of James and Laura Gass; husband of Marjorie Edith Gass, of New Eltham, London.

GIBBONS, Third Radio Officer, WILLIAM AUSTIN, S.S. Lackenby (West Hartlepool). Merchant Navy. 25th January 1943. Age 17. Son of Henry A. and Nora Kathleen Gibbons, of Chorlton-cum-Hardy, Manchester.

GORHAM, Fireman and Trimmer, JOSEPH, S.S. Lackenby (West Hartlepool). Merchant Navy. 25th January 1943. Age 60.

GRAY, Chief Steward, JAMES, S.S. Lackenby (West Hartlepool). Merchant Navy. 25th January 1943. Age 40. Son of Joseph and Catherine Gray; husband of Lily Florence Gray, of Cleadon Park, South Shields, Co. Durham.

HARVEY, Able Seaman, WILLIAM JOHN, S.S. Lackenby (West Hartlepool). Merchant Navy. 25th January 1943. Age 25. Son of William John and Whilimena Harvey, of Jarrow, Co. Durham.

HEWITT, Fireman and Trimmer, ARTHUR JAMES, S.S. Lackenby (West Hartlepool). Merchant Navy. 25th January 1943. Age 29.

JACKSON, Assistant Steward, ALEXANDER, S.S. Lackenby (West Hartlepool). Merchant Navy. 25th January 1943. Age 22. Son of Alexander and Ethel Jackson, of South Shields, Co. Durham.

JONES, Third Officer, OWAIN GLYN, S.S. Lackenby (West Hartlepool). Merchant Navy. 25th January 1943. Age 30. Son of Evan Ernest and Dorcas Hughes Jones, of Caernarvon.

KARLSON, Carpenter, JOHN, S.S. Lackenby (West Hartlepool). Merchant Navy. 25th January 1943. Age 63. Husband of Thomasina Karlson, of South Shields, Co. Durham.

KEY, Petty Officer, HARRY, C/JX 190598, S.S. Lackenby, Royal Navy. 23 January 1943. Age 21. Son of Alfred Ernest and Amelia Key, of Walworth, London.

LODGE, Second Officer, ALFRED, S.S. Lackenby (West Hartlepool). Merchant Navy. 25th January 1943. Age 66. Husband of Hannah Jane Lodge.

LUCAS, First Radio Officer, ALBERT JAMES, S.S. Lackenby (West Hartlepool). Merchant Navy. 23rd January 1943. Age 27. Son of George and Mabel Edith Lucas, of Errol, Perthshire.

LUPTON, Able Seaman, JAMES TONY, P/JX 291864. H.M.S. President III. Royal Navy. (lost in S.S. Lackenby). 23rd January 1943. Age 29. Son of George and Alice Lupton; husband of Amy Lupton, of Edgeware, Middlesex.

MELVILLE, Gunner, DAVID, 901207, 5/3 Maritime Regt., Royal Artillery. 23 January 1943. Age 20. Son of George Ironside Melville and Alice Melville.

MORRIS, Fireman and Trimmer, HARRY ALBERT, S.S. Lackenby (West Hartlepool). Merchant Navy. 23rd January 1943. Age 35.

MULLEN, Ordinary Seaman, THOMAS, S.S. Lackenby (West Hartlepool). Merchant Navy. 23rd January 1943. Age 19.

MUSGROVE, Second Engineer Officer, WILLIAM, S.S. Lackenby (West Hartlepool). Merchant Navy. 25th January 1943. Age 42. Son of Thomas and Mary Musgrove; husband of Jane Musgrove, of South Shields, Co. Durham.

McMANUS, Able Seaman, WILLIAM HENRY CARNEY, S.S. Lackenby (West Hartlepool). Merchant Navy. 25th January 1943. Age 28. Son of Alfred McManus, and of Louisa McManus, of Boldon Colliery, Co. Durham.

NEWTON, Assistant Steward, PETER, S.S. Lackenby (West Hartlepool). Merchant Navy. 23rd January 1943. Age 17.

PHILLIPS, Third Engineer Officer, EDWARD, S.S. Lackenby (West Hartlepool). Merchant Navy. 25th January 1943. Age 26.

PHIPPS, Able Seaman, BEN, S.S. Lackenby (West Hartlepool). Merchant Navy. 25th January 1943. Age 23. Son of Fred and Williamina Phipps, of Hebburn, Co. Durham.

ROWE, Able Seaman, VICTOR HENRY, S.S. Lackenby (West Hartlepool). Merchant Navy. 25th January 1943. Age 47.

RUSSELL, Gunner, ERNEST LESLIE LLOYD, 5673605, 5/3 Maritime Regt., Royal Artillery. 23 January 1943.

SHIELDS, Ordinary Seaman, JOHN THOMAS, S.S. Lackenby (West Hartlepool). Merchant Navy. 25th January 1943. Age 19.

SMITH, Ordinary Seaman, JOSEPH GRAHAM, S.S. Lackenby (West Hartlepool). Merchant Navy. 25th January 1943. Age 22. Son of Joseph Graham Smith and Margaret Smith, of South Shields, Co. Durham.

STEEL, Chief Officer, ALFRED JAMES, S.S. Lackenby (West Hartlepool). Merchant Navy. 25th January 1943. Age 27. Son of Ivor and Minnie Steel; husband of Phyllis E. Steel, of Cardiff.

STORY, Fourth Engineer Officer, GEORGE CARLTON, S.S. Lackenby (West Hartlepool). Merchant Navy. 25th January 1943. Age 21. Son of Thomas Rudd Story and Emily Story, of West Hartlepool, Co. Durham.

SWANSON, Boatswain, CECIL, S.S. Lackenby (West Hartlepool). Merchant Navy. 25th January 1943. Age 31. Son of Mary Swanson, of Tyne Dock, South Shields, Co. Durham.

THOMPSON, Able Seaman, JACK, P/JX 334325. H.M.S. President III. Royal Navy. (lost in S.S. Lackenby). 23rd January 1943. Age 19. Son of William and Hannah Maria Thompson, of Leeds, Yorkshire.

WATKINS, Fireman and Trimmer, WILLIAM RIGHT, S.S. Lackenby (West Hartlepool). Merchant Navy. 25th January 1943. Age 26.

WELLS, Fireman and Trimmer, ERNEST VIVIAN, S.S. Lackenby (West Hartlepool). Merchant Navy. 25th January 1943. Age 22. Son of Ernest Vivian and Mary Jane Wells, of Whitburn, Co. Durham.

WILSON, Cook, ANDREW CHARLES, S.S. Lackenby (West Hartlepool). Merchant Navy. 25th January 1943. Age 35.

WOOLLER, Second Radio Officer, RONALD, S.S. Lackenby (West Hartlepool). Merchant Navy. 25th January 1943. Age 17.

SS Maltby

ALI HASAN, Fireman. S.S. Maltby (West Hartlepool). Mercantile Marine. Drowned, as a result of an attack by an enemy submarine, 26th February 1918.

DAVISON, Third Engineer, ALFRED, S.S. Maltby (West Hartlepool). Mercantile Marine. Drowned, as a result of an attack by an enemy submarine, 26th February 1918. Age 30. Son of Anthony and Mary Ann Davison (nee Dwyer), of 7, Victoria Place, Hartlepool, Co. Durham. Born at Hartlepool.

HASAN ABDULLAH, Fireman. S.S. Maltby (West Hartlepool). Mercantile Marine. Drowned, as a result of an attack by an enemy submarine, 26th February 1918.

HUSAN FARAH, Fireman & Trimmere. S.S. Maltby (West Hartlepool). Mercantile Marine. Drowned, as a result of an attack by an enemy submarine, 26th February 1918.

SS Mansepool

DICKIE, Second Engineer Officer, JAMES NORRIE, S.S. Mansepool (West Hartlepool). Merchant Navy. 24th February 1941. Age 55. Son of Henry and Margaret Dickie.

WALSH, Sailor, JAMES, S.S. Mansepool (West Hartlepool). Merchant Navy. 24th February 1941. Age 19.

SS Otterpool

ANNANDALE, Third Engineer Officer, ALEXANDER HENRY RALPH, S.S. Otterpool (West Hartlepool). Merchant Navy. 20th June 1940. Age 34. Son of Alexander Henry and Sarah Annie Annandale, of Edinburgh.

BROWN, Fireman and Trimmer, ALEXANDER, S.S. Otterpool (West Hartlepool). Merchant Navy. 20th June 1940. Age 56.

COOPER, Corporal, WILLIAM, PLY/16528. H.M.S. President III. Royal Marines. lost in S.S. Otterpool. 20th June 1940. Age 45. Son of Joseph and Martha Cooper; husband of Maggie Cooper, of Nantwich, Cheshire.

DAVIES, Greaser, WILLIAM, S.S. Otterpool (West Hartlepool). Merchant Navy. 20th June 1940. Age 47. Husband of Edith Davies, of Adamsdown, Cardiff.

DAVIS, Second Officer, HARRY HARDY, S.S. Otterpool (West Hartlepool). Merchant Navy. 20th June 1940. Age 24. Son of Leopold G. and Jane Davis, of West Hartlepool, Co. Durham.

GLENN, Fireman and Trimmer, RAYMOND, S.S. Otterpool (West Hartlepool). Merchant Navy. 20th June 1940. Age 25. Son of Samual and Lavinia Glenn; husband of Thelma Louisa Glenn, of Canton, Cardiff.

HANTMAN, Fireman and Trimmer, HENRY, S.S. Otterpool (West Hartlepool). Merchant Navy. 20th June 1940. Age 30.

JONES, Fireman and Trimmer, JOHN, S.S. Otterpool (West Hartlepool). Merchant Navy. 20th June 1940. Age 51. Husband of M. Jones, of Cardiff.

MELVIN, Steward, WILLIAM MICHAEL, S.S. Otterpool (West Hartlepool). Merchant Navy. 20th June 1940. Age 40.

MILLARD, Fireman and Trimmer, THOMAS, S.S. Otterpool (West Hartlepool). Merchant Navy. 20th June 1940. Age 53.

MOGENSEN, Cook, JEAN VIGGO ODWARD, S.S. Otterpool (West Hartlepool). Merchant Navy. 20th June 1940. Age 54.

McGEE, Donkeyman, CHARLES EDWARD, S.S. Otterpool (West Hartlepool). Merchant Navy. 20th June 1940. Age 35. Son of John George McGee, and of Margaret McGee, of North Shields, Northumberland.

McREYNOLDS, Fireman and Trimmer, THOMAS, S.S. Otterpool (West Hartlepool). Merchant Navy. 20th June 1940. Age 53.

O'SHEA, Fireman and Trimmer, TIMOTHY, S.S. Otterpool (West Hartlepool). Merchant Navy. 20th June 1940. Age 22. Son of Peter O'shea, and of Mary O'shea, of Cardiff.

PETERSON, Greaser, LESLIE, S.S. Otterpool (West Hartlepool). Merchant Navy. 20th June 1940. Age 25. Son of Mrs. L. Peterson, of Cleethorpes, Lincolnshire.

PRINCE, Master, THOMAS, S.S. Otterpool (West Hartlepool). Merchant Navy. 20th June 1940. Age 38. King's Commendation for Brave Conduct. Son of Captain W. and Mrs. Prince, of Northallerton, Yorkshire.

RATTER, Third Officer, JOHN CHRISTOPHER, S.S. Otterpool (West Hartlepool). Merchant Navy. 20th June 1940. Age 29. Son of James and Christina J. Ratter, of Brae, Zetland.

RUDD, Sailor, ALFRED, S.S. Otterpool (West Hartlepool). Merchant Navy. 20th June 1940. Age 34.

ROBB, Second Engineer Officer, ALBERT, S.S. Otterpool (West Hartlepool). Merchant Navy. 20th June 1940. Age 44.

SINCLAIR, Able Seaman, ALEXANDER, S.S. Otterpool (West Hartlepool). Merchant Navy. 20th June 1940. Age 49. Son of David and Jemima Sinclair.

TICKLE, Fourth Engineer Officer, ARTHUR, S.S. Otterpool (West Hartlepool). Merchant Navy. 20th June 1940. Age 61. Husband of Esther Christina Tickle, of Grange Town, Cardiff.

WEST, Chief Engineer Officer, THOMAS, S.S. Otterpool (West Hartlepool). Merchant Navy. 20th June 1940. Age 58. Son of George and Mary Ann West; husband of Lydia West, of Norton, Stockton-on-Tees. Co. Durham.

YEARWOOD, Boy, LEWIS, S.S. Otterpool (West Hartlepool). Merchant Navy. 20th June 1940. Age 19.

SS Pikepool

BOUCHERON, Mess Room Boy, PAUL JAMES, S.S. Pikepool (West Hartlepool). Merchant Navy. 22nd November 1940. Age 22.

CROOK, Boatswain (Bosun), REGINALD, S.S. Pikepool (West Hartlepool). Merchant Navy. 22nd November 1940. Age 35. Son of David and Elizabeth Crook; husband of Annie May Crook, of Barry, Glamorgan.

CUTLER, Able Seaman, WILLIAM, S.S. Pikepool (West Hartlepool). Merchant Navy. 22nd November 1940. Age 28.

DAWSON, Second Officer, VINCENT WILLIAM, S.S. Pikepool (West Hartlepool). Merchant Navy. 22nd November 1940. Age 45. Husband of Dorothy Dawson, of Wingate, Co. Durham.

DONNELLY, Fireman and Trimmer, ROBERT, S.S. Pikepool (West Hartlepool). Merchant Navy. 23rd November 1940. Age 53. Buried Milford Haven Cemetery.

GALL, Able Seaman, GEORGE DAVID, S.S. Pikepool (West Hartlepool). Merchant Navy. 22nd November 1940. Age 46.

GREEN, Donkeyman, WILLIAM, S.S. Pikepool (West Hartlepool). Merchant Navy. 22nd November 1940. Age 47. Husband of M. Green, of Northenden, Lancashire.

HABBERSHAW, Third Engineer Officer, GEORGE CLARK COMMON, S.S. Pikepool (West Hartlepool). Merchant Navy. 22nd November 1940. Age 39.

HAYDEN, Able Seaman, SIDNEY FRANK, P/J 28067. H.M.S. President III. Royal Navy. (Lost in S.S. Pikepool). 22nd November 1940. Age 44. Son of William and Helen Hayden.

HAZEL, Third Officer, LESLIE, S.S. Pikepool (West Hartlepool). Merchant Navy. 22nd November 1940. Age 28. Son of Ernest Hazel, and of Clarissa Hazel, of Beverley, Yorkshire.

HOLT, Ordinary Seaman, HERBERT, S.S. Pikepool (West Hartlepool). Merchant Navy. 22nd November 1940. Age 19. Son of Wilfred and Mary Emily Holt, of South Shore, Blackpool, Lancashire.

LEWIS, Steward, THOMAS JOHN, S.S. Pikepool (West Hartlepool). Merchant Navy. 22nd November 1940. Age 28. Son of Gomer and Annie Lewis; husband of Elsie Lewis, of Splott, Cardiff. Buried Bude Haven (St. Michael) Churchyard.

McCUAIG, Fireman and Trimmer, ANGUS, S.S. Pikepool (West Hartlepool). Merchant Navy. 22nd November 1940. Age 36. Son of Angus and Janet McCuaig, of Glasgow.

McGREGOR, Chief Engineer Officer, WILKIE, S.S. Pikepool (West Hartlepool). Merchant Navy. 22nd November 1940. Age 72.

RICHARDS, Cabin Boy, PETER FRANK, S.S. Pikepool (West Hartlepool). Merchant Navy. 22nd November 1940. Age 17. Son of Thomas George and Bessie Richards, of Town Hill, Swansea.

SMITH, Second Engineer Officer, JOHN VINCENT, S.S. Pikepool (West Hartlepool). Merchant Navy. 22nd November 1940. Age 67.

STOTT, Able Seaman, CHARLES, S.S. Pikepool (West Hartlepool). Merchant Navy. 22nd November 1940. Age 28. Son of James and Julia Stott; husband of Ellen Stott, of Oldham, Lancashire.

VICKERS, Second Radio Officer, JAMES FREDERICK, S.S. Pikepool (West Hartlepool). Merchant Navy. 22nd November 1940. Age 47. Husband of Clara Elizabeth Vickers, of Toronto, Ontario, Canada.

SS Reedpool

ANDERSON, Donkeyman (Assistant), JOSEPH, S.S. Reedpool (Stockton-on-Tees). Merchant Navy. 20th September 1942. Age 23. Son of George and Bridget Anderson, of Primrose, Jarrow. Co. Durham.

GUILFOYLE, Fireman, THOMAS, S.S. Reedpool (Stockton-on-Tees). Merchant Navy. 20th September 1942. Age 22. (Canadian)

McMULLEN, Fireman, WILLIAM, S.S. Reedpool (Stockton-on-Tees). Merchant Navy. 20th September 1942. (Canadian)

PARDOE, Fireman and Trimmer, THOMAS GEORGE, S.S. Reedpool (Stockton-on-Tees). Merchant Navy. 20th September 1942. Age 32.

PATTERSON, Second Officer, WILSON, S.S. Reedpool (Stockton-on-Tees). Merchant Navy. 20th September 1942. Age 23. Son of William and Sarah Elizabeth Patterson, of Backworth, Northumberland.

TIPP, Third Engineer Officer, ROBERT, S.S. Reedpool (Stockton-on-Tees). Merchant Navy. 20th September 1942. Age 32.

SS Romanby
(Died in captivity. Milag Nord PoW Camp)

NICHOLSON, Master, HARRY, S.S. Romanby (West Hartlepool). Merchant Navy. 28th December 1942. Age 47. Son of John Ralph and Jane Nicholson, of West Hartlepool, Co. Durham; husband of Constance Isabel Nicholson, of West Hartlepool. Buried Becklingen War Cemetery.

SS Roxby

ANDERSON, Chief Officer, ARTHUR JAMES, S.S. Roxby (West Hartlepool). Merchant Navy. 7th November 1942. Age 36. Husband of Annie Anderson, of Sunderland, Co. Durham.

CELMS, Donkeyman, PRICIS, S.S. Roxby (West Hartlepool). Merchant Navy. 7th November 1942. Age 44.

CONNOLLY, Cook, JOHN JOSEPH, S.S. Roxby (West Hartlepool). Merchant Navy. 7th November 1942. Age 44.

COYLE, Deck Boy, JOHN E., S.S. Roxby (West Hartlepool). Merchant Navy. 7th November 1942. Age 18.

CRONIN, Able Seaman, PATRICK, S.S. Roxby (West Hartlepool). Merchant Navy. 7th November 1942. Age 33. Son of James and Nora Cronin; husband of Jane Cronin, of Ely, Cardiff.

CUNNINGHAM, Fireman and Trimmer, WILLIAM, S.S. Roxby (West Hartlepool). Merchant Navy. 7th November 1942. Age 34.

DEW, Able Seaman, BERTRAM GEORGE, P/JX 336996. H.M.S. President III. Royal Navy. (lost in S.S. Roxby). 7th November 1942. Age 19. Son of Bertram Alfred and Ceta Dew, of Fakenham, Norfolk.

DYER, Fireman and Trimmer, GEORGE HENRY, S.S. Roxby (West Hartlepool). Merchant Navy. 7th November 1942. Age 26. Stepson of William John Gully, of Port Tennant, Swansea.

EDWARDS, Able Seaman, JOHN, S.S. Roxby (West Hartlepool). Merchant Navy. 7th November 1942. Age 59.

ELLIOTT, Cook, ALBERT, S.S. Roxby (West Hartlepool). Merchant Navy. 7th November 1942. Age 32. Son of Mr. and Mrs. William Brown Elliott; husband of Jane Ann Elliott, of Dinas Powis, Glamorganshire.

ELLIS, Third Engineer Officer, THOMAS ARTHUR, S.S. Roxby (West Hartlepool). Merchant Navy. 7th November 1942. Age 22. Son of Frank Ellis, and of Annie Mariah Ellis, of Balby, Doncaster, Yorkshire.

FARRELL, Fireman and Trimmer, THOMAS MICHAEL, S.S. Roxby (West Hartlepool). Merchant Navy. 7th November 1942. Age 22. Son of Michael Farrell, and of Florence Mary Farrell, of Grangetown, Glamorgan.

GILLIS, Fireman, RODERICK JAMES, S.S. Roxby (West Hartlepool). Merchant Navy. 7th November 1942. Age 29. (Canadian)

HARRISON, Able Seaman, JAMES, C/JX 313457, S.S. Roxby, Royal Navy. 7 November 1942. Age 20. Son of George and Mary Harrison, of Laughton, Yorkshire.

HAINES, Donkeyman, WILLIAM EDWARD, S.S. Roxby (West Hartlepool). Merchant Navy. 7th November 1942. Age 39. Husband of L. M. Haines, of Grangetown, Cardiff.

GILLIS, Fireman, RODERICK JAMES, S.S. Roxby (West Hartlepool). Merchant Navy. 7th November 1942. Age 29. (Canadian)

HANNAH, Fireman and Trimmer, GEORGE, S.S. Roxby (West Hartlepool). Merchant Navy. 7th November 1942. Age 20. Son of Robert Hannah, and of Jeanie Hume Hannah, of Glasgow.

HEDGES, Able Seaman, WILLIAM RONALD, S.S. Roxby (West Hartlepool). Merchant Navy. 7th November 1942. Age 25. Son of Richard Thomas Hedges and Florence Maud Hedges.

HUGGETT, Able Seaman, JOSEPH HOUSLEY, S.S. Roxby (West Hartlepool). Merchant Navy. 7th November 1942. Age 55.

JONES, Ordinary Seaman, EDWARD LLOYD, S.S. Roxby (West Hartlepool). Merchant Navy. 7th November 1942. Age 20.

KILLOPS, Leading Seaman, THOMAS, D/JX 204718. H.M.S. President III. Royal Navy. Lost in S.S. Roxby. 7th November 1942. Age 29. Son of Robert and Anna Killops, of Killyleagh, Co. Down, Northern Ireland; husband of Rebecca Killops, of Killyleagh.

KINNES, Third Officer, WILLIAM JAMES, S.S. Roxby (West Hartlepool). Merchant Navy. 7th November 1942. Age 31. Son of William and Edith Kinnes; husband of Johanna Mary Kinnes, of Ely, Cardiff.

LEWIS, Second Engineer Officer, OSWALD, S.S. Roxby (West Hartlepool). Merchant Navy. 7th November 1942. Age 51. Son of Thomas and Mary Ann Lewis.

MATTHEWS, Carpenter, JOSEPH, S.S. Roxby (West Hartlepool). Merchant Navy. 7th November 1942. Age 60.

MAYES, Boatswain, GEORGE, S.S. Roxby (West Hartlepool). Merchant Navy. 7th November 1942. Age 48.

HARRISON, Able Seaman, JAMES, C/JX 313457, S.S. Roxby, Royal Navy. 7 November 1942. Age 20. Son of George and Mary Harrison, of Laughton, Yorkshire.

McLAREN, First Radio Officer, GEORGE ALEXANDER INNIS, S.S. Roxby (West Hartlepool). Merchant Navy. 11th November 1942. Age 36.

McMANUS, Fireman and Trimmer, JOHN, S.S. Roxby (West Hartlepool). Merchant Navy. 7th November 1942. Age 34.

O'CONNELL, Fireman and Trimmer, MICHAEL ALBERT, S.S. Roxby (West Hartlepool). Merchant Navy. 7th November 1942. Age 30.

PRICE, Second Radio Officer, HUGH MONTAGUE, S.S. Roxby (West Hartlepool). Merchant Navy. 7th November 1942. Age 22. Son of Montague W. Price, and of Ethel May Price, of Weston-super-Mare, Somerset.

RYAN, Able Seaman, ROBERT, D/JX 198434. H.M.S. President III. Royal Navy. Lost in S.S. Roxby. 7th November 1942

SALIBA, Sailor, FRANCIS, S.S. Roxby (West Hartlepool). Merchant Navy. 7th November 1942. Age 27. Son of Joseph Saliba and of Angela Saliba (nee Portelli), of Gozo, Malta, G.C.

SPENCER, Fireman and Trimmer, JOHN, S.S. Roxby (West Hartlepool). Merchant Navy. 7th November 1942. Age 46. (served as TAYLOR, Albert James).

THOMAS, Sailor, GLYN, S.S. Roxby (West Hartlepool). Merchant Navy. 7th November 1942. Age 18. Son of James and Jane G. Thomas, of Senghenydd, Glamorgan.

VINCENT, Fireman and Trimmer, EDWARD GEORGE, S.S. Roxby (West Hartlepool). Merchant Navy. 7th November 1942. Age 48.

SS Rudby

DORE, Able Seaman, ARTHUR CHARLES, S.S. Rudby (West Hartlepool). Merchant Navy. 29th June 1941. Age 28. Son of Walter James Dore, and of Elizabeth Ethel Dore, of Grimsby. Buried Grimsby (Scartho Road) Cemetery.

OSHIGIN, Ordinary Seaman, WILLIAM, S.S. Rudby (West Hartlepool). Merchant Navy. 29th June 1941. Age 18.

PRATT, Deck Boy, KENNETH WILLIAM, S.S. Rudby (West Hartlepool). Merchant Navy. 29th June 1941. Age 17. Son of James William and Elizabeth Pratt, of 69, Yarborough St., Grimsby. Buried Grimsby (Scartho Road) Cemetery.

WHARTON, Able Seaman, HENRY, S.S. Rudby (West Hartlepool). Merchant Navy. 29th June 1941. Age 47. Son of Mr and Mrs Charles Wharton, of 121 Hilda St., Grimsby. Buried at sea. (At the time of writing, Mr Wharton has no official commemoration with the Commonwealth War Graves Commission. In 2007 I submitted Henry Wharton's details surrounding his death to the CWGC who accepted my findings and his name is to added to the Tower Hill Memorial addenda section when the next update is installed)

SS Stagpool
(Non-war dead looked after by the CWGC)

COOK, Third Mate, JOHN FREDERICK, 405528. S.S. Stagpool. Merchant Navy. 21st December 1941. Age 63. Buried Khartoum War Cemetery.

SS Samsuva

CRAIB, Second Engineer Officer, GILBERT SIMPSON, S.S. Samsuva (London). Merchant Navy. 29th September 1944. Age 41

GILES, Donkeyman, WILLIAM, S.S. Samsuva (London). Merchant Navy. 29th September 1944. Age 20.

HENRY, Fireman, JOHN, S.S. Samsuva (London). Merchant Navy. 29th September 1944. Age 20. Son of John and Isabella Henry, of Benwell, Newcastle-on-Tyne.

SS Sedgepool WWI

BURVILLE, Fireman, JAMES, S.S. Sedgepool (West Hartlepool). Merchant Marine. 10th February 1919. Buried Terlincthun British Cemetery, France.

WILLIAMSON, Able Seaman, M, S.S. Sedgepool (West Hartlepool). Mercantile Marine. 27th October 1918. Buried Staglieno Cemetery, Genoa. (Non-war dead looked after by CWGC).

SS Sedgepool

BAINE, Second Officer, CYRIL, S.S. Sedgepool (West Hartlepool). Merchant Navy. 19th October 1940. Age 37. Son of Thomas Percival and Florence Beatrice Baine; husband of Harriet Baine, of Hull.

THOMPSON, Third Engineer Officer, JAMES HUDSON, S.S. Sedgepool (West Hartlepool). Merchant Navy. 19th October 1940. Age 38. Husband of Barbara Ann Thompson, of South Shields, Co. Durham.

WITTEN, Master, ROBERT BELL, S.S. Sedgepool (West Hartlepool). Merchant Navy. 19th October 1940. Age 43.

SS Stonepool

AGATE, Deck Boy, GORDON, S.S. Stonepool (West Hartlepool). Merchant Navy. 11th September 1941. Age 17. Son of Thomas and Matilda Agate, of West Croydon, Surrey.

BASS, Gunner, THOMAS, 1588844, 7/4 Maritime Regt., Royal Artillery. 11 September 1941. Age 29.

BILLOT, Second Engineer Officer, EDWARD, S.S. Stonepool (West Hartlepool). Merchant Navy. 11th September 1941. Age 40.

BIRCH, Cabin Boy, RONALD, S.S. Stonepool (West Hartlepool). Merchant Navy. 11th September 1941. Age 16. Son of John and Caroline Birch, of Birmingham.

BRIDGES, Boy, CYRIL JAMES, S.S. Stonepool (West Hartlepool). Merchant Navy. 11th September 1941. Age 18.

BROADHURST, Gunner, GEORGE, 1566850, 7/4 Maritime Regt., Royal Artillery. 11 September 1941. Age 26. Son of George and Alice Broadhurst, of Ashton-under-Lyne, Lancashire.

BROOKES, Able Seaman, ARTHUR COLE, S.S. Stonepool (West Hartlepool). Merchant Navy. 11th September 1941. Age 32.

BROWN, Fourth Engineer Officer, HENRY GEORGE, S.S. Stonepool (West Hartlepool). Merchant Navy. 11th September 1941. Age 21. Son of Charles and Annie Matilda Brown, of Canton, Cardiff.

BOWMAN, Able Seaman, JOSEPH, D/JX 181601. H.M.S. President III. Royal Navy. Lost in S.S. Stonepool. 11th September 1941. Age 36. Husband of Mabel Bowman, of Belfast, Northern Ireland.

CANE, Bombardier, DONALD ANTHONY, 1478540, 7/4 Maritime Regt., Royal Artillery. 11 September 1941. Age 20. Son of Robert Henry and Jessie Cane; husband of Sybil Joan Cane, of Paignton, Devon

COATES, Steward, GEORGE WILLIAM, S.S. Stonepool (West Hartlepool). Merchant Navy. 11th September 1941. Age 43. Son of John Shotton Coates and Caroline Coates.

COOKE, Gunner, ERNEST, 1566823, 7/4 Maritime Regt., Royal Artillery. 11 September 1941. Age 26. Son of Ernest and Frances Annie Cooke, of Altrincham, Cheshire.

CORNEY, Third Officer, LEONARD ARTHUR, S.S. Stonepool (West Hartlepool). Merchant Navy. 11th September 1941. Age 25. Son of Harry John and Jessie Eveline Corney, of Whitchurch, Glamorgan.

DE BONO, Fireman and Trimmer, JOSEPH, S.S. Stonepool (West Hartlepool). Merchant Navy. 11th September 1941. Age 33.

DORAN, Sailor, FRANK, S.S. Stonepool (West Hartlepool). Merchant Navy. 11th September 1941. Age 38.

DOWNES, Fireman and Trimmer, ERNEST, S.S. Stonepool (West Hartlepool). Merchant Navy. 11th September 1941. Age 55.

DOYLE, Boy, PATRICK, S.S. Stonepool (West Hartlepool). Merchant Navy. 11th September 1941. Age 18.

FLETCHER, Cook, WILLIAM BRANSBY, S.S. Stonepool (West Hartlepool). Merchant Navy. 11th September 1941. Age 22. Son of William and Elizabeth Fletcher, of Whitby, Yorkshire.

FREEMAN, Cabin Boy, CYRIL, S.S. Stonepool (West Hartlepool). Merchant Navy. 11th September 1941. Age 18. Son of Albert Edward Freeman, and of Leah Freeman, of Bushbury, Wolverhampton.

FURBER, Fireman and Trimmer, JACK, S.S. Stonepool (West Hartlepool). Merchant Navy. 11th September 1941. Age 19. Son of Reginald and Elizabeth Furber, of Bristol.

GANDER, Able Seaman, WILLIAM CLEMENT, P/JX 261573. H.M.S. President III. Royal Navy. (Lost in S.S. Stonepool) 11th September 1941. Age 27. Son of David and Rosemary Annie Gander, of Battle, Sussex; husband of Lillian Mary Gander, of Battle, Sussex.

HOWELL, Able Seaman, REES, C/JX 249314, S.S. Stonepool, Royal Navy. 11 September 1941. Age 27. Son of Thomas and Gwenllian Howell; husband of Gladys May Howell, of Port Talbot, Glamorgan.

JAMES, Donkeyman, CHARLES, S.S. Stonepool (West Hartlepool). Merchant Navy. 11th September 1941. Age 41.

JONES, Sailor, ERNEST GRENVILLE, S.S. Stonepool (West Hartlepool). Merchant Navy. 11th September 1941. Age 21.

KEMPFF, Boatswain, JOHN HENDRICK, S.S. Stonepool (West Hartlepool). Merchant Navy. 11th September 1941. Age 41. Husband of Lily Kempff, of Plasmarl, Swansea.

KNIGHT, Second Officer, JOHN WILLIAM, S.S. Stonepool (West Hartlepool). Merchant Navy. 11th September 1941. Age 32. Son of James Thomas Knight and Betsy Knight.

LAING, First Radio Officer, ALEXANDER, S.S. Stonepool (West Hartlepool). Merchant Navy. 11th September 1941. Age 19. Son of David and Helen Man Laing, of Cortachy, Angus.

LEAR, Fireman and Trimmer, BERT PHILIP, S.S. Stonepool (West Hartlepool). Merchant Navy. 11th September 1941. Age 51.

LUKINS, Fireman and Trimmer, WESLEY, S.S. Stonepool (West Hartlepool). Merchant Navy. 11th September 1941. Age 20. Son of Charles Albert and Florence Lilian Lukins, of Shirehampton, Bristol.

McAULEY, Fireman and Trimmer, MICHAEL, S.S. Stonepool (West Hartlepool). Merchant Navy. 11th September 1941. Age 37.

MOORE, Lance Bombardier, GEORGE SHEPHERD, 1567248, 7/4 Maritime Regt., Royal Artillery. 11 September 1941. Age 27. Son of Martha Moore, of West Hartlepool, Co. Durham.

NICHOLSON, Master, JOSEPH HEWITSON, S.S. Stonepool (West Hartlepool). Merchant Navy. 11th September 1941. Age 49. Son of Capt. J. Nicholson and Rebecca Nicholson; husband of Catherine W. Nicholson, of Carlisle.

OVERBURY, Greaser, WILLIAM HENRY, S.S. Stonepool (West Hartlepool). Merchant Navy. 11th September 1941. Age 65. Son of Mr. and Mrs. Leonard Overbury; husband of Florence Annie Overbury, of Bristol.

POLKINGHORNE, Ordinary Seaman, RANDOLPH, S.S. Stonepool (West Hartlepool). Merchant Navy. 11th September 1941. Age 23. Son of Elizabeth Polkinghorne, of Ventonleague, Hayle, Cornwall.

POUNTAIN, Third Radio Officer, CLAUD ERIC, S.S. Stonepool (West Hartlepool). Merchant Navy. 11th September 1941. Age 31.

ROSS, Chief Officer, JOHN STEVENS, S.S. Stonepool (West Hartlepool). Merchant Navy. 11th September 1941. Age 29. Son of Dr. Ross, and of Mrs. M. E. Ross, of Tudhoe, Co. Durham; husband of Margaret Ann Ross, of Spennymoor, Co. Durham. Master Mariner, Merchant Navy.

SAVEGE, Second Radio Officer, RONALD MAXWELL, S.S. Stonepool (West Hartlepool). Merchant Navy. 11th September 1941. Age 18.

SEYMOUR, Third Engineer Officer, WILLIAM HENRY, S.S. Stonepool (West Hartlepool). Merchant Navy. 11th September 1941. Age 32.

SHERMON, Fireman and Trimmer, CLIFFORD, S.S. Stonepool (West Hartlepool). Merchant Navy. 11th September 1941. Age 18. Son of Mr. and Mrs. Frederick Shermon, of Southville, Bristol.

SIMPSON, Chief Engineer Officer, THOMAS YOUNG, S.S. Stonepool (West Hartlepool). Merchant Navy. 11th September 1941. Age 48. Husband of Dorothy M. Simpson, of Toronto, Ontario, Canada.

WEAKLEY, Fireman and Trimmer, THOMAS WILLIAM, S.S. Stonepool (West Hartlepool). Merchant Navy. 11th September 1941. Age 49. Husband of C. Weakley, of Bristol.

WHELAN, Fireman and Trimmer, CHARLES, S.S. Stonepool (West Hartlepool). Merchant Navy. 11th September 1941. Age 65.

SS Swiftpool

ANDERSON, Carpenter, MAGNUS, S.S. Swiftpool (West Hartlepool). Merchant Navy. 5th August 1941. Age 63.

ARNOLD, Chief Officer, WILLIAM HENRY, S.S. Swiftpool (West Hartlepool). Merchant Navy. 5th August 1941. Age 46. Son of Mr. and Mrs. John Herbert Arnold; husband of Lilian Arnold, of Low Fell, Gateshead, Co. Durham.

BAIN, Chief Engineer Officer, ALEXANDER, S.S. Swiftpool (West Hartlepool). Merchant Navy. 5th August 1941. Age 41.

BONES, Ordinary Seaman, HARRY, S.S. Swiftpool (West Hartlepool). Merchant Navy. 5th August 1941. Age 33. Senr. Husband of Laura Bones, of Crookes, Sheffield.

BURDEN, Ordinary Seaman, CYRIL HARRIS, V/2340, S.S. Swiftpool., Royal Canadian Navy Volunteer Reserve. 5 August 1941. Age 20. Son of Mr. and Mrs. Richard Burden, of Saint John, New Brunswick.

BENTON, Able Seaman, GEORGE ERNEST, C/JX 239483, S.S. Swiftpool, Royal Navy. 5 August 1941. Age 26. Son of George Percy and Minnie Benton; husband of Gladys Susan Benton, of Lewisham, London.

CHAPPLE, Chief Steward, NORMAN JAMES, S.S. Swiftpool (West Hartlepool). Merchant Navy. 5th August 1941. Age 40. Son of Robert James Chapple and Elizabeth Chapple; husband of Dorothea Helen Chapple, of Beer, Devon.

CLARK, Master, HARRY RAYMOND, S.S. Swiftpool (West Hartlepool). Merchant Navy. 5th August 1941. Age 50. Son of Edward and Mary E. Clark; husband of Jane Clark, of Shiptonthorpe, Yorkshire.

CRAVEN, Fireman and Trimmer, OWEN, S.S. Swiftpool (West Hartlepool). Merchant Navy. 5th August 1941. Age 33. Husband of Annie Craven, of Birkenhead.

CUSWORTH, Fourth Engineer Officer, ALFRED ERNEST, S.S. Swiftpool (West Hartlepool). Merchant Navy. 5th August 1941. Age 25.

CUTAJAR, Greaser, JOHN, S.S. Swiftpool (West Hartlepool). Merchant Navy. 5th August 1941. Age 35.

DAYCOCK, Third Officer, ROBERT WALKER, S.S. Swiftpool (West Hartlepool). Merchant Navy. 5th August 1941. Age 21.

DONALD, Gunner, JAMES, 1594201, 4/2 Maritime Regt., Royal Artillery. 5 August 1941. Age 30. Son of Peter and Mary Donald; husband of Jessie Donald, of Alyth, Perthshire.

FARRUGIA, Fireman and Trimmer, NICHOLAS, S.S. Swiftpool (West Hartlepool). Merchant Navy. 5th August 1941. Age 35. Son of Carmelo Farrugia and of Nicolina Farrugia (nee Gutajar); husband of Paula Farrugia (nee Attard), of St. Paul's Bay, Malta, G.C.

FAWCETT, Sailor, JOHN RICHARD, S.S. Swiftpool (West Hartlepool). Merchant Navy. 5th August 1941. Age 21. Son of Mr. and Mrs. Sidney Fawcett, of Scarborough, Yorkshire.

FIELDING, Second Officer, CYRIL, S.S. Swiftpool (West Hartlepool). Merchant Navy. 5th August 1941. Age 24.

GALASSO, Able Seaman, ALBERT HERBERT, S.S. Swiftpool (West Hartlepool). Merchant Navy. 5th August 1941. Age 22. Son of Joseph Henry and Rachel Galasso, of Walton, Liverpool.

GIRLING, Third Engineer Officer, ALBERT CHARLES, S.S. Swiftpool (West Hartlepool). Merchant Navy. 5th August 1941. Age 44.

HALL, Fireman and Trimmer, FRANK, S.S. Swiftpool (West Hartlepool). Merchant Navy. 5th August 1941. Age 26. Son of John William Hall, and of Clara Hall, of Preston, Lancashire.

HANNATH, Ordinary Seaman, CHARLES LEONARD, S.S. Swiftpool (West Hartlepool). Merchant Navy. 5th August 1941. Age 15. Son of Leonard and Mary Ann Hannath, of Cleethorpes, Lincolnshire.

HARTLING, Fireman, HAROLD, Swiftpool (West Hartlepool). Merchant Navy. 5th August 1941. (Canadian)

HEATLEY, Second Engineer Officer, REGINALD ANDREW, S.S. Swiftpool (West Hartlepool). Merchant Navy. 5th August 1941. Age 60. Son of Marshall Davis Heatley and Lavinia Heatley, of Hamilton, Tasmania; husband of Florence Emily Heatley, of Albany, West Australia.

HEFFY, Mess Room Boy, HERBERT ANTHONY, S.S. Swiftpool (West Hartlepool). Merchant Navy. 5th August 1941. Age 16. Son of Annie Heffy, of Walton, Liverpool.

HOGAN, Ordinary Seaman, GERARD, S.S. Swiftpool (West Hartlepool). Merchant Navy. 5th August 1941. Age 18. Son of Michael and Ellen Hogan, of Liverpool.

KELLY, Able Seaman, WILLIAM, S.S. Swiftpool (West Hartlepool). Merchant Navy. 5th August 1941. Age 49.

LOFTUS, Assistant Cook, JAMES, S.S. Swiftpool (West Hartlepool). Merchant Navy. 5th August 1941. Age 20. Son of John and BridgeLoftus, of Speke, Liverpool.

MADDOCKS, Assistant Steward, JOHN, S.S. Swiftpool (West Hartlepool). Merchant Navy. 5th August 1941. Age 27.

MONTIGO, Able Seaman, PHILIP ANTHONY, S.S. Swiftpool (West Hartlepool). Merchant Navy. 5th August 1941. Age 24. Son of Catherine Montigo, of Liverpool.

MURPHY, Fireman and Trimmer, MICHAEL, S.S. Swiftpool (West Hartlepool). Merchant Navy. 5th August 1941. Age 51.

MUNROE, Fireman, ALAN, S.S. Swiftpool (West Hartlepool). Merchant Navy. 5th August 1941. (Canadian)

McCRORIE, Greaser, HENRY, S.S. Swiftpool (West Hartlepool). Merchant Navy. 5th August 1941. Age 34.

McLAUGHLIN, Able Seaman, JOHN, S.S. Swiftpool (West Hartlepool). Merchant Navy. 5th August 1941. Age 20. Son of M. McLaughlin, and of Kathleen McLaughlin, of Shrove, Co. Donegal, Irish Republic.

REYNOLDS, Able Seaman, ERNEST, S.S. Swiftpool (West Hartlepool). Merchant Navy. 5th August 1941. Age 23.

RICHARDSON, Boatswain, WILLIAM, S.S. Swiftpool (West Hartlepool). Merchant Navy. 5th August 1941. Age 37. Husband of M. Richardson, of Scarborough, Yorkshire.

RICHMOND, Gunner, JACK FRED, 1625955, 4/2 Maritime Regt., Royal Artillery. 5 August 1941. Age 27. Son of John Henry and Alice Jane Richmond, of Oldham, Lancashire.

ROACH, Able Seaman, SIDNEY, D/JX 188305. H.M.S. President III. Royal Navy. lost in S.S. Swiftpool. 5th August 1941.

ROGAN, Fireman and Trimmer, THOMAS, S.S. Swiftpool (West Hartlepool). Merchant Navy. 5th August 1941. Age 36.

SIDAWAY, First Radio Officer, ALWYN, S.S. Swiftpool (West Hartlepool). Merchant Navy. 5th August 1941. Age 30.

TASKER, Fireman and Trimmer, ARTHUR WILLIAM, S.S. Swiftpool (West Hartlepool). Merchant Navy. 5th August 1941. Age 35. Son of Mr. and Mrs. George Tasker; husband of Lily Rose Tasker, of Hull.

TAYLOR, Second Radio Officer, ERIC PETER, S.S. Swiftpool (West Hartlepool). Merchant Navy. 5th August 1941. Age 19. Son of Charles Joseph and Enid May Taylor, of Crouch End, Middlesex.

WILLIAMS, Fireman and Trimmer, THOMAS JAMES, S.S. Swiftpool (West Hartlepool). Merchant Navy. 5th August 1941. Age 30.

ZENOPHON, Donkeyman, DEMETRIUS, S.S. Swiftpool (West Hartlepool). Merchant Navy. 5thAuust 1941. Age 56. (may have been named XENOPHON).

SS Teespool

BLANCHARD, Fourth Engineer Officer, JAMES WILLIAM, S.S. Teespool (West Hartlepool). Mercantile Marine. Killed, as a result of an attack by an enemy submarine, 19th October 1917. Age 22.
Son of Melville Blanchard and Susannah Blanchard (nee Newby), of 65, Hylton Rd., Sunderland. Born at Easington, Co. Durham.

HANSEN, Fireman, MARTIN, S.S. Teespool (West Hartlepool). Mercantile Marine. Killed, as a result of an attack by an enemy submarine, 19th October 1917. Age 23. Born in Norway.

MELLON, Able Seaman, ANTOINE GASTON, S.S. Teespool (West Hartlepool). Mercantile Marine. Killed, as a result of an attack by an enemy submarine, 19th October 1917. Age 28. Son of the late Nacelie Mellon. Born in Seychelles.

MOORE, Assistant Cook, HENRY, S.S. Teespool (West Hartlepool). Mercantile Marine. Killed, as a result of an attack by an enemy submarine, 19th October 1917. Age 16. Son of John and Margaret Moore, of 21, Adelaide St., Durham. Born at South Shields.

SS Therese Heymann

ALLARDICE, Third Engineer, WILLIAM NICOLL, S.S. Therese Heymann (London). Mercantile Marine. Presumed drowned 25th December 1914. Age 23. Son of George Allardice, of 85, Hilltown, Dundee, and the late Mary Ann Allardice.

BLAKEY, Fireman and Trimmer, THOMAS, S.S. Therese Heymann (London). Mercantile Marine. Presumed drowned 25th December 1914. Age 42. Son of the late Thomas and Mary Ann Blakey. Born at South Shields.

BROWN, Mess Room Steward, THOMAS WILLIAM, S.S. Therese Heymann (London). Mercantile Marine. Presumed drowned 25th December 1914. Age 33. Son of George Rutherford Brown, and Mary Brown (nee Turnbull), of 37, Dent St., Fulwell, Sunderland. Born at South Shields.

CLYNE, Fireman, GEORGE, S.S. Therese Heymann (London). Mercantile Marine. Presumed drowned 25th December 1914. Age 31. Born at Helsingford.

CRUICKSHANKS, First Mate, JOHN, S.S. Therese Heymann (London). Mercantile Marine. Presumed drowned 25th December 1914. Age 34. Son of the late John and Charlotte Cruickshanks (nee Davidson); husband of Grace Mary Cruickshanks (Nee Littlejohn), of 16, Queen St., Montrose, Forfar. Born at Johnshaven.

EVANS, Master, THOMAS, S.S. Therese Heymann (London). Mercantile Marine. 25th December 1914. Age 52. Son of Thomas and Catherine Evans, of Laura, Aberarth; husband of Annie E. Evans, of Awelfa, Aberarth.

EWART, Second Engineer, GEORGE ROBERT, S.S. Therese Heymann (London). Mercantile Marine. Presumed drowned 25th December 1914. Age 52. Son of Harriett Ewart, and the late George Robert Ewart; husband of Sarah Jane Ewart (nee Allon), of 25, Mariner's Cottages, South Shields. Born at South .Shields.

HILSON, Sailor, ALBERT WILLIAM, S.S. Therese Heymann (London). Mercantile Marine. Presumed drowned 25th December 1914. Age 34. Born at Plymouth.

JOHANSEN, First Engineer, A, S.S. Therese Heymann (London). Mercantile Marine. Presumed drowned 25th December 1914. Age 38.

Husband of Phylis Johansen, of 24, Roseberry Avenue, South Shields. Born in Sweden.

KESSELI, Sailor, A, S.S. Therese Heymann (London). Mercantile Marine. Presumed drowned 25th December 1914. Age 22. Born in Switzerland.

LARGE, Steward, FRANK, S.S. Therese Heymann (London). Mercantile Marine. Presumed drowned 25th December 1914. Age 27. Son of the late Frank and Jane Large; husband of Eliza Jane Large, of 166, Studley Rd., West Hartlepool. Born at West Hartlepool.

MANGER, Donkeyman, WALTER GEORGE, S.S. Therese Heymann (London). Mercantile Marine. Presumed drowned 25th December 1914. Age 46. Son of the late Richard and Elizabeth Ann Manger; husband of Jessie Manger (nee Jordan), of 31, Seymour St., Dunston-on-Tyne. Born in Jersey.

MARR, Able Seaman, FRANCIS, S.S. Therese Heymann (London). Mercantile Marine. Presumed drowned 25th December 1914. Age 46. Son of the late Thomas and Kathleen Marr; husband of Mary Alice Marr (nee Cottrill), of 4, Bank St., Sunderland. Born at Aberdeen.

PEPLER, Second Mate, JAMES, S.S. Therese Heymann (London). Mercantile Marine. Presumed drowned 25th December 1914. Age 50. Husband of Margaret A. Pepler, of 6, Queen's Crescent, Sunderland. Born in London.

PETERSON, Boatswain (Bosun), J, S.S. Therese Heymann (London). Mercantile Marine. Presumed drowned 25th December 1914. Age 26. Born in Sweden.

PIKKA, Fireman and Trimmer, ALBERT, S.S. Therese Heymann (London). Mercantile Marine. Presumed drowned 25th December 1914. Age 20. Born in Russia.

RAHIKAIN, Sailor, OSCAR, S.S. Therese Heymann (London). Mercantile Marine. Presumed drowned 25th December 1914. Age 22. Born in Russia.

ROBINSON, Ship's Cook, ROBERT WILLIAM, S.S. Therese Heymann (London). Mercantile Marine. Presumed drowned 25th December 1914. Age 33. Son of the late Thomas William and Isabell Robinson. Born at Liverpool.

SHILSON, Fireman and Trimmer, JOHN WILLIAM, S.S. Therese Heymann (London). Mercantile Marine. Presumed drowned 25th December 1914. Age 41. Son of the late John and Barbara Shilson; husband of Hannah Shilson (nee Lazenby), of 8, Linden Terrace, Ferry Hill, Co. Durham. Born at West Hartlepool.

STALBERG, Sailor, J, S.S. Therese Heymann (London). Mercantile Marine. Presumed drowned 25th December 1914. Age 23. Born in Sweden.

TURNBULL, Fireman and Trimmer, GEORGE, S.S. Therese Heymann (London). Mercantile Marine. Presumed drowned 25th December 1914. Age 47. Son of the late Henry and Ann Turnbull; husband of Rebecca Turnbull (nee Emms), of 115, John Williamson St., South Shields. Born at Sunderland.

SS Thirlby WWI

GARTHSHORE, Fireman and Trimmer, ROBERT, S.S. Thirlby (West Hartlepool). Mercantile Marine. Killed, as a result of an attack by an enemy submarine, 2nd July 1917. Age 18. Son of the late Neil and Janet Garthshore. Born at Coatbridge.

MARTIN, Third Engineer, JAMES ALEXANDER, S.S. Thirlby (West Hartlepool). Mercantile Marine. Killed, as a result of an attack by an enemy submarine, 2nd July 1917. Age 25. Son of George and Jessie Martin (nee Reid), of 87, Westburn Rd., Aberdeen. Born at Aberdeen.

SS Thirlby

CRAIG, Assistant Steward, JAMES, S.S. Thirlby (West Hartlepool). Merchant Navy. 10th April 1941. Age 30. Son of James and Catherine Craig, of Bearsden, Dunbartonshire.

GHALEB ALI, Fireman and Trimmer, S.S. Thirlby (West Hartlepool). Merchant Navy. 10th April 1941. Age 37.

GILLESPIE, Fireman, JAMES, S.S. Thirlby (West Hartlepool). Merchant Navy. 23rd January 1942. Age 41. Son of James Gillespie, and of Sarah Jane Gillespie, of Belfast, Northern Ireland; husband of Mary Gillespie.

HUISH, Greaser, ALBERT FREDERICK, S.S. Thirlby (West Hartlepool). Merchant Navy. 23rd January 1942. Age 17.

O'REILLY, Fireman, CHARLES T., S.S. Thirlby (West Hartlepool). Merchant Navy. 23rd January 1942. Age 34.

SS Thornaby

BAUMAN, Fireman, TOM, S.S. Thornaby (West Hartlepool). Mercantile Marine. Killed by mine 28th February 1916. Age 23. Born at Windan.

BLAXLAND, Pilot, THOMAS, Cinque Ports Pilot S.S. Thornaby (West Hartlepool). Mercantile Marine. Drowned, as a result of a mine explosion, 28th February 1916.

CARO, Boatswain (Bosun), LUIS, S.S. Thornaby (West Hartlepool). Mercantile Marine. Killed by mine 28th February 1916. Age 23. Son of Jose Caro, of Torrevieja, Alicante, Spain. Born at Alicante, Spain.

CLARK, Ship's Cook, ROBERT, S.S. Thornaby (West Hartlepool). Mercantile Marine. Killed by mine 28th February 1916. Age 60. Husband of the late Elizabeth Jane Clark (nee Johnson). Born at Sunderland.

CLUNE, Fireman, ARTHUR, S.S. Thornaby (West Hartlepool). Mercantile Marine. Killed by mine 28th February 1916. Age 47. Born at Glasgow.
COTT, Mess Room Steward, GERALD, S.S. Thornaby (West Hartlepool). Mercantile Marine. Killed by mine 28th February 1916. Age 19. Son of the late David and Mary Cott.

DUIFF, Deck Hand, JOHANNE, S.S. Thornaby (West Hartlepool). Mercantile Marine. Killed by mine 28th February 1916. Age 24. Son of Thomas Andreas Duiff. Born at Rotterdam.

EARL, Second Engineer, FREDRIC HARRY, S.S. Thornaby (West Hartlepool). Mercantile Marine. Killed by mine 28th February 1916. Age 25. Son of Elizabeth Earl, and the late Frederick Earl; husband of Blodwen Gwenlian Earl (nee Jones), of 82, Kildare St., Middlesbrough. Born at Middlesbrough.

EVANS, Master, DAVID, S.S Thornaby (West Hartlepool). Mercantile Marine. Drowned, as a result of a mine explosion, 28th February 1916. Husband of M. A. Evans, of 3, Harries Avenue, Old Rd., Llanelly.

GREIG, Third Engineer, ROBERT WILLIAM, S.S. Thornaby (West Hartlepool). Mercantile Marine. Killed by mine 28th February 1916. Age 22.

Son of the late David Pattison Greig and the late Jane Greig (nee Herron). Born at West Hartlepool.

HOPKINS, Able Seaman, H, S.S. Thornaby (West Hartlepool). Mercantile Marine. Killed by mine 28th February 1916. Age 53. Born in London.

LEYS, Boatswain P, S.S. Thornaby (West Hartlepool). Mercantile Marine. Killed by mine 28th February 1916. Age 40. Son of Mr. Leys, of Baesrode, Belgium.

McHUGH, First Engineer, GEORGE, S.S. Thornaby (West Hartlepool). Mercantile Marine. Killed by mine 28th February 1916. Age 41. Son of James McHugh and the late Isabella McHugh; husband of Margaret Hopper McHugh (nee Hind march), of 10, Romilly St., South Shields. Born at South Shields.

OFSTHUN, First Mate, PAUL, S.S. Thornaby (West Hartlepool). Mercantile Marine. Killed by mine 28th February 1916. Age 58. Husband of A. Jensen Oftshun, of 15, Hangeveien, Bergen, Norway. Born at Bergen, Norway.

PROSEN, Able Seaman, JOHN HERMANN ERNEST, S.S. Thornaby (West Hartlepool). Mercantile Marine. Killed by mine 28th February 1916. Age 40. Husband of Matilda Prosen (nee Stothard), of 4, Sussex St., Sunderland. Born in Switzerland.

SODERMAN, Able Seaman, EBBLE, S.S. Thornaby (West Hartlepool). Mercantile Marine. Killed by mine 28th February 1916. Age 37. (may have been surnamed SODERHAM, or forenamed EBEL). Born at Aland.

VAN DER HARST, Fireman and Trimmer, ARIE, S.S. Thornaby (West Hartlepool). Mercantile Marine. Killed by mine 28th February 1916. Age 34. Son of Arie van der Harst, of 4, Brandery St., Flushing, Netherlands. Born at Flushing.

VINEY, Fireman and Trimmer, JAMES, S.S. Thornaby (West Hartlepool). Mercantile Marine. Killed by mine 28th February 1916. Age 31. Son of Margaret Ann and the late William Viney, husband of Margaret Ann Viney (nee Penn), of 1, Mordey St., Sunderland. Born at Sunderland.

WAPENAAR, Fireman and Trimmer, CLAUDIUS BARTHELOMENS, S.S. Thornaby (West Hartlepool). Mercantile Marine. Killed by mine 28th

February 1916. Age 31. Son of Hendrik Albertus Wapenaar, of Calitzdorp, C.P., South Africa, and the late Magdalena Catherina Wapenaar.

SS Troutpool

ABDUL ALI, Fireman and Trimmer, S.S. Troutpool (West Hartlepool). Merchant Navy. 20th July 1940. Age 39.

AHMED, Fireman and Trimmer, SHIEF, S.S. Troutpool (West Hartlepool). Merchant Navy. 20th July 1940. Age 40. Husband of Margaretta Ahmed, of Glasgow. Buried Bangor Cemetery.

AWLED MOHAMED, Fireman and Trimmer, S.S. Troutpool (West Hartlepool). Merchant Navy. 20th July 1940. Age 40.

BECKETT, Carpenter, THOMAS SMITH, S.S. Troutpool (West Hartlepool). Merchant Navy. 20th July 1940. Age 32. Son of Archibald and Margaret Beckett, of Glasgow. Buried Bangor Cemetery.

CALEB, Fireman and Trimmer, MUCKLELE, S.S. Troutpool (West Hartlepool). Merchant Navy. 20th July 1940. Age 43.

CONNELL, Boy, ALEXANDER, S.S. Troutpool (West Hartlepool). Merchant Navy. 20th July 1940. Age 19.

DEMARI SALEH AHMED, Fireman and Trimmer, S.S. Troutpool (West Hartlepool). Merchant Navy. 20th July 1940. Age 41.

MURRAY, Ordinary Seaman, WILLIAM GEORGE, S.S. Troutpool (West Hartlepool). Merchant Navy. 20th July 1940. Age 25. Son of William Murray, and of Anne Murray, of Hopeman, Morayshire.

MacDOUGALL, Ordinary Seaman, DONALD ANDREW, S.S. Troutpool (West Hartlepool). Merchant Navy. 20th July 1940. Age 17. Son of Donald and Theresa MacDougall, of Castlebay, Isle of Barra.

McGRATH, Able Seaman, JOHN, S.S. Troutpool (West Hartlepool). Merchant Navy. 20th July 1940. Age 53. Son of Hugh and Margaret McGrath.

McNEILL, Able Seaman, DONALD, S.S. Troutpool (West Hartlepool). Merchant Navy. 20th July 1940. Age 41. Son of Neil McNeill, and of Catherine McNeill, of Port Charlotte, Isle of Islay.

SS Ullapool

BURROUGH, Fourth Engineer Officer, JOHN PHILIP, S.S. Ullapool (West Hartlepool). Merchant Navy. 13th March 1941. Age 24. Son of Hedley Arthur and Mary Ellen Burrough, of South Shields, Co. Durham.

CORKISH, Able Seaman, ARTHUR ALEXANDER HUGHSON I., S.S. Ullapool (West Hartlepool). Merchant Navy. 13th March 1941. Age 38. Son of Mr. and Mrs. John Corkish; husband of Grace Corkish, of South Shields, Co. Durham.

FARNIE, Steward, HENRY, S.S. Ullapool (West Hartlepool). Merchant Navy. 13th March 1941. Age 40. Son of Mark Frederick and Eliza Farnie; husband of E. M. Farnie, of Sunderland, County Durham.

FLANNIGAN, Fireman and Trimmer, JOHN, S.S. Ullapool (West Hartlepool). Merchant Navy. 13th March 1941. Age 26. Son of James and Joan Flannigan; husband of Margaret Flannigan, of Finsbury Park, Middlesex.

GRAY, Fireman and Trimmer, PETER SCOTT, S.S. Ullapool (West Hartlepool). Merchant Navy. 13th March 1941. Age 35. Husband of W. Gray, of South Shields, Co. Durham.

JOICEY, Fireman and Trimmer, ALBERT HECTOR, S.S. Ullapool (West Hartlepool). Merchant Navy. 13th March 1941. Age 33. Son of George and Phillis Hopper Joicey, of North Shields, Northumberland.

KERR, Second Engineer Officer, PATRICK GEORGE, S.S. Ullapool (West Hartlepool). Merchant Navy. 13th March 1941. Age 60.

LAKE, Cook, HERBERT, S.S. Ullapool (West Hartlepool). Merchant Navy. 13th March 1941. Age 26. Son of Herbert Thomas Lake, and of Annie Lake, of West Hartlepool, Co. Durham.

LOGAN, Deck Boy, ALEXANDER RUSSELL, S.S. Ullapool (West Hartlepool). Merchant Navy. 13th March 1941. Age 15.

McKAY, Fireman and Trimmer, JOHN, S.S. Ullapool (West Hartlepool). Merchant Navy. 13th March 1941. Age 52.

PATTERSON, Fireman and Trimmer, JOHN COMMON, S.S. Ullapool (West Hartlepool). Merchant Navy. 13th March 1941. Age 19.

PAYTON, Radio Officer, JOSEPH ALFRED WILLIAM, S.S. Ullapool (West Hartlepool). Merchant Navy. 13th March 1941. Age 32. Son of Joseph Fletcher Payton and Hannah Prudence Payton, of Pembroke Dock.

SCOTT, Second Officer, FREDERICK HARRY, S.S. Ullapool (West Hartlepool). Merchant Navy. 13th March 1941. Age 24. Son of Frederic and Hilda Scott, of West Hartlepool, Co. Durham.

STEPHENSON, Second Radio Officer, JAMES ALEXANDER, S.S. Ullapool (West Hartlepool). Merchant Navy. 13th March 1941. Age 20.

THWAITES, Master, WILLIAM JEWITT, S.S. Ullapool (West Hartlepool). Merchant Navy. 13th March 1941. Age 56. Son of Charles Jewitt Thwaites and Isabella Jewitt Thwaites; husband of M. E. Thwaites, of South Shields, Co. Durham.

WENLOCK, Sergeant, GEORGE HENRY PERCIVAL, PLY/21836. H.M.S. President III. Royal Marines. Lost in S.S. Ullapool. 13th March 1941. Age 49.

SS Warlaby

ABDUL MOHAMED, Fireman and Trimmer, S.S. Warlaby (West Hartlepool). Merchant Navy. 12th February 1941. Age 44.

ANDERSON, Fireman and Trimmer, JAMES GERALD, S.S. Warlaby (West Hartlepool). Merchant Navy. 12th February 1941. Age 24.

BAMBRO, Third Officer, GEORGE, S.S. Warlaby (West Hartlepool). Merchant Navy. 12th February 1941. Age 25. Husband of Catherine M. Bambro, of Whitley Bay, Northumberland.

BATCHELER, Chief Yeoman of Signals, CHARLES, C/230728, S.S. Warlaby, Royal Navy. 12 February 1941. Age 52. Son of Charles Henry and Ellen Batcheler; husband of Julia Emily Batcheler, of Aylesbury, Buckinghamshire.

BLACK, Able Seaman, ARTHUR, S.S. Warlaby (West Hartlepool). Merchant Navy. 12th February 1941. Age 25.

BLACKBOURN, Second Officer, FREDERICK, S.S. Warlaby (West Hartlepool). Merchant Navy. 12th February 1941. Age 28. Son of Fredrick and Jennie Blackbourn, of Cleethorpes, Lincolnshire.

BOLAND, Steward, JOSEPH PATRICK, S.S. Warlaby (West Hartlepool). Merchant Navy. 12th February 1941. Age 27.

BRANNAN, Fireman and Trimmer, THOMAS, S.S. Warlaby (West Hartlepool). Merchant Navy. 12th February 1941. Age 26. Son of James and Charlotte Brannan.

BRAY, Fireman and Trimmer, GEORGE FREDERICK, S.S. Warlaby (West Hartlepool). Merchant Navy. 12th February 1941. Age 36. Son of Thomas Jackson Bray and Gavilla Bray, of Halling, Yorkshire.

BROOKS, Donkeyman, J, S.S. Warlaby (West Hartlepool). Merchant Navy. 12th February 1941. Age 38.

BROWN, Second Engineer Officer, ROBERT, S.S. Warlaby (West Hartlepool). Merchant Navy. 12th February 1941. Age 42.

COPLAND, Third Engineer Officer, GEORGE, S.S. Warlaby (West Hartlepool). Merchant Navy. 12th February 1941. Age 28. Son of George and Hellen Copland, of Northfield, Aberdeen.

DAVISON, Second Radio Officer, RONALD, S.S. Warlaby (West Hartlepool). Merchant Navy. 12th February 1941. Age 18. Son of Robert Davison, and of Catherine E. Davison, of Chester-le-Street, Co. Durham.

FEARN, Able Seaman, CHARLES, S.S. Warlaby (West Hartlepool). Merchant Navy. 12th February 1941. Age 36. Son of Charles and Elizabeth Fearn.

FITZMAURICE, Fireman and Trimmer, STANLEY ALAN ROBIN, S.S. Warlaby (West Hartlepool). Merchant Navy. 12th February 1941. Age 34. Husband of Sanchia Fitzmaurice, of Sloane Square, London.

GILLEN, Fourth Engineer Officer, JAMES, S.S. Warlaby (West Hartlepool). Merchant Navy. 12th February 1941. Age 41. Son of James and Mary Gillen; husband of Amy Gillen, of Swinefleet, Yorkshire.

GILMOUR, Galley Boy, JOHN, S.S. Warlaby (West Hartlepool). Merchant Navy. 12th February 1941. Age 17. Son of Thomas and Annie Reid Gilmour, of Barrow-in-Furness, Lancashire.

GRACE, Signalman, GEORGE SAMUEL, D/MD/X 529. H.M.S. President III. Royal Naval Volunteer Reserve. Lost in S.S. Warlaby. 12th February 1941. Age 30. Son of Peter and Frances E. Grace, of Liverpool.

GRAY, Sailor, VIVIAN, S.S. Warlaby (West Hartlepool). Merchant Navy. 12th February 1941. Age 25.

HAYES, Deck Hand, JOSEPH, S.S. Warlaby (West Hartlepool). Merchant Navy. 12th February 1941. Age 48.

HEDDITCH, Mess Room Boy, FRANCIS TOM, S.S. Warlaby (West Hartlepool). Merchant Navy. 12th February 1941. Age 20. Son of Mr. and Mrs. F. T. Hedditch, of Port Mulgrave, Yorkshire.

HOLBOROW, Able Seaman, ULRICK RATCLIFFE, S.S. Warlaby (West Hartlepool). Merchant Navy. 12th February 1941. Age 36.

HUNTER, Carpenter, ARTHUR, S.S. Warlaby (West Hartlepool). Merchant Navy. 12th February 1941. Age 23.

JACKSON, Donkeyman, SYDNEY, S.S. Warlaby (West Hartlepool). Merchant Navy. 12th February 1941. Age 26.

MITCHELSON, Cabin Boy, STOREY, S.S. Warlaby (West Hartlepool). Merchant Navy. 12th February 1941. Age 18. Son of Storey and Hannah Lizzie Mitchelson, of North Shields, Northumberland.

MURRAY, Master, SEPTIMUS HOWARD, S.S. Warlaby (West Hartlepool). Merchant Navy. 12th February 1941. Age 35. Son of John William and Frances Annie Murray; husband of Lily Osborne Murray, of Carrshields, Northumberland.

NEVILLE, Deck Boy, GEORGE ARTHUR, S.S. Warlaby (West Hartlepool). Merchant Navy. 12th February 1941. Age 18. Son of Mr. and Mrs. S. J. Neville, of Hornchurch, Essex.

NICHOLSON, First Radio Officer, STANLEY GEORGE, S.S. Warlaby (West Hartlepool). Merchant Navy. 12th February 1941. Age 21. Son of George William and Florence May Nicholson.

OBAD MOSSELEH, Fireman and Trimmer, S.S. Warlaby (West Hartlepool). Merchant Navy. 12th February 1941. Age 47.

RAWES, Deck Boy, GEORGE JAMES, S.S. Warlaby (West Hartlepool). Merchant Navy. 12th February 1941. Age 17. Son of Reginald and Jessie Rawes, of King's Cross, London.

ROBERTS, Fireman and Trimmer, JOHN WILLIAM COWELL, S.S. Warlaby (West Hartlepool). Merchant Navy. 12th February 1941. Age 29.

ROCHA, Able Seaman, JOHN, S.S. Warlaby (West Hartlepool). Merchant Navy. 12th February 1941. Age 53.

SAHLMAN, Boatswain, ARTHUR, S.S. Warlaby (West Hartlepool). Merchant Navy. 12th February 1941. Age 47. Son of Henry Bernard Sahlman and Mary Sahlman; husband of Eleanor Carlisle Sahlman, of Wallsend, Northumberland.

SANDERSON, Chief Engineer Officer, PERCY GEORGE, S.S. Warlaby (West Hartlepool). Merchant Navy. 12th February 1941. Age 55. Son of John and Sarah Sanderson; husband of Annie Sanderson, of Linthorpe, Middlesbrough, Yorkshire. Formerly Lieut.-Comdr., R.N. His son George Charles Peter also fell.

SMITH, Donkeyman, WILLIAM, S.S. Warlaby (West Hartlepool). Merchant Navy. 12th February 1941. Age 47.

THOMPSON, Fireman and Trimmer, FREDERICK, S.S. Warlaby (West Hartlepool). Merchant Navy. 12th February 1941. Age 32. Son of Ellen Thompson; husband of L. Thompson, of Leeds, Yorkshire.

WHEATLEY, Deck Boy, JAMES SMITH, S.S. Warlaby (West Hartlepool). Merchant Navy. 12th February 1941. Age 20. Son of James Smith Wheatley and May Elizabeth Wheatley, of North Shields. Northumberland.

YEARDSLEY, Fireman and Trimmer, ROBERT WILLIAM, S.S. Warlaby (West Hartlepool). Merchant Navy. 12th February 1941. Age 31.

"Full sacrifice has been their lot, they faced the test most bravely. Come light a way, out debt repay to the men of the Merchant Navy. "
(Wm McAdam 1942)

Bibliography

Britain's Sea Wars: A Diary of Ships Losses 1939-1945. (John M. Young)

British & Commonwealth Merchant Ship Losses to Axis Submarines 1939-1945. (Alan J. Tennent)

The Allied Convoy System 1939-1945: it's Organisation, Defence & Operation. (Arnold Hague)

Milag: Captives of the Kriegsmarine Merchant Navy Prisoners of War. (Gabe Thomas)

The Fourth Service: Merchantmen at War 1939-1945. (John Slader)

The Red Duster at War. (John Slader)

The Worlds Merchant Fleets 1939-1945. (Roger W. Jordan)

Axis Submarine Successes. (Rohwer Jurgen)

The Atlantic Star. (W.H. Allen)

Attack & Sink (Bernard Edwards)

The Fighting Tramps: The Merchant Navy Goes to War (Bernard Edwards)

No Longer Required: My War in the Merchant Marine. (Bill Linskey)

The Empire Ships second edition. (W.H. Mitchell & L.A. Sawyer)

The Ropner Story. (Ian Dear)

Ropner Shipping Co. 1874-1974. (World Ship Society)

Ropner's Record: Eighty Years on the Seven Seas. (Craig J. M. Carter)

Lloyds War Losses. The First World War

Lloyds War Losses. The Second World War Vol. 1

Lloyds War Losses. The Second World War Vol. 2

Life Line, The Merchant Navy at War 1939-1945 (Peter Elphik)

Travels of the Tramps: Twenty Tramp Fleets Vol. III (Norman L. Middlemiss)

The National Archives, Kew. BT372, BT373, BT381, BT382 & BT389

An HMSO Publication: Casualties & Medical Statistics 1972 (Mellors)

mna

The Merchant Navy Association®
from ship to shore, from past to present

Leading the Way for 16 years
National Chairman - Captain J.M.R.Sail MNI
National Secretary _ T.Brant Tel:- +44 (0)1472 851130

Athenia - The first allied Merchant ship to be sunk in 1939 in the first day of WW2 with the Avondale Park being the last ship sunk on the 7th May 1945 brining the total to 2535 sunk in action.

- The Merchant Navy association is the oldest established organisation with a regional and branch structure, overseas support and a continuous line of activity lobbying for over 16 years.
- An organisation run by members, for and on behalf of members.
- Members receive a FREE quarterly magazine "Full Ahead".
- Executive members attend meetings with Ministers, MP's, MEP's and other seafaring organisations.
- Regularly engaged with the MOD and the Veterans Policy Unit.
- Meetings with the Merchant Navy Welfare Board.
- Members of the Sea Vision and the NVCO.
- Local Organisers and Sponsors of the MNA memorial stone at the National Arboretum.
- Lead organisers and Sponsors of the MN Day Commemorative Services and Re-union.
- Lead Organisers and sponsors of the MN Falklands Trust to build the new MN Falkland memorial at Tower Hill.

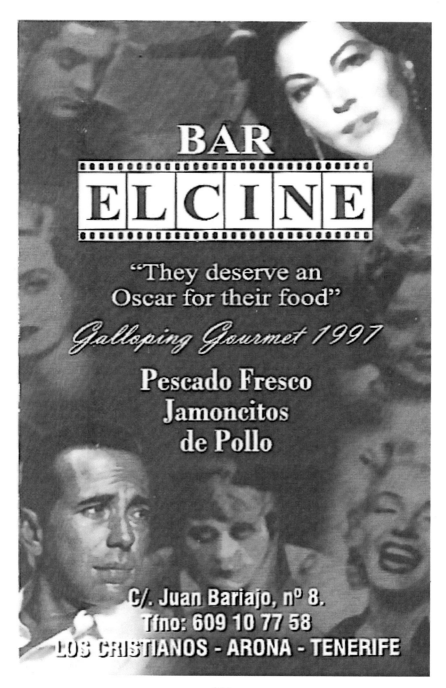

BAR

ELCINE

"They deserve an
Oscar for their food"

Galloping Gourmet 1997

**Pescado Fresco
Jamoncitos
de Pollo**

C/. Juan Bariajo, nº 8.
Tfno: 609 10 77 58
LOS CRISTIANOS - ARONA - TENERIFE

Welcome to the Spinnaker Hotel, Gourock, Scotland.

The Spinnaker is a small, family run hotel in Gourock, Scotland's classic seaside holiday town. With Glasgow Airport less than half an hour away, it's a convenient stopover before you hop on to the ferry to tour the Highlands and Islands.

But first , why not linger a while and enjoy sailing, fishing and many other attractions of the Clyde Coast!

Here's a friendly, welcoming place by the sea. The Spinnaker offers good quality accommodation at reasonable prices, and has picture postcard views across the Firth of Clyde.

The Hotel is located in a listed sandstone Victorian terrace in Albert Road, which runs along the coast midway between two ferry terminals at Gourock. The view is quirte simply stunning, looking out across the water to the Holy Loch, with mountains of Argyll rising up behind Dunoon and Kilcreggan to mark the start of the Highlands. All year round you'll see fishing trawlers puffing up and down the Clyde - perhaps even the odd submarine. During the yachting season, the view if filled with sleek sailboats, their brightly coloured spinnakers catching the wind.

The Spinnaker is owned by Stewart McCartney and his wife Julie, who will personally make sure your stay is everything you expect. A recent expansion programme has resulted in substantially upgraded facilities, including Bar and the Dining Room..

The Spinnaker, 121 Albert Road, Gourock, PA19 1BU. Tel: 01475-633107

Hartlepool Marina is the venue for the 2010 Tall Ships Race when an estimated one million visitors will come to Hartlepool for the biggest sailing event in the Tall Ships calendar. In addition to the spectacle of seeing the old sailing ships enter the Marina visitors can take in the Historic Quay, Maritime Museum, and the two resident ships the "Wingfield Castle" and HMS Trincomalee. For a unique dining experience visitors will be able to dine at Krimo's, Portofino and Casa del Mar - part of the Krimo triangle on the Marina.

Krimos

Krimo's opened on 4th May 1985 with a mere £250 at the seaside resort of Seaton Carew (Hartlepool) in the North-East of England. The restaurant was put on the map with the help of immensely dedicated staff, a few of whom are still with us. From the very start, we realised that Krimo's was a runaway success because we were booked up weeks in advance due to the format of "your table for the night" At one time, there wasn't one free table on Saturdays for 16 weeks. In July 1990, we moved out of the first-floor flat and doubled the seating. In April 2000, we opened the new **Krimo's**, our new self-designed 80-seater restaurant on Hartlepool Marina. Whilst retaining quite a few of the old menu's favourites, we encourage the chefs to experiment with new dishes and as a result the menu now contains some exciting additions. Over the last two years we have added also a few Algerian dishes. These have been proved very popular. **Krimo's** has remained as popular as ever and, although we may now have the odd free table mid-week, we still refuse people on Saturdays. The same format remains and so does the quality of ingredients. A truly delightful oasis now offering superb Mediterranean and Algerian cuisine in the idyllic setting of Hartlepool Marina.. We have built this restaurant by listening to our customers and therefore your views and comments are greatly valued; please take the time to send us an email with your comments and suggestions. Hartlepool Marina has brought a new breath of fresh air to the town. The Historic Quay, the replica of an 18th century port was voted best tourist attraction in 2000. HMS Trincomalee, attracts thousands of visitors.

Portofino

In October 1998 Portofino was opened and its reputation has grown rapidly due to its beautifully prepared meals, mainly of Mediterranean style. **Krimo** places considerable emphasis on customer care and service ensuring that the recipes are produced exactly as they should by an energetic young team. Visitors to this happy bistro cannot help but be thrilled by the buzzing atmosphere created by the décor and carefully compiled music. The restaurant is placed in a pleasant setting overlooking the **Historic Quay** and **Hartlepool Marina.**

Casa del Mar

Is the latest addition to the Krimo "triangle" on Hartlepool Marina. Offering more than 50 authentic tapas dishes.

Consistency

The common ingredient in all our restaurants is consistency.

www.krimos.co.uk   **01429 266120**
www.portofino.co.uk   **01429 266166**
www.casabar.co.uk   **01429 222223**

For all the latest news from Krimo log onto his blog at
www.krimosrestaurant.blogspot.com